CHINA'S ECONOMIC CHALLENGE

Smashing the Iron Rice Bowl

Neil C. Hughes

AN EAST GATE BOOK

M.E. Sharpe

Armonk, New York
London, England

An East Gate Book

Copyright © 2002 by Neil C. Hughes

Photographs by Neil C. Hughes.

Library of Congress Cataloging-in-Publication Data

Hughes, Neil C., 1936–
   China's economic challenge : smashing the iron rice bowl / Neil C. Hughes.
      p. cm.
   Includes bibliographical references and index.
   ISBN 0-7656-0808-1 (alk. paper); ISBN 0-7656-0809-X (pbk. : alk. paper)
   1. China—Economic policy—1976–2000. 2. China—Economic policy—2000–
   3. China—Economic conditions—1976–2000. I. Title.

HC427.9.H867 2001
338.951—dc21   2001049909

Printed in the United States of America

BM (c)   10   9   8   7   6   5   4   3   2   1
BM (p)   10   9   8   7   6   5   4   3   2   1

For Kathleen

CHINA'S ECONOMIC CHALLENGE

CHINA'S ECONOMIC CHALLENGE

*Smashing
the Iron Rice Bowl*

Neil C. Hughes

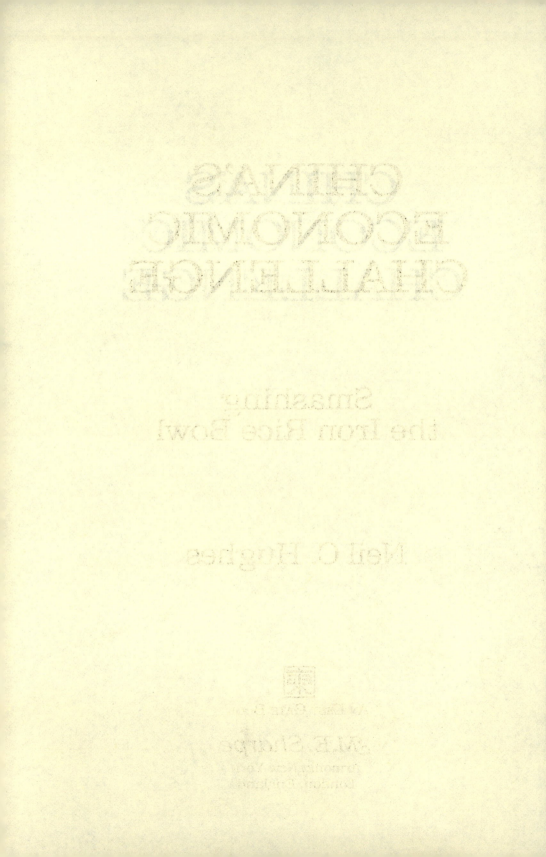

M.E.Sharpe
Armonk, New York
London, England

Contents

Preface

I became involved in China's reform process during its most exciting phase—after Deng Xiaoping made his southern tour in the fall of 1992 and proclaimed that "to get rich is glorious," starting a gold rush in which millions of Chinese took this advice literally.

In many ways China was unique in my experience: the sheer numbers of its people; its size and geophysical diversity; the oldest continuous written history of any nation; a tradition of civil administration that was at least two thousand years old; the formality of its social relations; the oldest and densest cities on earth; and the destructive force of its natural disasters.

Above all, I was fascinated by the risks China's leaders were taking in opening up China to economic forces the leaders could not control. Those who held power in China had started a revolution that could end their careers and even destroy the Communist Party. What had prompted them to discard the legacy of the Great Helmsman, Mao Zedong, and to urge their citizens to embark on the unpredictable seas of market economics?

I knew that China's reformers under Deng Xiaoping understood that to change from a centrally planned economy to one that followed market principles, they had to shatter the iron rice bowl that symbolized the Communist Party's commitment to provide cradle-to-the-grave security for all its citizens. I decided that the focus of my book should be to find out whether the iron rice bowl had really been broken.

But first I had to consider the matter of change. Could I understand what the current changes meant without studying earlier changes? I came upon Jonathan Spence's statement that "China's history illuminates its present." Like Spence, I believe that only by studying the past can we get a sense of how China's problems have arisen and how well equipped China is to solve them.

I found this approach essential to understanding Chinese behavior, which so often seems to confound and contradict what the West deems appropriate. It also provided a way of taking a second look at the preconceived notions that often dominate the current debate about who the Chinese are and what they want.

I have tried to see things from a Chinese perspective, to comprehend better the magnitude of the task facing China's leaders. I tried to imagine what it would be like to run a country that has 7 percent of the world's land mass and 22 percent of its population. How does any government manage a country of 1.3 billion people? If I were China's president, what would I do to improve the lot of 800 million rural Chinese who live on about one-fourth the income of their urban counterparts? How would I deal with the 100–120 million people who have already left the farm and live on the margins of China's cities without permanent shelter or jobs? I tried to imagine what it must have been like forty years ago to live in the center of Guangzhou where over fifty-seven thousand people were packed into a single square kilometer. I asked myself how 30 million people could have died of hunger and disease from Mao Zedong's failed experiment to make a great leap forward in the economy.

It is easy to become obsessed by numbers in China. There are so many people who have to be accounted for and classified in so many ways. The government depends on numbers in setting its economic policy priorities and assessing its economic performance. The Chinese love to use numbers as guides to action. "The four modernizations" guided economic policy for decades. "The three represents" are supposed to keep the Communist Party in power. This book also depends on numbers to tell its story, but what it tries to do is get behind the numbers.

I considered how best to capture the essence of China's effort to modernize. Industry and finance were obvious choices, with state enterprises and their symbiotic relationship with state banks playing a central role. A discussion of agriculture was also essential as 69 percent of China's population still lives outside cities. China's cities have been the focal point of China's modernization efforts, and it was essential to have a separate chapter devoted to them. China's showcase project, the Three Gorges Dam, also merited a separate chapter because it epitomizes China's preference for applying engineering solutions to complex problems of development and raises difficult environmental issues. Telecommunications has its own chapter because the digitalized information superhighway is revolutionizing the way information is exchanged in China, and this sector best illustrates the contradictions that have arisen as China opens its "socialist market economy" to domestic and foreign competition. The premise of the final chapter is that although in the last 100 years China has changed more than any other nation on Earth, the values of China's leaders are still tied to the past.

U.S. secretary of state Colin Powell has said that "free markets promote free societies." He made this statement in the context of discussing how exposure to a rules-based international marketplace is changing China for the better because it forces China to see that it needs to adapt to the rest of the world. Powell's statement reflects a widely held belief that by exposure to other nations, China will become like them. Adopting the same set of economic rules will require behavior modification, but when behavioral change conflicts with fundamental values, resistance is almost inevitable. Values have to change before fundamental changes in behavior can take place. In the past 100 years China has suffered foreign occupation, the overthrow of the last imperial dynasty, a weak republican government, regional separatism, foreign invasion, civil war, and the Communist triumph, and now it is undergoing an economic revolution. Yet, China's leaders still share cultural values that characterized Qing Dynasty autocrats 100 years ago. The Communist Party's best chance for survival is to part with these beliefs.

Acknowledgments

I am deeply grateful to my wife, Kathleen. Without her encouragement, wise counsel, and guidance, I could never have produced this book.

I am very grateful to Tom Mathews, who encouraged me to reach as high as possible, and then showed me the way. My heartfelt thanks to Martha Baine, who worked so hard to format the manuscript and proofread the final version.

I am profoundly thankful for having editors like Douglas Merwin, Patricia Loo, Eileen Maass, and Angela Piliouras of M.E. Sharpe, Inc. I thank them for giving me the opportunity to publish this book and for being a constant source of good advice and support.

William Mularie gets a special vote of thanks for assisting me through the intricacies of the information superhighway and for reviewing chapter 6, "Cyberspace Gatekeeper." Many, many thanks to Jack Fritz, who reviewed chapter 4, "Cities Without Walls," and provided many insightful comments and suggestions. Many thanks also to Albert Nyberg, who reviewed chapter 3, and gave me valuable insights about "The Good Earth." Thanks also to Alain Bertaud, who allowed me to cite his unpublished manuscript, "China—Urban Land Use Issues." I owe a debt of gratitude to Han Suyin, whose elegant and insightful writing about China opened my eyes to the country and its possibilities.

My thanks to *Foreign Affairs,* which graciously gave me permission to reprint chapter 1, "Smashing the Iron Rice Bowl," portions of which appeared in the July–August 1998 issue.

The Fletcher Forum of World Affairs has allowed the reprinting of chapter four, "Cities Without Walls," parts of which appeared in the fall 1999 issue.

Thanks also to Estelle James for allowing me to cite her article, "How Can China Solve Its Old Age Security Problems? The Interaction Between Pension, SOE, and Financial Market Reform." *Journal of Pension Economics and Finance* 1 (1) 2002.

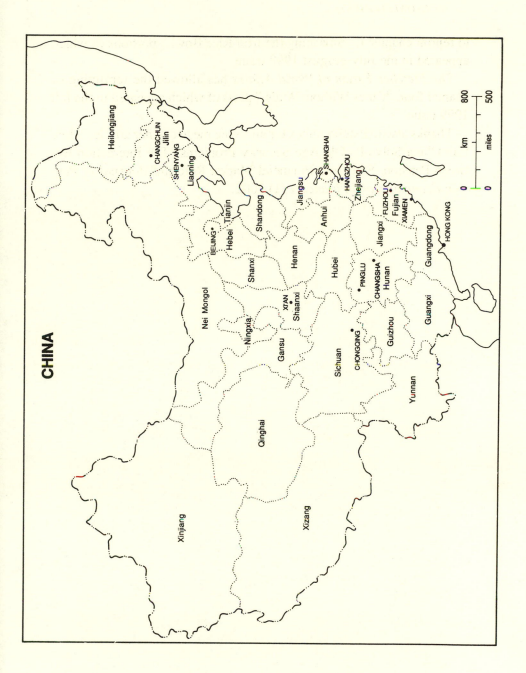

CHINA

Heilongjiang

CHANGCHUN
Jilin
SHENYANG
Liaoning
Tianjin
BEIJING
Hebei
Shandong
Jiangsu
SHANGHAI
HANGZHOU
Zhejiang
FUZHOU
Fujian
XIAMEN
Anhui
Henan
Shanxi
Hubei
Jiangxi
PINGLU
CHANGSHA
Hunan
XI'AN
Shaanxi
Nei Mongol
Ningxia
Gansu
CHONGQING
Guizhou
Guangxi
Guangdong
HONG KONG
Sichuan
Yunnan
Qinghai
Xizang
Xinjiang

km   800
miles   500

CHINA'S
ECONOMIC
CHALLENGE

Chapter One

Smashing the Iron Rice Bowl

Making steel and pollution, Chongqing. A 1958 Soviet-built electric arc furnace emits bright flames, and a cloud of glowing ashes rises into the atmosphere. This furnace is scheduled to shut down at the end of 2002.

Symbols have played an important part in Chinese life since the beginning of its recorded history. For centuries, the Chinese have performed their rituals, celebrated their holidays, and adorned their personal effects with images of good fortune, long life, and prosperity. During the Communist era, symbols and slogans continue to play an important part in providing an easily remembered litany of the Communist party's ideological themes and objectives. Rice has been China's staple food for thousands of years, and the most important symbol of the party's economic policies was an unbreakable iron rice bowl, which stood for the party's commitment to provide cradle-to-the-grave security for all its citizens. When Deng Xiaoping began in 1978 to transform China from a centrally planned and controlled economy to a more open market–oriented economy, his supporters insisted that the iron rice bowl must be smashed if China was to achieve this economic transformation.

China's dilemma is that it is afraid to smash the iron rice bowl because it fears that the social stability that has sustained its reform program will be threatened. The government is still relying on subsidies to keep redundant workers off the streets and finance its core group of large state enterprises. It is also desperately looking for buyers for thousands of smaller state enterprises, but they are hard to find and many enterprises have to be almost given away. Time is running out because the government cannot afford to continue such massive subsidies indefinitely, and World Trade Organization (WTO) membership is putting even greater competitive pressure on these enterprises.

Forging the Iron Rice Bowl

Li Hongzhang, governor general of Hebei Province and commissioner of the northern ports under the Qing empress dowager Cixi, almost single-handedly established China's first industrial enterprises. He founded a cotton mill in Shanghai in 1878 to compete with foreign imports and established armaments factories in Tianjin in the 1880s to help modernize China's army.[1] Establishing an industrial base began in earnest in the 1890s when foreign governments that had been granted concession rights in major Chinese cities began building railways, ports, and factories to produce and transport iron and steel and export goods.

Industrialization varied according to local circumstance and the vigor of foreign and local initiative. In Wuhan, for example, a mining and iron and steel complex was established in the 1890s that employed 10,000 workers. Conservative forces were opposed to development, but strong opposition all but ceased after the Boxer uprising was put down in 1900. Chinese-owned industry really began to grow only in the second decade of the twentieth century. By 1913, there were 700 Chinese factories employing 270,000 workers. By 1920, 1,700 factories employed 500,000 workers. By 1920, 7,000 foreign firms were registered in China, and Shanghai had become the center of the textile industry with 100,000 workers.[2]

For the next two decades, industry continued to be centered in zones of foreign influence like Shanghai, Wuhan, Canton (Guangdong), and Tianjin, and foreigners still owned important parts of major industries. The Japanese invasion of 1937 changed all that. The nationalist Guomindang government fled Nanjing for the comparative safety of Chongqing in Sichuan Province. Most industries stayed in place, but a great deal of machinery and equipment was carried on the backs of people or animals across hundreds of miles of rugged terrain to Chongqing or to the Communist base at Yan'an in Yunnan Province.

After the Communist regime took power in 1949, they borrowed the Soviet Union's model for industrial development, which was based on a series of five-year plans focusing on capital-intensive investments in heavy industry. Most of the resources to finance industry came from agriculture and mining, either directly through the budget or indirectly through subsidized prices for food and inputs. China's planners decided that to maintain the growth level of industry in the future, agricultural production had to be increased. There was considerable debate between those who believed that farmers should be given more economic incentives and those who believed in mass mobilization of the peasantry through appeals to self-reliance and Communist ideals. Mao Zedong was at the forefront of the latter group. He worried that as the Revolution became more and more institutionalized, individual commitment and the appeal of revolutionary ideology would be lost.

The Great Leap Forward was launched in 1957 with great fanfare, centralized allocation and planning were shelved, and new industrial production was decentralized to the commune. Based on the principle of achieving self-reliance, more than 1 million "backyard" iron and steel furnaces were built. The quality of the metal produced was atrocious and the unit cost incalculable. Agricultural production was disrupted, but no official was willing to make any report that revealed the true situation. The famine that followed in the wake of the Great Leap Forward claimed 30 million lives. Children especially suffered, as reflected in mortality data showing the median age at death, which fell from 17.6 years of age in 1957 to 9.7 years of age in 1963. One-half of the people dying in China were under ten years old, and the Great Leap Forward had turned inward upon itself and was devouring its children.[3]

By 1964, China faced a hostile Soviet Union on its northern borders, and Mao Zedong was worried about a possible invasion from Taiwan and of being drawn into the Vietnam War. He decided to establish a "Third Front" of heavy industry deep in the heart of China. Widely dispersed industrial complexes located in remote areas would provide, thought Mao, a strategic reserve production base if China had to go to war. For the next twelve years, this effort absorbed a large part of China's entire national investment. Annual expenditures for Third Front factory complexes and transportation networks in the provinces of Sichuan, Guizhou, Yunnan, Qinghai, Gansu, and Ningxia from 1964 to1975 ranged from 38 to 53 percent of China's entire national investment budget.[4]

In spite of China's great leap backward, the Maoists remained unrepentant, and Daqing, a large, isolated industrial complex at an oil field in northern Heilongjiang Province, became a symbol of the virtues of self-reliance and hard work. "Learn from Daqing!" became a rallying cry for industrial workers all over China. The entire Chinese leadership agreed that China's primary economic goal should be to carry out the "four modernizations" of agriculture, industry, science and technology, and national defense; but it was difficult to reach agreement over how to do it. In the early 1970s, a group of reformers, led by Zhou Enlai and including Deng Xiaoping, tried to promote the acquisition of foreign technology and technical assistance, including the importation of whole industrial plants. Although initially successful, these efforts were thwarted by the apostles of self-reliance, many of whom were in the ascendancy during the Cultural Revolution of 1968 to1976. It was not until after Mao's death in 1976 that Deng Xiaoping and other reformers were able to proceed with the modernization of industry by reforming existing structures and opening the country to outside influences.

Economic Reform Versus the Iron Rice Bowl

In 1978, collective farming was abandoned and replaced with the household-responsibility system, which gave farmers the right to income from the crops sold from their land, introduced informal markets, and allowed farm prices to rise over a support price. These actions appeared to signal the end of the iron rice bowl. However, similar bold initiatives were not undertaken to reform state enterprise in urban areas, where the government approached tackling the more complex and contentious problem of industrial reform with much debate and more caution, first experimenting on a small scale before undertaking major reforms—"crossing the river by feeling for each stone," as Deng Xiaoping put it.

At the Fourteenth Communist Party Congress, which took place in October 1992, China was still emerging from the shadow of the Tienanmen massacre of 1989. Deng's spokesman, party secretary-general Jiang Zemin, reiterated China's commitment to the reform begun in 1978 and launched a bold innovation by adopting market competition as official policy under the ideological banner of a socialist market economy with Chinese characteristics. Deng had put an end to the debate. The market was to be the main instrument for making investment decisions and allocating resources. In March 1993, the Chinese constitution was amended by the party's Central Committee to include the concept of a socialist market economy, and the concept of a planned economy under public ownership was deleted.[5]

In November 1993, the Third Plenary Session of the Fourteenth Party Congress issued the "Decision on Issues Concerning the Establishment of a Socialist Market Economic System," whose agenda featured the creation of a modern enterprise system by the year 2000, in which state enterprises would be incorporated under new legislation, usually called the company law. Government administration would be separated from day-to-day operations and enterprise managers given operational responsibility. It also encouraged diversified forms of enterprise ownership, especially privately owned, individually owned, and foreign-invested enterprises; but public ownership (broadly defined in the constitution to include enterprises owned by national, provincial, municipal, township, and village governments) would continue to be the dominant form of ownership in the economy.

If the socialist market economy was to be the central arch supporting the new economic edifice, the modern enterprise system embodying state enterprise reform would be its keystone. In 1994, major steps were begun to implement the modern enterprise system. Internationally based accounting practices were adopted. The company law was enacted, providing the legal basis for separating ownership control from the management of state enterprises and substituting a corporate legal and administrative structure for the centralized command and control system. The tax system was reformed to clarify the distinction between taxes due to the government and profits to be retained by the enterprise (lumped together prior to the reform). Direct subsidies through the budget were largely eliminated, but indirect subsidies continued to be made through the banking system. "Pillar industries" were identified, and key enterprises in these industries were incorporated at the provincial or city level to form the core of the modern enterprise system. Enterprises in the same line of business were encouraged to consolidate into large group companies—a Chinese version of the Japanese *keiretsu* and Korean *chaebol*—to reduce overhead costs and eliminate redundant production lines.

These reforms represented real but gradual progress, and much remained to be done. Many state enterprises remained mired in the wasteful use of resources and low productivity. They continued to depend upon outmoded and often polluting technologies and could not afford to replace obsolete equipment. They carried far too many workers on their payrolls and were obligated to provide a wide array of social services to their employees. Enterprise managers in most cases lacked sufficient autonomy and had not been given any incentives to respond to signals from the market.

Group consolidation proved to be a double-edged sword, for while it enabled enterprises with a clear view of where they wanted to go to restructure themselves to a more economical scale, others with more intractable problems came to depend on the group to solve them. Enterprise groups received tax benefits, access to loans from government banks and local governments, and central government support when needed. In return, enterprises with strong balance sheets were required to join forces with less successful ones, with the group providing an umbrella for those who could not survive on their own.

Prior to the Fifteenth Party Congress in September 1997, there was a good deal of speculation as to whether the issue of state enterprise reform was going to be dealt with more substantively. In Secretary-General Jiang's speech to the Congress, he reiterated the major economic themes of the Fourteenth Congress, now enshrined under the great banner of Deng Xiaoping theory, but emphasized that reforms of medium and large state enterprises would be accelerated to complete the transition to the modern enterprise system by the year 2000.

Jiang proposed two new initiatives, major layoffs of state workers and divestiture of state enterprise. But distinctions are critical: laid-off workers in China are not unemployed; they maintain links with their work unit and receive minimal salaries. Divestiture applies only to the smaller state enterprises, which will be merged, leased, sold off, or in some cases closed down through bankruptcy. Jiang sought to maintain a consistent ideological stance and insisted that divestiture is not privatization, it is rather a necessary part of the primary stage of social-ism, which China is still undergoing. Subsequently, the government in-dicated its willingness to divest itself of larger-scale state enterprises, and stated that more than 10,000 of China's 13,000 medium and large state enterprises would be sold off. The goal was to reduce the number of state enterprises to a core of large group companies. This was a major admission by the government that it would no longer be the dominant force in industry. By the end of 1998, the government had approved 2,472 large enterprise groups with total assets of US$806 billion, or over one-half the total assets of all state enterprises.[6] China was on its way to following the Japanese and Korean example of a mixed public-private economy in which state enterprises have the advantage of politi-cal backing, access to state funding, and high-level *guanxi* contacts (relationships based on exchange of favors).

Jiang insisted that reform was only possible because of stability: "Without stability, nothing could be achieved. . . . [We] must uphold the leadership of the party and the people's democratic dictatorship."[7] Jiang's message is clear: Only the party can guarantee stability and carry off the reform program. But can it? Selling off state enterprises and accepting that many workers will lose their jobs and benefits in the process repre-sents an enormous gamble for Jiang.[8]

At the Ninth National People's Congress, which met in March 1998, Zhu Rongji was sworn in as China's new premier. He put his reputation on the line by assuring the delegates that the accelerated reform would indeed be completed by 2000. Outgoing premier Li Peng, in his report on government, announced a giant step backward: a return to massive direct subsidies to try to reverse the unprofitability of China's key industries, beginning with its most troublesome industry, textiles. This was a first step in the government's plan to modernize China's key industries and bring into being the modern enterprise system by the year 2000.

In the textile industry in 1996, there were 4,031 state-owned firms, (including 280 enterprises that were "restructured" and merged to form 100 group companies), employing 4 million workers and operating 41.7

million spindles. Since 1993, the industry had suffered continuing deficits, amounting to US$1.28 billion in 1996 and US$963 million in 1997. The situation was so serious in 1997 that one government official stated that 40 percent of these enterprises were "on the brink of bankruptcy."[9]

It is ironic but instructive that China is the world's biggest exporter of textile products, which amount to one-fourth of all China's exports. China's textile exporters are competing in the international market in one of the most fiercely competitive industries in the world, while a much larger number of enterprises producing for the domestic market is mired in obsolescence, inefficiency, and gross overcapacity. The government's strategy was to reduce overcapacity and obsolescence by providing subsidies for enterprises that agreed to eliminate up to an aggregate of ten million spindles. For every 10,000 spindles taken out of production, enterprises received US$600,000 in a blend of cash and low-interest loans. In addition, the government as owner swapped debt for equity by buying up bad loans from these enterprises. In 1997, US$1.2 billion in debt was converted to equity in 555 state textile enterprises, and double this amount was allocated for the same purpose in 1998. About 9.06 million spindles were taken out of production, and 1.16 million workers became redundant. But some of the spindles found their way back into production again (there were twenty such instances in the first six months of 2000).[10] In 1999, the government claimed that the textile industry as a whole had finally become profitable. About 2,000 textile enterprises were declared to be of national significance, thus ensuring they would continue to receive the bulk of government subsidies.

The textile industry is one of the most forward-looking in terms of using the Internet. An industry website was established in 1997 to obtain product and marketing information, improve inventory control, and carry out on-line transactions. In 2000, the China Textile Network Company was established as a focal point for information flows from government agencies, industry associations, and each of the 2,000 national companies, with the objective of speeding up the application of information technology to the textile industry.

Debt–Equity Swaps: The Last Supper for State Banks and Their Borrowers?

In 1999, the government launched a major publicity campaign to promote debt–equity swaps as the solution to the problem of eliminating the debt burden of state enterprises as well as the nonperforming loans made by state banks to those same enterprises. As the discussion above indicates, there was nothing new in this approach except that this time the government seized on it as the way to reach its goal of resolving the difficulties of large state enterprises and establishing the modern enterprise system by 2000. In 1999, the government established four asset-management corporations (AMCs), each with an initial capital of RMB 132.5 billion, to purchase nonperforming loans from the four state banks that dominate commercial banking. In return, the banks received cash or bonds issued by the AMCs while the enterprises reduced their liabilities and issued a like amount of shares to them. In addition, The People's Bank of China agreed to provide five- to ten-year interest-free loans to the AMCs. By the end of 2000, all four AMCs had reduced the nonperforming debt of state enterprises by US$168 billion.[11]

Cleaning up financial statements is only the beginning of the process, yet the role of the AMCs has not been well defined. The AMCs have become major enterprise shareholders, but it is unclear what their level of responsibility and involvement is in the affairs of the enterprise. Since AMC managers are told by the government what enterprises they are to assist and as most are led by government bureaucrats who have little experience in finance or understanding of how to run a manufacturing plant, their role seems to be limited to channeling funds.

No quid pro quo is being required of either the banks or the enterprises. There is no linkage between receiving a swap and successful bank or enterprise restructuring. The swap is seen by the government as a means of transforming enterprises from unprofitable to profitable and thus establishing the enterprise's financial viability (however short-lived) and providing access to additional sources of financing. Turning financial statements from red to black gives enterprises a year, perhaps two, to try to deal with the more fundamental problem of survival in a rapidly changing and highly competitive market.

One expert takes the view that the debt–equity swap program provides an extraordinary window into the Chinese debate over the nature of markets and the policy-making process. The Chinese view markets as providing incentives for enterprises to behave more profitably and efficiently. Their vision is one of all firms' responding positively to profit incentives and all being drawn upward like ships on a rising tide. What is lacking is an understanding of the competitive nature of markets and that competition results in winners and losers. In 1984, when the government decided to shift from financing state enterprises through direct subsidies to bank loans, it expected that if the enterprises had to pay interest to obtain financing, they would have to improve performance. The government did not understand, however, that attaching a price to capital and requiring that the capital be repaid would separate state enterprises into those that could pay the price and those that could not—and that this was really the market at work. The government is still laboring under this misapprehension and fails to grasp that the inability to repay debt is not simply because the debt is too large but because too often it is symptomatic of more fundamental problems such as the enterprise's inabililty to realize a satisfactory return on invested capital.[12] This is why, when something happens to an enterprise, the government believes it is the system—not the enterprise—that is at fault and therefore the government must intervene to fix the system.

For debt–equity swaps, the government uses a top down approach in which the State Economic and Trade Commission makes the initial selection from among top performers that have demonstrated the potential to stand on their own feet. Final approval is provided by the State Council, China's highest governing body (roughly equivalent to the U.S. cabinet). It is the government, not the enterprise, that is the agent of change. The government will often appoint new management or even a new board of directors and require the enterprise to go through a new round of cost-cutting and staff downsizing. New general managers are usually appointed from the bureaucracy and are provided with operational targets and expected to meet them. They have little room for independent judgment because the manager's career depends on carrying out the government's wishes.

Dai Xianglong, governor of the People's Bank of China, said he told the banks that "the debt–equity swap is the last supper for them. . . . There will be no midnight snack and no breakfast for tomorrow."[13] The banks are getting away with only a stern admonition that this is their last bailout. Herein lies the weakness of the program: The banks lose the incentive to recover bad debts, and enterprises no longer make an effort to repay them. The program can be successful in the long term only if the enterprise becomes the agent of change. The debt–equity swap should become a reward for individual state enterprises that assume responsibility for achieving a successful outcome as demonstrated in an approved feasibility and restructuring plan containing a timetable and specific monitorable steps that it will take to reach this goal.

In January 2001, the government declared victory and claimed that

China has basically attained its goal of introducing a modern enterprise system and bringing the majority of deficit-ridden large- and medium-sized state enterprises back into the black within three years. Seventy percent of the country's 6,599 large and medium state enterprises that were in the red three years earlier reported profits. The government also noted that during this time, 2,000 other medium and large state enterprises had slipped into the red, with special mention of the problems of coal mines and enterprises formerly run by the military.[14] This result was possible only because of the debt forgiveness program, and some outside observers believe it also involved a massive massaging of enterprise financial figures.[15] The government subsequently admitted that only 30 percent of the improved performance of state enterprises was the result of increased efficiency.[16]

State Enterprises Are Different

In 1995, there were 8 million industrial enterprises in China, about 6 million of which were referred to as family or individually owned because they had fewer than eight employees. There were also fewer than 50,000 enterprises classified as "other," including enterprises called private businesses if they employed more than eight, and joint ventures between Chinese and foreign enterprises. The rest were publicly owned as defined by the constitution but with important differences. Only about one hundred eighteen thousand were owned by government at the national, provincial, and municipal level and were classified as state-owned enterprises. Within this group were roughly thirteen thousand medium and large state enterprises that effectively accounted for most of the output of this category.

The rest of the publicly owned enterprises (approximately one million nine hundred thousand) were owned by townships and villages and were classified as collectively owned enterprises. They were largely unregulated, had little access to the banking system, and relied on local savings and entrepreneurial skills. Yet, the output share of the collectives grew rapidly and, according to the government, accounted for 40 percent of total industrial output in 1994, while the share of the state-owned had declined to just 34 percent of output.[17]

Nevertheless, state-owned enterprises dominated most major mining and manufacturing sectors such as coal, ferrous and nonferrous metals, chemicals, textiles, pharmaceuticals, machine tools, capital goods, fertilizers, motor vehicles, and defense. But output was not the whole story. In 1994, state enterprises still accounted for 72 percent of fixed industrial assets, 70 percent of industrial employment and bank credit, and 65 percent of industrial income tax revenues.[18]

The fact that state enterprises tied up over two-thirds of industrial assets while contributing about one-third of output made for very wasteful use of resources. Many state enterprises (especially those in traditional heavy industries) were dependent upon technology that was thirty, forty, or even fifty years old. Their plants were obsolete, inefficient, and highly polluting. They survived by receiving fiscal subsidies and subsidized credit both through the financial system and from local governments. Worker productivity was low, stagnant, or growing slowly. Many plants had not been built to economic scale, and without fundamental restructuring could not become efficient. Investment had been heavily skewed to favor heavy industry. Overcapacity as reflected in underutilization of existing productive capacity had become a grave problem, and large inventories were piling up in many enterprises. A government industrial census in 1996 revealed that almost one-half of the 900 major industrial products surveyed came from factories that were operating on average at less than 60 percent of their installed capacity.[19]

Collective, individual, family, private, and joint-venture enterprises located in townships and villages were lumped together as "township and village enterprises." They were held up by some as an example for state enterprises to follow as they were largely unregulated and grew so fast during the first two decades of reform that they were considered to embody the virtues of capitalism. Between 1978 and 1996, township and village enterprises created more than five million new jobs every year.[20] Much of the initial dynamism from this group came from collective enterprises that were founded by groups of entrepreneurs in rural areas who usually invited the local government to share control rights. In return, they gained access to land and capital, transport and infrastructure services, and government protection of property rights. But sharing of ownership rights blurred responsibilities and weakened management controls, and recently their dynamism has waned. They generated 17 million new jobs in 1993 but only 1.4 million in 1994 and 1995, while private and individually owned enterprises created 6.6 million new jobs.[21] In 1997, township and village enterprises as a group, *lost* 5 million jobs. Increasing competition is putting as much pressure on these enterprises as it is on state enterprises, but unlike the latter, most do not have access to credit from state banks, and with profit margins drying up, township and village enterprise bank borrowing fell from 8 percent of total bank borrowing in the early 1990s to just 3 percent in the late 1990s.[22]

Others see the uncontrolled growth of township and village enterprises as a major source of labor exploitation, as workers at these enterprises receive no benefits, and working conditions often are as bad and wages as low as the seemingly endless flow of jobless rural migrants looking for work at any price will bear.[23] In Shenzhen on the mainland across from Hong Kong, for example, some workers receive as little as the equivalent of 60 U.S. cents a day. Many of these unregulated enterprises pose a serious threat to their workers and the environment. In Wenzhou in Zhejiang Province, a teenage girl works eighteen hours every day in a shoe factory with no ventilation to remove the toxic stench of chemical dyes and glues. In Shenzhen, eighty-one workers died in a toy factory fire because all windows and exits had been sealed to prevent theft.

The Rise of the Private Sector

Private enterprise ownership has risen remarkably in recent years, and employment in private enterprises has increased from 26.5 million in 1985 (38 percent of total township and village enterprise employment) to 75.6 million in 1996 (56 percent of total township and village enterprise employment).[24] The International Finance Corporation, the World Bank's private investment subsidiary, has estimated that the private sector (excluding agriculture) accounted for 27 percent of China's gross domestic product (GDP) in 1998.[25] The real contribution of the private sector is undoubtedly even more significant, because many thousands of private enterprises are registered as collectives to gain the support of local governments, get better access to credit, and avoid the prejudices against private ownership that still exist throughout China.

In 1999, private ownership was legitimized in an amendment to China's constitution that recognized that private enterprises are "an important part of the socialist market economy." The government finally recognized that the private sector had become an important source of jobs for unemployed workers and fiscal revenue for the state. The private sector has also become important to the success of the government's strategy of divesting itself of smaller state enterprises. In recent years, in Jiangsu Province alone, 30,000 township and village enterprises were auctioned to private investors.[26]

The Heavy Burden of Social Welfare

A state enterprise was not just a workplace. It was a community that tried to provide its workers and their families with the care and services they needed to lead productive and healthy lives. State enterprises employed about 76 million workers by the end of 1993, of which 20 percent—15 million—were officially estimated by the government to be redundant. As direct subsidies to enterprises were reduced (from 6 percent of gross domestic product in 1990 to 4 percent in 1994), enterprises had to depend more on their own resources, which were often insufficient to finance these costs. The problem was especially serious for traditional industries with large aging-worker populations. These enterprises tended to be unprofitable, so the problem was compounded. These enterprises could no longer afford to pay pension, housing, medical, child care, education, food, recreation, and transportation expenses for workers and their families. Their employees found their benefits reduced and they were left with the option of paying the difference themselves or foregoing vital services.

State enterprises made determined efforts to spin off some of their welfare functions as separate service enterprises and have sold off most housing units to workers. But even at discounted prices, the cost is beyond the capacity of most workers to finance without a mortgage lending system in place (see chapter 4). Enterprises are also working with local governments to place schools and clinics under local administration. National medical insurance is another major government priority, but in 1996 only 7 percent of workers and their families were covered by medical insurance.

The lucky ones are those who, under an arrangement known as one family, two systems, are able to depend upon housing, health, and other benefits provided by other family members who work as government civil servants or with enterprises capable of funding these expenditures. The unlucky ones are like a twenty-seven-year-old woman from Hainan Province who went to Beijing to have a difficult tumor removed after her own hospital was unable to do so. In Beijing, she was requested to make a RMB 10,000 deposit (about $1,200), but she had only RMB 800. The hospital refused to admit her, and she will probably die.

With longer life expectancies and a one-child-per-family policy, China's population is aging rapidly, and pension obligations are growing commensurately. In 1990, 9 percent of China's population was over the age of 65, and by 2030, 22 percent of Chinese are expected to be over 65.[27] Pension payments to retired workers come out of an enterprise's cash flow, and many state enterprises making the difficult transition to market-oriented operations are in arrears in their pension payments. In just the first four months of 2000, state enterprise pension arrears amounted to US$175 million.[28] Cities that are centers of declining traditional industries are being hard hit, because they not only have many pensioners but a more rapidly aging workforce.

In the mid-1980s, the government began to shift the responsibility for managing pension funds from state enterprises to county, municipal, and prefecture governments. This pooling of pensions was intended to break the link between individual worker and enterprise, spread the risk, and ensure that payments would be made to pensioners at state enterprises with a heavy pension load. Pooling requires each participating work unit to contribute according to its wage bill, and shortfalls arising from enterprises whose contributions were exceeded by their pension obligations were expected to be made up from the surplus arising from other enterprise contributions. Pooling has not worked because enterprises with a higher proportion of retirees were often required to contribute more—and could not—while enterprises with few pensioners were unwilling to make the contributions asked of them. This situation is exacerbated by high payroll deduction rates, generally exceeding 20 percent, which further discourages enterprises from contributing to the pool. All of which has led to widespread evasion at the local level, followed by weak enforcement by pension authorities. The system also suffered from mismanagement of funds by local government officials and limited coverage of nonstate enterprises. Pay-as-you-go funding coupled with contribution evasion and exemptions resulted in wide disparities between costs and the funding necessary to create a viable system. Because pension funds had to be 80 percent invested in government bonds and 20 percent in bank deposits, and the rates of return on these investments were below the rate of inflation and the growth rate of wages, the pension system could not become financially sustainable over the long term. As a result, unfunded pensions have reached crisis proportions, and are a major cause of worker unrest.

Pension reform is critical to maintaining social stability and moving the reform process forward, and the government is attempting to put together a national social insurance system that would unify existing pension systems. Yet the task is so massive and complex that the government is having great difficulty in moving ahead. The basis for the current reform was laid in 1997, when the state council issued its decree, "Unification of the Basic Pension Insurance for Enterprise Workers." The main objectives of the reforms are to reduce the necessity for sharp increases in pension contribution rates, prevent reduction in pension benefits, complete pooling arrangements, separate pension administration from individual work units, and extend coverage to non-state enterprises. The new system is based on "three pillars." The first pillar provides a basic benefit equal to 0.6 percent per year of the average wage of covered service. On this basis, a worker with 40 years of service would receive a basic pension that replaced 24 percent of his or her wages. This would be financed by enterprise contributions of 9 percent of the wage bill. The second pillar provides mandatory individual accounts for workers that would be fully funded equally by workers and enterprises, with a combined contribution of 8 percent, resulting in a wage replacement rate of about 35 percent. Thus pillars 1 and 2 would provide an aggregate pension of about 60 percent of the worker's wage for a worker with 40 years of service.[29] The third pillar consists of an optional commercial, private, and group life insurance scheme. In 1998, the government combined labor and social security functions into a single Ministry of Labor and Social Security, in an attempt to strengthen the institutional basis for carrying out the reform.

Making the transition from a pay-as-you-go system to a fully funded one has so far not been successful. Establishing the second pillar means that a significant portion of pension contributions can no longer be used to meet current pension expenditures, but are to be invested. This creates a financial gap that has to be filled, but most local governments need all their contributions just to meet current expenditures. Current expenditures are very high because of the absence of specific provisions to cover the cost of pension liabilities that existed prior to the new reforms. Since 1997, pension deficits have continued to grow, and on a national basis, contributions are about one-half of what they should be. In 1998 and 1999, both central and local governments' pension systems experienced cash flow deficits, and in 1997–1999, the Ministry of Finance transferred US$4 billion to help twenty-five municipal governments meet their pension obligations.[30] In desperation, local governments have turned to the sale or leasing of state assets to raise the necessary funds. Without dramatic improvement, however, pension deficits and claims on the central government are likely to grow larger, and could eventually lead to a collapse of the new pension system.

Some experts believe that the central government should step in and assume responsibility for payment of pre-1997 pension system liabilities. This would significantly reduce payroll deductions and therefore reduce evasion of contributions. It would also provide an incentive to nonstate enterprises to join the pension system, thus helping broaden the system's coverage.[31]

The simplest way for the central government to make payments to persons already retired and to capitalize the individual accounts of persons employed under the old system who are still working would be to issue state bonds with the same maturities as these liabilities. However, this would mean that responsibility for paying pensions remains a government liability, which would have to be honored out of future taxes or borrowing. Alternatively, the proceeds from the sale of state assets such as real estate leases or state enterprise shares could also be used for this purpose. In 2001, the government announced that 10 percent of the proceeds of future initial public stock offerings by state enterprises will be contributed to a new National Social Security Fund. In return, the enterprise is allowed to sell a portion of its state shares to private investors, However, state enterprise share prices are extremely high, because they are not traded and are driven by shareholder demand rather than underlying values of the equities involved. In fact, state enterprises that have sold shares under this scheme have seen their share prices decline, leading to considerable concern about the effect of further sales on the market as a whole. China's securities markets are simply too risky for pension fund investors, because they are undeveloped and not yet properly regulated.

The government finds itself in an extremely difficult position and time is running out. It is planning to establish a national lottery and use the proceeds to finance the pension system, to advance the retirement age by five years, and index pensions to consumer prices rather than wages. These actions will all help, but they will not be enough. There appears to be no alternative but for the government to accept responsibility for payment of pre-1997 pension liabilities.

Who Is in Charge?

In the late 1950s, decision making in state enterprises was regulated by the factory director responsibility system under party committee leadership, in which real power to manage the enterprise was exercised by the party secretary. In 1984, the director responsibility system was adopted, and management responsibility was shifted to the enterprise director, while the party secretary was given a supervisory role and was supposed to make sure the enterprise adhered to the party line. Nevertheless, since most directors are party members, they are subject to party discipline administered by the party secretary. This awkward situation is somewhat mitigated by the fact that under the reform, their respective roles have become more complementary, with the role of the party secretary focusing on political actions that will ensure that the enterprise follows through in carrying out the reform program. An arrangement that is becoming more and more common is for one individual to hold both positions, but this subverts the government's goal of separating the party from operational responsibility.

The State Council is the ultimate owner of state enterprises. The National Bureau of State Owned Property was created to implement State Council directives, and it, in turn, is at the top of a hierarchical structure comprising state asset supervisory committees, state asset management bureaus, and state asset operating companies, each acting out particular roles as representatives of the state. In parallel with this structure are very large group companies under the central government, which manage state assets directly. Although this structure replaced the national ministries and local line bureaus, many of the same people who were in the ministries and line bureaus are now found in asset-management institutions.

According to the World Bank, this multitiered network is burdened by conflicts of interest because lines of authority are unclear and asset-management organizations act not only as owner of the assets but retain the role of administrator of the enterprises.[32] It is difficult to see that any fundamental change in function has really taken place. In addition, the central government retains a virtual veto power over the investments of these enterprises under its national planning function, in which it determines whether such investments are consistent with the objectives of the current five-year plan. As long as state enterprises are subject to the national five-year planning cycle, they will not be free to plan their own futures.

On the Horns of an Environmental Dilemma

State enterprises are caught on the horns of an environmental dilemma. They strive to attain ever higher production, which by law must be environmentally sustainable. Yet in reaching this goal they are dependent on polluting fuels and production equipment that emits vast amounts of dust and gases, liquid effluents, and toxic wastes. A big part of the problem is that industrial enterprises are dependent on coal as an energy source. Government statistics indicate that in 1995, use of industrial coal accounted for 35 percent of all coal burned in China, 39 percent of all sulfur dioxide emissions, 37 percent of particles emitted into the atmosphere, and 28 percent of total carbon dioxide emissions (equal to 30 percent of total greenhouse gas emissions from energy consumption in China). The efficiency rate of Chinese industrial boilers is 60 to 65 percent, compared with 80 to 90 percent in the West, and coal quality measured by ash and sulfur contents varies greatly.[33]

One reason pollution is such a big problem in China is that factories were often built right in the middle of a city or town where infrastructure was readily available, and workers' housing was built close to the factory. As the cities expanded, even plants outside urban areas were engulfed by new housing developments. In the city of Changzhou in Jiangsu Province, a chemical plant is just twenty-five meters from an elementary school, and a factory nearby has been built right up against a hospital.

Similar situations exist in every Chinese city, and the health of millions of their residents has been affected. The best solution would be to eliminate the proximity to population of polluting enterprises such as cement and chemical plants and pulp, paper, and steel mills, by relocating them outside of residential areas on land set aside as industrial parks. However, China's present rapid urbanization is gobbling up agricultural land at the rate of 1.5 percent per year of China's total agricultural land, and the government has instituted a freeze on the use of agricultural land for nonagricultural purposes.

At the national level there is complete agreement that pollution must be controlled, and all the necessary legislation and bureaucratic infrastructure is in place. Yet, at the provincial, city, township, and village levels, where most enterprise ownership is really exercised, the conflict of interest between the state as owner of polluting enterprises and the state as regulator of pollution has often been decided in favor of the enterprise, as reflected in lack of enforcement. Monitoring compliance of state enterprises with environmental protection regulations is the responsibility of local environmental protection bureaus, but these entities have neither the resources nor the clout to pursue and punish polluters adequately. Fines paid are usually a negotiated portion of the fine assessed, and enterprises regard them as part of the cost of doing business. This was the situation until several years ago, when the central government began to take a stronger hand in dealing with pollution. Beginning in 1998, the central government began crafting a policy that is truly revolutionary in scope—to establish a national program to replace coal with much cleaner energy sources, such as natural gas, liquefied petroleum gas, and fuel oil (see chapter 4).

Accountability Is a Foreign Concept

China adopted internationally accepted accounting standards in 1993, and state enterprises were given until 1995 to integrate these into their own accounting practices. Yet, the concept of accountability remains foreign to most Chinese. The new standards for preparation of accounting information give as much priority to meeting the requirements of government macroeconomic control as to those of enterprise management and interested third parties. Consequently, preparation of financial statements continues to be viewed as a necessary reporting exercise to a higher authority, and data are often manipulated to paint a financial picture that best serves the interest of the enterprise.

As long as preparation of financial statements is seen as a reporting function rather than a diagnostic tool for discerning the financial health of the enterprise, determining the financial viability of an enterprise will not be possible. While state enterprises remain a part of a highly structured institutionalized hierarchy, it is unlikely that this reporting culture will change.

Chinese financial statements reflect these difficulties. Establishing asset values is highly complicated, as many enterprises have revalued their assets one or more times, and overvaluation of assets is compounded by the use of depreciation systems that give much longer life to assets than is generally acceptable in the West. Assets are often classified on a balance sheet into categories that make little sense to a Western accountant, so identification of individual assets becomes very difficult. This makes tracking asset transfers a problem, as they may be kept on one enterprise's balance sheet even after transfer to another entity.

Trying to establish the real costs of production is often even more difficult than valuing assets. Accounting for production costs is fundamental to determining the factor productivity of an enterprise at each stage of production and for determining the final unit costs of production for each product. However, costs are not assigned to categories that might enable such calculations to be made (the problem of classification once again), and costs are usually determined according to standard cost formulas rather than actual market prices, making it extremely difficult to arrive at a useful judgment as to whether assets have been used productively.

Poor Profitability Is Just the Tip of the Iceberg

China's premier, Zhu Rongji, stated publicly in 1997 that 40 percent of state enterprises were not profitable. The World Bank believed that 50 percent was more realistic,[34] and other estimates were even higher (60 percent). In spite of the government's protestation that this problem now has been solved for most state enterprises, it is an intractable one. Enterprise profitability is often overstated because discussions about profitability refer to net profit (or loss) after deducting enterprise costs, without taking into consideration taxes due to the government or interest and principal payments due to lenders. Many enterprises are in arrears in their tax payments, and overdue debt is often simply rolled over (the maturity date is extended again and again in lieu of payment) because many state enterprises cannot generate sufficient revenue to meet payments that have accumulated over time. Inter-enterprise debts are a further problem. Enterprises are caught in a cycle of triangular debt in which the enterprise receives at best partial payment from a customer and is therefore able to pay only a portion of its own suppliers. The triangular debt relationship is separate from the relation between an enterprise and its banks. It involves an enterprise, its suppliers, and its customers. Many state enterprises are caught in the triangular debt trap, which was estimated to have amounted to about US$24 billion in 1994.[35] Not only enterprises suffered. Between 1978 and 1992, fiscal revenues declined from 31.2 percent of GDP to 9.5 percent.[36] Almost two-thirds of this decline was directly attributable to lower tax receipts from state enterprises with declining profits.[37]

Reform and Corruption Go Hand in Hand

Corruption in China is woven into the social fabric of society. What is causing the government most concern now is that corruption has been spreading at an alarming rate. Two factors explain this. Decentralization of economic decision making from the national to local governments in the late 1970s and early 1980s presented local officials with opportunities for personal gain. Lack of clarity about who actually represents the government as asset owner and who is accountable for asset use and disposition, provided incentives for opportunistic behavior such as asset removal that has become a major concern of the government. This involves the stripping of state assets through "spontaneous privatization" by managers and employees of state enterprises, often aided and abetted by local government officials. In Sichuan Province and Shanghai municipality, many of the new limited liability companies are in the financial sector; this fact suggests the widespread creation of shell companies to drain off assets.[38] Without a clear concept of property rights to define ownership, increasing autonomy simply allows economic actors to pursue their own ends on a grander scale and with less risk of getting caught. The government itself has estimated the annual cost to the nation at RMB 50 billion over the past fifteen years. The formation of large company groups as holding companies, the increasing popularity of mergers, and the rapid growth of joint ventures with foreign firms has led to massive movements of assets, and opportunities for fraud arise whenever assets are transferred. Corruption is therefore not so much a new phenomenon as one that has shifted down the hierarchy, and the tradition of *guanxi* to obtain necessary approvals and other favors has simply been adapted to the new economic relationships.[39] In fact, the opening up of markets has actually encouraged *guanxi* as a way of minimizing market risk.

Corruption has also been fostered by China's fiscal crisis. Declining revenue from state enterprises had an enormous impact on government budgets clear down the bureaucratic hierarchy. With insufficient tax revenues to finance their activities, governments from the village level to Beijing resorted to creating new taxes and demanding kickbacks when payment was not forthcoming. The government says it is getting corrupt behavior under control, but a recent massive corruption scandal in Hainan Island indicates the opposite. One individual was able to smuggle goods worth US$3 billion over four years with impunity because he bought off everyone who could have stopped him. This makes a lie of the government's boast that the legal system plus the party's controls are sufficient to deal with the problem.[40] If *everyone* can be bought off, then no system is going to work.

Why Reform Is Failing to Change Economic Behavior

Explanations as to why Chinese reforms are failing are usually couched in terms of orthodox economic theories applied to other economies in transition. The debate is often polarized between those who believe in the Russian–East European massive one-time privatization and those who support China's gradualism as an expression of China's unique circumstances. However, the limited success of gradualism after twenty years has put the latter group on the defensive. Yet, the proponents of one-time reform are also on the defensive. Privatized firms in Russia, Poland, and Czechoslovakia are behaving much as they did under the old system of state socialist ownership. Why is it that state firms in transitional systems respond so poorly to the new incentive structures created by free markets? One view is that there is too much emphasis on transferring property rights (the rationale behind mass privatizations), which either do not exist, are unclear, or are unenforceable in transitional economies.[41] Economic behavior can be changed only in a system in which economic rights and obligations are defined and recourse is available against those who are accountable but fail to observe such rights and obligations. Chinese reforms are only beginning to address this issue.

A study of large steel-producing Chinese state enterprises indicates that when rights and responsibilities are unclear, economic behavior must be constrained to avoid massive abuses of the system. In the case of big steel, regardless of whether the command or reform system was in place, the most serious excesses occurred when there were no financial constraints to prevent collusion among government officials, enterprise managers, and bankers in providing virtually unlimited credit for nonproductive state enterprise investment. Because there was no accountability, local officials sought to extract as much tax revenue as possible, bankers granted loan after loan, and enterprise managers fudged profitability data to keep the cycle going. Reform in the context of an economy in transition must therefore be understood "not as a granting of rights but as a varying of constraints for economic actors."[42]

However, the problem extends beyond property rights and constraints. Twenty-three years of reform have greatly increased personal freedom but have done little to make individuals responsible for their actions. Although hundreds of national laws and local regulations governing economic activity have been put in place, important loopholes exist, and enforcement has been sporadic and inconsistent. Also, ensuring the rights of individuals while holding them responsible for their actions requires much more than a new legal structure because in China it goes against traditional behavior patterns. Throughout China's history, individual rights have been subordinated to the collective rights of society as represented by the Confucian state or more recently by the Communist Party. Such ingrained behavior is not easily changed. Like the emperors who preceded them, the leaders of the Chinese Communist Party consider the party above the law and view the legal system as an instrument of control rather than as guarantor of individual rights and obligations. As a start to genuine reform, the rule of law must be made supreme, and the party must be subordinated to it.

State Enterprises Are on the Block

Fierce competition due to declining demand, huge unsold inventories, and low-priced imports has forced state industrial enterprises to respond by reducing output, lowering prices, laying off workers, eliminating layers of administrative and managerial staff, linking wages and bonuses to output, reducing per unit production costs, and shifting to more value-added production lines. For most, cost-cutting has become as important an objective as maximizing profits. In short, they are acting like their Western counterparts. However, state enterprises are ill equipped to win this competition. They need to modernize by importing new technologies, but they lack capital, and their high levels of debt severely hinder their ability to borrow more. They cannot shed excess workers because worker mobility is limited by their ties to enterprise-specific welfare benefits, and many excess workers are marginally skilled, so their reemployment prospects are dim. The burden of social expenditures is so heavy for many state enterprises that they have no surplus left for investment purposes. The government is establishing a national welfare system to make social benefits portable. But for a national system to work, local governments, enterprises, and workers must all contribute, so there is no solution in sight for chronic loss-making enterprises, for neither the enterprises nor their workers will be able to pay for the new system and they will continue to need government subsidies.

Ironically, state enterprises find it is not so easy to compete in other markets because barriers to the free movement of goods still exist. Provincial and even municipal boundaries are a barrier because local politicians try to protect enterprises in their own jurisdictions from outside competition. Also, existing supplier–enterprise–client relationships are often based on political considerations (e.g., they were under the same ministry, are located in the same city or province), and such ties are cemented by intercompany liabilities. These ties still bind, making it difficult for state enterprises to enter into new business relationships. The physical transport of goods can be difficult because an intercity road system does not yet exist and because of barriers to inter-provincial commerce (see chapter 4). Cities in the interior are especially isolated unless they are located on a railroad.

The government established a nationwide network of thirty-six property rights transactions centers to facilitate mergers and acquisitions both among state enterprises and between state and other enterprises. It has also promoted the so-called administrative merger in which a profitable enterprise absorbs a money loser. The government encourages this form of merger with moratoriums on interest payments due from the unprofitable partner and conversion of inter-enterprise debts into equity share capital. Nevertheless, this type of merger has generated a lot of opposition from viable enterprises, but the merger often is completed at the insistence of the government (which is, after all, owner of both).

With China's accession to the WTO, the merger process has taken on a new urgency. The government would like the best performers to absorb more of the weaker enterprises before they are faced with foreign competition that could spell their demise. The government has targeted the airline, automobile, and electric power industries. China has thirty-nine airlines, most of which are unprofitable. Last year, the government established controls over ticket prices to prevent the airlines from undercutting each other and driving some out of business. It wants the three largest and strongest carriers to absorb other carriers, but they are reluctant to accept the weakest ones. There are about ninety automobile and truck manufacturers, although the ten largest producers dominate the industry. The government would like to reduce the number of manufacturers to ten, which effectively means the ten majors will absorb everybody else. In the electric power industry there are hundreds of enterprises, and the government wants to reduce the number to two dozen.[43] Whether the government will ultimately be successful is hard to say, but the process will take years. Because the government owns these enterprises, forced marriages cannot be avoided. Nevertheless, negotiations are often protracted, especially when a merger means taking on a sizable debt burden or many redundant workers. Most recently, to make the merger more appealing, the government has offered to swap the debt of both prospective partners for equity.

Although a bankruptcy law became effective in 1988 and the government officially supports liquidation of perennial money-losing enterprises, bankruptcy is avoided until it becomes a last resort. Fewer than two-tenths of 1 percent of the total number of state enterprises initiated bankruptcy proceedings between 1993 and 1995 (almost all were small enterprises whose aggregate impact is limited). In 1997, the number of state enterprises declaring bankruptcy rose to just six-tenths of 1 percent of the total state enterprises.[44]

Foreign Investors Are Having Their Problems Too

Many foreign investors are having almost as many difficulties as the state enterprises in navigating the swift and unpredictable currents of China's socialist market economy. Major problems experienced include incompetent or corrupt joint-venture partners, product copying and counterfeiting, demand for kickbacks, lack of legal structure regarding foreign investment, weakness in enforcing contract and property rights legislation, and an ineffective court system for conflict resolution. In the telecommunications sector (see chapter 6) lack of clear limits on the kinds of activities that could receive foreign financing caused the government to abrogate forty-five foreign joint ventures in which China Unicom was involved. In defense of the government, the foreign partners showed little hesitation in investing in an activity in which it was not clear that foreign participation was legal and demonstrated naïveté in assuming that if there were a problem it would be resolved by their local partner through *guanxi* connections.

Although the Chinese are criticized for not understanding how markets function, many foreign firms have also shown a marked lack of acumen in assessing market potential and risks in China. In the mid-1990s, economic prosperity and rising incomes led to very rapid increases in beer consumption. In 1981, beer production totaled one billion liters. By 1994, newly affluent Chinese were buying beer in increasing numbers, production soared to 13 billion liters, and China overtook Germany as second to the United States in beer consumption.[45] Many foreign brewers rushed to get a foothold in this market. There are over five hundred beer producers in China selling mostly in local and regional markets. Premium beer, which was the niche sought by foreign producers, represented only 5 percent of the total market. Soon there were far too many producers competing for this small share of the market. Overproduction led to price wars, declining sales, and plummeting profits. Losses mounted, and world-renowned names like Fosters, Bass, and Carlsberg beat a hasty retreat. China's largest brewer, Tsingtao Beer, was right behind, buying up plant after plant at fire-sale prices. In 1999 alone, Tsingtao acquired fifteen new breweries, increasing its output capacity by 90 percent.[46] Does Tsingtao know something that nobody else does? The rush to build cars in China also fell victim to grave miscalculations about market potential. Both the French producer Peugeot and Daimler-Chrysler have pulled out of their Chinese ventures.

One expert estimates that only one-third of the 354,000 companies with foreign investment in China are turning a profit. Large multinationals, which have the most money and influence, do somewhat better. A 1999 American Chamber of Commerce in China survey revealed that while 58 percent of its members had lower profit margins in China than elsewhere, 88 percent had plans to expand.[47] This indicates that most U.S. companies are in China for the long haul. Perhaps their global reach is such that losses in China are more than compensated for by profits elsewhere, and their bottom line is not affected.

China views foreign investors with mixed feelings. After all, China was under the domination of foreign powers from 1840 to 1945. Regarding foreign investment, the argument usually boils down to asking why support foreigners instead of helping our own domestic producers. Coca-Cola Company is such a big presence in China that it is a magnet for antiforeign sentiment. In response, the company commissioned a joint study by Peking University, Tsinghua University, and the University of North Carolina to determine the multiplier effect of Coca-Cola's investment. The study determined that in employment terms, its presence resulted in the direct hiring of 14,000 employees and the creation of 414,000 jobs outside the company.[48]

State Enterprises Get Preferential Access to Financing

The government has officially stated that one-fifth of the total of all state-owned specialized bank portfolios are made up of overdue loans to state enterprises. According to the World Bank, the capital of these banks is therefore already negative.[49] Nevertheless, the government continues to provide financing to state enterprises through the four state-owned specialized commercial banks. State enterprises are also the major beneficiaries of China's capital markets. The amount of funds that can be raised on Chinese equity markets is established by the government for each of China's mainland stock exchanges in Shanghai and Shenzhen.

These exchanges are characterized by doubtful valuations and great volatility in share price. Enterprise listing is a government monopoly, enforcement of securities regulations is being strengthened but is still weak, the role of underwriting is limited, and there is minimal disclosure of information about the enterprise issuing shares or bonds. Bureaucrats-turned-entrepreneurs have appropriated large amounts of shares. These markets are still in a formative stage and are driven by investor demand looking for a higher return rather than long-term appreciation of equities. Prices are sky high, and the average price-to-earnings ration is 60:1. At the end of 1994, only 170 companies were listed on the Shanghai Stock Exchange and 110 on the Shenzhen Stock Exchange. In 1995, the government began a major effort to channel individual savings into financing state-owned enterprises, and in the latter half of the 1990s, it listed many of its larger core enterprises. By the year 2000, 1,133 enterprises—90 percent state owned—had been listed on both exchanges, with a total capitalization of US$590 billion—the second largest in Asia—and the participation of 60 million investors. In addition, more than 100 mainland companies were registered on the Hong Kong exchange.

A significant shift in attitude is taking place within the government, which involves opening up capital markets to private investment and bringing in institutional investors. The quota system favoring state enterprises is being phased out, and foreign joint ventures and Chinese private companies have been given the opportunity of becoming listed. At the same time, the government is beginning to crack down on market manipulation and insider trading, and one firm has been delisted. The government is also allowing selected state enterprises to sell a limited portion of their government-owned shares to private investors. Since government shares are not traded, their valuation is artificial, and share prices have dropped for those state enterprises that have sold shares to the public. There is real concern among some experts that selling significant quantities of state shares could not only result in a substantial drop in their share value but have a negative on the market as a whole.

By promoting mutual funds and allowing insurance companies and eventually pension funds to own securities, the government hopes to introduce a whole new clientele to capital markets. This would provide a more stable investor base, since these entities will take a longer-term view about matching assets against liabilities and in balancing risk with return on investment. Even so, it is a long stretch to imagine that institutional investors, who themselves are learning their craft, can bring more stability to a market in which the value of equities is subject to manipulation, speculation, and suspect accounting. These institutions will be subjecting themselves to considerably greater risk without the benefit of experience to assess it. On the other hand, in China investors have a built-in safety net, because the government is staking its prestige on the development of a real capital market, and, as owner of state enterprises, it will stand behind them.

Unemployment Is a Bad Word

The urban workforce is estimated at 190 million of which 76 million are employed by state enterprises. This does not include 100 million to 120 million rural workers who have left their farms for the towns and cities. These migrants can be seen on the street corners of any major city waiting for the chance to make a few *yuan* carrying goods suspended from their bamboo poles, collecting garbage, or doing just about any other job that urban dwellers are unwilling to do. This diaspora of rural migrants has not yet created a major political problem for the government because they left little behind and had everything to gain by seeking opportunity in urban areas. However, along with government civil servants, state-enterprise workers are the privileged elite of China's workforce. They have everything to lose if they are forced to leave their enterprises. They will not go quietly.

This is why the government has avoided an uncontrolled increase in the number of unemployed by creating the category of laid-off workers. Such workers are not separated from their work unit and receive a minimal stipend, usually augmented by the municipal government. At the end of 1997, the number of unemployed urban workers rose to about 6.5 million, equal to an unemployment rate of 3.4 percent, while the numbers of laid-off workers at the end of 1997 was estimated by a government official to be eleven million. Sensing big trouble, the Communist Party Central Committee in 1998 issued a circular announcing that solving the problem of laid-off workers had become the party's highest priority. It sternly admonished cadres to make sure that minimum living standards were provided and reemployment opportunities assured. Central and local governments joined with enterprises in providing laid-off workers with a minimum income. In spite of the government's entreaties, the number of laid-off workers rose to between sixteen and eighteen million by the end of 1999.[50] In June 2001, Qinghua University's Research Center reported that during 1996–2000 state enterprises and the civil service had laid off 28 percent of their workforce, while township and village enterprises had let go over one-half their workers. As a result, 46 million jobs had been lost. By contrast, only 15 million jobs had been created by the fast-growing private sector and foreign joint ventures.[51]

As the privileged of China's working population, state enterprise workers are the least likely to accept a reduction in status or loss of income. They are represented by the All-China Federation of Trade Unions, which is controlled by the Communist Party. When factories are closed or workers stop receiving subsidies, they find that the Federation turns a deaf ear in most cases. Independent unions are not allowed, and the workers have no other place to turn. They have resorted to public protest, so far mostly nonviolent. The government's response has been conciliatory—up to a point. It usually will give in to some demands, especially by restoring, at least temporarily, funding that has not been forthcoming. What is presently alarming the government is that protests have become much more frequent and are turning violent. The target of the workers' anger is often the enterprise manager. In Anhui Province, for example, there were sixty officially acknowledged attacks against enterprise managers from 1997 to 1999. In Fujian Province, there were just four mass protests in 1998, but in the first six months of 1999, there were thirty-one.[52] Worker discontent is an accurate barometer of the parlous and worsening situation in many state enterprises. Local governments everywhere have constructed reemployment centers, but new industrial jobs cannot be created fast enough to meet the demands of the centers, and the government has been relying on investment in public works and services to create new jobs. The government's urgency in trying to resolve the problem of redundancy is compounded by the fact that each year 6 million new entrants come into the job market.

The Government's Dilemma

WTO membership is placing additional strains on most state enterprises. The government is relying on its core 1,500 to 2,000 large state enterprises and an expanding private sector to meet the challenge of foreign competition. The government is divesting itself of its smaller state enterprises, but many are not attractive investments and can be unloaded only at bargain prices. Government-administered mergers between strong and weak enterprises serve to hide the problems of the weaker enterprise, which are bound to surface later.

The government continues to rely on direct subsidies to stimulate better performance of the core enterprises. Although subsidies can help in the short term, as demonstrated by debt–equity swaps, they will not solve the deeper structural problems of individual enterprises, and it is likely that another fiscal fix will be required in the future.

The government is facing a terrible dilemma for which there is no easy resolution. It should close down hundreds of obsolete state enterprises that have no chance of surviving, now that China has joined the WTO. But there are already far too many redundant urban workers and rural migrants searching for too few urban jobs. From the government's viewpoint, closing down enterprises and putting workers on the street would simply create a far bigger problem, for which there is no immediate solution. So the government continues to protect state enterprises from competition by subsidizing core state enterprises and requiring that they keep weaker enterprises afloat.

The government really has no choice, because it would amount to political suicide for it simply to close down failing state enterprises, since alternative employment opportunities do not exist. But its policy of keeping the iron rice bowl intact while limiting access to it is not working. Workers' protests are multiplying because state enterprises are failing to meet pension, salary, and laid-off subsistence payments. WTO membership is putting even greater pressure on state enterprises. Massive reeducation and job retraining programs for redundant workers are crucial but are not enough. The primary source of new jobs is going to have to be the private sector. The government has recognized the importance of the private sector, but it must do more—it must do everything it can to enable the private sector to flourish. This means making sure that private business has equal access to the factors of production, is an equal beneficiary of government policy, and has equal protection under the law.

The time has also come for new initiatives to be taken at the national level. One possibility would be to explore the "guest worker" approach, by establishing formal worker exchanges with more developed nations in which Chinese workers would contract to perform work for which there is a shortage of local workers. Although large-scale migrations of

Chinese looking for work have been going on since China's rapid population increases of the eighteenth and nineteenth centuries, this effort
was never supported—indeed, it was usually prohibited or discouraged—
by successive Chinese governments. With full government backing and
financial support, this could provide a viable employment alternative
for many Chinese. Another possibility could be for the government to
adopt a nationwide program of labor-intensive public works targeted to
reemploying redundant workers along the lines of the Civilian Conservation Corps established in the United States during the Great Depres-
sion. What would be required is a nationally based program with a strong
identity and clear objectives, publicly supported and endorsed by China's
leaders and financed and run by the central government. Such a program would be costly, but it would create jobs rather than maintain redundant workers as wards of the state.

Chapter Two

Like Stones Dropped in the Sea

Two men fishing, Beijing. In the background, polluted air forms a haze over the walls and moat protecting the Forbidden City.

Twenty years ago, China had only one real bank, and state enterprises had no debt. Now, the government is bailing out heavily indebted state enterprises that cannot repay their loans and is recapitalizing insolvent state banks. China's leading financial newspaper has stated that a considerable number of loans extended by the banks have disappeared like stones dropped in the sea.[1] How did this all come about?

The national credit plan was the primary means the government used in the allocation of investment financing. The lending volume of each state bank was spelled out, including how much was to be allocated for different types of lending and, depending on priorities established in the current five-year plan, the amount to be lent to specific sectors, subsectors, and even individual enterprises. As long as the central government was responsible for making all investment decisions, Chinese banks simply acted as conduits for moving money. Interest rates were low, simply representing a transfer cost. Since the state was banker, state enterprises had privileged access to funds. All this was financed by individual savers who, despite low interest rates, had no alternative places to invest their funds and thus kept immense sums of money in the banks. They had faith that the government would stand behind the banks.

Under the "socialist market economy" initiated by Deng Xiaoping, banks are supposed to take charge of their own destiny. Yet, they have not done so. What is at stake is the viability of China's banking system. On top of China's banking pyramid sits the People's Bank of China, the central bank. Below, four huge specialized banks control about three-fourths of all bank deposits. Next are three policy banks, created to make "directed credit" loans on behalf of the government, thus supposedly freeing the specialized banks to operate on a true commercial basis. Although smaller in size, eleven "shareholding" commercial banks are providing competition to their larger brethren. Hundreds of urban credit cooperatives have been amalgamated into eighty-eight city cooperative banks. At the bottom of the pyramid are many nonbank financial institutions including thousands of urban and rural credit cooperatives and hundreds of specialized financial entities like trust and investment companies, securities companies, and leasing and insurance companies. Many of these are the offspring of banks, which use them to get around credit ceilings established by the government.

The state banks are not required to publish audited financial statements, and most do not even prepare consolidated accounts that include their subsidiaries. Lax regulation and failure to allow outside scrutiny of banks' financial conditions encourages fraud, corrupt business practices, and politically motivated lending. The result is that far too many loans have been made without any assurance they can be repaid, especially to state-owned enterprises, whose dire predicament, discussed in chapter one, is mirrored in the banks' own financial statements. In fact, since the mid-1990s, the government has admitted that one-fifth of the loans made by the state banks cannot be repaid. With the fortunes of state enterprises in sharp decline, this percentage is rising. Regulation is a new phenomenon in China, and the People's Bank does not have sufficient authority or independence to supervise the banking system adequately.

In the late 1990s, Nicholas Lardy[2] concluded that lack of capital market development coupled with state domination of the banking system led to underpricing of loans to state enterprises, and this has encouraged borrowing far in excess of the enterprises' capacity to repay. He pointed to four danger signs that indicated the seriousness of the debt problem:

- The level of debt of state enterprises rose on average to five times the amount of their equity capital; a level that is simply unsustainable
- With 40 percent of industrial capacity lying idle (see chapter 1), much of the debt financed unutilized assets that cannot generate income to meet repayments
- During the real estate boom of the 1990s, too many loans were made on speculation rather than any assessment of demand, with the result that empty office buildings and luxury apartments cannot provide the revenue required to repay the banks
- The rapid build-up of "nonperforming" loans with long overdue interest or principal payments amounted to one-fourth of the total loans of China's four largest state banks

The debt problem is symptomatic of Chinese reforms that have not gone far enough in creating a modern financial system. China has not really made the tough decisions required, especially to ensure the banks' independence and viability and to provide real authority for the People's Bank. Bailouts are a temporary solution, and unless structural reform is carried through to the end, other bailouts will be necessary.

Strings of Cash and Silver Dollars

About 1000 B.C., along the southern coast of China, cowry shells strung in decimal units began to substitute for standard units of silk or grain as a medium of exchange. In the fifth century B.C., metal coinage came into widespread use, and each state under the Zhou dynasty (1122–256 B.C.) had its own coinage in the shape of small bronze spades or knives inscribed with the name of the state or city and in some cases individuals. Under the first Yellow Emperor of Qin, who unified China in 221 B.C., coins were circular with a hole in the middle for stringing on cords and became the standard measure of value for all China. A monetary unit was adopted of a string of 1,000 copper coins (or cash as they later became known) equal to one bushel of grain or a bolt of silk. The string of cash continued as China's measure of value and unit of exchange for 1,800 years.

Still, barter remained the main form of economic exchange, but in A.D. 1065, government cash revenues surpassed commodity revenues for the first time in Chinese history.[3] As more and more commerce came to depend on cash, the government was unable to mint sufficient copper coins to keep up with demand. Paper money was first used in Sichuan around the year A.D. 1000 and, in response to the chronic shortage in coinage, was adopted in A.D. 1023 as the official medium of exchange by the Sung dynasty (A.D. 960–1127). Paper currency was essentially a promise to pay a certain amount of strings of cash. It was also a substitute for the much bulkier coins that merchants began to keep on deposit with trading houses. The receipts the merchants received were used in lieu of cash in exchanges with other merchants.

By the time of the Song dynasty, therefore, China had an incipient money market with paper promissory notes linked to a metallic monetary unit, a system of cash deposits, and negotiable paper. China also had some of the basic problems of modern money markets. By the twelfth century A.D., printing of paper notes that were not backed by strings of cash became commonplace as the needs of successive emperors exceeded their ability to tax the population to pay for the large armies they needed to protect China's frontiers. As more and more paper notes pursued fewer goods, prices skyrocketed. Eventually merchants would not accept the notes and insisted on cash or barter. The Yuan dynasty (A.D. 1271–1368) reverted to paper currency, banned metallic coinage from circulation, and promulgated regulations governing the issuance of paper currency and its circulation. The Ming dynasty (A.D. 1368–1644) terminated the use of paper currency and later tried to reinstate it but could keep it in circulation only by requiring that certain taxes be paid with it. Paper currency returned to general use only in the nineteenth century.

In the sixteenth century, Spanish silver minted in Spain's South American colonies made its way into Asian trade. Silver coins were specially minted in Mexico for the China trade and became standard currency on China's south coast. Soon silver became a new unit of exchange with one ounce (*tael*) of silver equal to one string of cash. China's peasants, who had previously been required to pay taxes in cash, were now required to pay taxes in silver. Since their income was received in cash or barter, this created major difficulties for the peasants whenever silver was in short supply and the rate of exchange changed in favor of silver. Because silver had to be imported, China's impoverished peasants were subject to foreign-exchange risk for the next 250 years! This created enormous hardships for the peasants, particularly during the severe silver shortages of the mid-seventeenth and mid-nineteenth centuries, when peasants had to pay 300 to 400 percent more cash to buy the amount of silver required to meet their tax liabilities.[4]

Banking became important only after foreign governments gained a foothold in China and established spheres of influence at the turn of the twentieth century. China's first notable bankers, the Kong family, began as owners of pawn shops in Shanxi Province in the eighteenth century, expanded into the remittance business, and eventually became banking agents for a number of foreign firms. The British established the first bank in China in 1845, when the Oriental Banking Corporation opened for business in Shanghai. More British banks and the banks of other western powers followed suit. Much of China's early growth in infrastructure and industry was financed by foreign banking consortia. The largest of these loans were destined for railway development. However, a high percentage of these foreign funds were siphoned off by officials in Beijing or by local warlords. In one famous instance, the entire amount of a Japanese loan of ¥120 million was appropriated by the local warlord. The loan was really a bribe so that Japanese interests would be favored.[5]

The first Chinese bank, the Imperial Bank of China, was established in 1897. This was followed by the Bank of the Board of Revenue in 1905. The bank was renamed Daqing Bank in 1908. By the end of the Qing dynasty in 1911, six provincial Chinese banks had been established, and by 1918 there were thirty-seven Chinese banks. China's first central bank was established by the nationalist Guomindang government in 1928 as was a new currency, the *fabi yuan*. Yet, throughout the 1920s and early 1930s, silver continued to serve as China's measure of value, and silver dollars or silver *yuan* with the same weight of silver were issued by the nationalist government, foreign concessions, and local warlords. In the 1940s, the nationalist government vastly increased the printing of paper money to pay for the costs of the war. The value of the nationalist *fabi* fell throughout the war, and when high inflation turned into hyperinflation in 1948, prices spiraled out of control and the *fabi* was essentially valueless.

From Monobank to Many Banks

For the first thirty years of the Communist regime, investment was financed through the budget, and most monetary transactions were carried out by a single, large "monobank." A new currency, the people's currency or *renminbi*, was introduced in 1949. The People's Bank carried out both central and commercial banking functions and had 15,000 branches and offices across China. It accounted for 80 percent of deposits and was the source of 93 percent of all loans. A subsidiary, the Bank of China, was responsible for foreign exchange transactions and international payments. A People's Construction Bank of China also existed, but it was part of the Ministry of Finance, acting simply as a transfer agent for funds channeled to investment projects under the state budget. The Agricultural Bank of China was created in 1951 and functioned both as an independent entity and as an agent of the People's Bank. It was closed down in 1965. A network of rural credit cooperatives completed the financial picture. For most of its existence, the People's Bank was under the Ministry of Finance, and its function was to make credit available for government-approved projects. When provincial governments were involved, they controlled the local branches of the People's Bank. People's Bank central banking functions included regulating other financial institutions, managing the money supply and the state's foreign exchange holdings, and setting interest rates. In practice, it had no independence in carrying out any of these tasks, and all major monetary decisions were made by the State Council, China's highest organ of government. As China's sole commercial bank, it had even less authority, as investment decisions were made according to a centrally approved plan.

After Deng Xiaoping succeeded Mao Zedong and began to reform the economy, one of the first steps taken by reformers was to reestablish the Agricultural Bank as a separate entity in 1979. In the same year, the independence of the Bank of China and the People's Construction Bank was enhanced by making them directly subordinate to the State Council. In 1980, the People's Construction Bank began to accept deposits and make loans. In that year, China became a member of the World Bank and the International Monetary Fund, and the China Investment Bank was established to handle World Bank lines of credit. On January 1, 1984, the People's Bank formally became China's central bank. The Industrial and Commercial Bank of China was created to take over the People's Bank's commercial banking responsibilities, and it instantly became China's largest financial institution. In 1985, the People's Bank also became responsible for managing the interbank flow of funds, promulgating credit targets, and setting reserve requirements for the specialized banks. Again, its independence in carrying out these functions was largely circumscribed since it acted under the instructions of the State Council. In 1986, the legal basis for the People's Bank to supervise other financial institutions was established. In 1988, the bank was given the authority to appoint and remove its own branch managers, but first it had to consult with provincial governments, which could effectively veto such appointments.

The Agricultural Bank, the People's Construction Bank, the Industrial and Commercial Bank, and the Bank of China each had quite separate functions, and they became known as the "four specialized banks." After 1985, however, the Bank of China was no longer allowed to monopolize foreign trade banking, and the other specialized banks entered this business. At the same time, the Bank of Communications and the China International Trust and Investment Company (CITIC) Industrial Bank were established as "national comprehensive banks" because they could operate anywhere in the country and, unlike the specialized banks, had no restriction on the type of banking business they could conduct. Yet CITIC Industrial Bank was the financial arm of one of China's largest holding companies, and its ability to expand outside the sphere of the CITIC group was limited. The Bank of Communications had been established in the early years of the twentieth century and was resurrected as a unique entity with a variety of shareholders, including the People's Bank, municipal governments, and state enterprises.

During the 1980s, tens of thousands of rural and urban credit coop-eratives and hundreds of trust and investment companies, finance com-panies, leasing firms, and securities and insurance companies were established. These institutions are lumped together as "nonbanking fi-nancial institutions" because they have specialized functions, cannot establish branches, and, except for the credit cooperatives, do not ac-cept deposits from the public. Urban credit cooperatives were the fast-est growing of these institutions, and by the end of 1987, there were 1,600 of them. Since almost all of their borrowers were collectively owned and private enterprises, they filled a desperate need for credit among these enterprises, which had been ignored by the state banks. A few trust and investment companies were authorized to raise funds on international capital markets, but many were established after the People's Bank in 1986 required all state banks to shift their trust and securities operations to separate entities that could be more rigorously super-vised. Local governments were also active in forming such compa-nies, which specialized in financing long-term investments financed by shareholders' equity and the sale of long-term bonds. Less impor-tant were finance companies, which were usually the financial arm of a single, large group company, and financial leasing companies, which were mostly joint ventures with foreign firms. Securities companies' trading stocks and government bonds did not become important or numerous until after the Shanghai and Shenzhen stock exchanges were established in 1990 and 1991.

The rise of nonbank lending institutions paralleled the rise of nonstate enterprises, the fastest growing segment of industry and com-merce during the 1980s and 1990s (see chapter 1). Many of the former were created by the banks themselves to bypass the credit limits estab-lished by the government in the national credit plan. In fact, the People's Bank was a leader in establishing urban credit cooperatives, and by 1995, it owned 1,813 (38 percent of the total).[6] Branches of the People's Bank established and operated trust and investment companies, as did the state banks and local governments. Regulators and politicians had become owners and operators. It is hardly surprising that trust and investment companies became a major source of banking irregulari-ties, to the extent that the State Council ordered many of them closed, and their numbers fell from a high of 1,000 in 1988 to 339 in 1989. One authoritative report issued in 1989 stated that only 40 percent of the funds invested by trust companies met government guidelines for the use of trust funds and the rest were diverted to other purposes.[7] By 1995, there were 391 trust and investment companies (47 percent owned by the specialized banks),[8] which included a substantial number of international trust and investment companies set up by provincial governments as a means of channeling foreign loans to finance provincial development projects. The ownership links among banks, local governments, and trust and investment companies had not been really severed, and these entities retained their political clout and influence at the local level.

In the late 1980s, the interbank market for funds became important. It was made up of forty-three regional short-term financing centers supervised by the People's Bank, and fifty local interbank markets operated by the specialized banks. In 1986, the volume of interbank transactions was RMB 30 billion; just two years later it reached RMB 520 billion. The market was essentially a local phenomenon, with little, if any, national supervision. For both lenders and borrowers, the interbank market was an effective way to circumvent the credit plan. There were few entry requirements, interest rates were set by the market and were higher than official rates, and short-term financing rapidly developed into long-term lending. Estimated net outflows from the banking system into the interbank market were RMB 46 billion in 1991, RMB 106 billion in 1992, and RMB 206 billion in 1993.[9]

Another phenomenon of the late 1980s was the rise of regional development and commercial banks in the prosperous coastal provinces: Shenzhen Development Bank and Merchants Bank in 1987; and Guangdong Development Bank, Fujian Xingye Bank, and Shanghai Pudong Development Bank in 1988. These banks have diverse ownership structures, geographic scope, and size. Merchants Bank was originally owned by the Shenzhen-based Merchants Group, but has sold shares to ninety-two additional shareholders and has 107 branches or offices all over the country. Shanghai Pudong Bank has moved into the neighboring provinces of Jiangsu and Zhejiang. All these banks have offices in Beijing. In addition, two experimental housing banks were established in Shandong and Anhui provinces in 1987 to help finance the transfer of ownership of enterprise housing to their occupants. Also in the late 1980s, foreign banks were allowed to set up branches but were restricted to a specific geographic area and could lend only to foreign-invested enterprises and individuals and were not allowed to do business in local currency.

State Banks Try to Rescue State Enterprises

The fiscal reforms initiated in the 1980s led to a steady decline in government revenues, and the government turned to the banks to finance the operations and new investments of the state enterprises. In 1984, banks were given responsibility for financing their working capital, and in 1986, their investments. And so began the process of indebtedness that was to lead banks and state enterprises to near collapse. This financing was carried out according to the government's annual credit plan. The financing needs of specific state investment projects were aggregated into regional credit plans and then screened at the national level before being included in the national plan. Each province or municipality with provincial standing[10] was given borrowing quotas, and the head office of each state bank was given a lending quota to be distributed to its branches. The basic problem for each bank was how to match the volume of deposits, which was determined by economic activity, with the volume of lending, which was determined by the credit plan. This situation required the People's Bank to provide financing and ensure that banks that had excess funds over their quotas would make funds available to banks that were unable to meet their credit quotas. This is evident in data that show that banks in provinces with the highest share of state-owned industrial output had much higher loan-to-deposit ratios than banks in less industrialized provinces. Guandong, Fujian, and Zhejiang provinces, for example, were among the provinces with the lowest share of industrial output produced by state enterprises and also the lowest in terms of the percentage of bank deposits that had been loaned out. The irony is that these three coastal provinces were the first, second, and fourth fastest growing provinces in China from 1984 to1994, and what the government was really doing was reallocating investment away from regions of high economic growth to regions of low economic growth.[11]

Because of the lending quotas established under the annual credit plans, state banks had a major incentive to make loans in ways that did not have to be reported as loans, and they did so. Discounting of commercial paper and repurchase of bills of exchange are not included as loans, although the former involves lending money against a pledge on receivables and the latter involves extending credit in exchange for government bonds. These operations grew dramatically in the 1990s. Loans made under trust agreements are not included because the bank simply acts as agent for the trustee and accepts no liability. This lending grew significantly for the specialized banks until 1992, after which the banks were no longer authorized to carry out trust operations. Banks also recorded loans as "other assets" on their balance sheets, and in the 1990s, this became a more important form of lending. In addition, bank loans to nonbank financial institutions channeled through the interbank market appear on bank balance sheets as interbank transactions rather than loans.

The 1990s also brought two new, smaller national comprehensive banks on the scene. Everbright Bank and Huaxia Bank, established in 1992, were both closely affiliated with a single industrial group. Irregularities arising from conflicts of interest between their banking roles and group objectives led to both being reorganized by the People's Bank in 1995. Everbright Bank became a joint stock bank and sold 1.37 billion new shares to a wide range of state enterprises, but the Everbright Group still retained 51 percent ownership. Huaxia Bank, originally owned by the Capital Iron and Steel (Shougang) Group Company, was converted into a joint stock commercial bank with more than thirty large enterprises as shareholders. At the instigation of the People's Bank, which was unhappy over the deterioration of the quality of the bank's assets under the stewardship of the Shougang group, several large group companies purchased enough shares to reduce the Shougang group share holding to one-fifth of the total.

The period 1979 through 1992 was a time of enormous growth and diversification of financial institutions and financial markets, which was not paralleled by commensurate development of the regulatory structure. When the economy overheated in the early 1990s, the flaws in the banking system became all too evident.

The Banking Crisis of 1993 Sparks Financial Reform

Deng Xiaoping's tour of southern China in September 1992, followed by his statement that it was glorious to get rich and that the rest of the country should emulate the economic dynamism of the southern coastal cities, began a new spurt of economic activity. In the same year, the money supply more than doubled, resulting in an overheated economy and rapidly rising inflation. A wave of speculation led to a massive outflow of funds from the banks—estimated to be at least RMB 105 billion —which were channeled illegally through the interbank market at high interest rates, mostly into real estate markets and the new stock exchanges at Shanghai and Shenzhen. In the first six months of 1993, capital investment grew an astounding 70.7 percent over the same period in the previous year. As inflation increased, depositors became reluctant to place new funds with the banks, and the banks found themselves squeezed for funds and had difficulty making payments. Banks were required by the People's Bank to maintain payment reserves to meet liquidity requirements and make settlement payments by keeping 13 percent of their deposits with the People's Bank and 5 to 7 percent in their own vaults. However, they were unable to do so.

In mid-June 1993, the government moved swiftly to cool down the economy, reassure depositors, and assert control over bank lending. Demand deposit interest rates were almost doubled. The lending authority of the regional branches of the People's Bank was abrogated, and loans to the specialized banks could be made only between the head offices of the People's Bank and the specialized banks. Local interbank markets were shut down, and the banks were given until August 15 to recall all their interbank loans. To tighten credit, lending rates were raised by 1.38 percent on average. The People's Bank lent a total of RMB 272.6 billion to the specialized banks in the second half of 1993 to ease their liquidity problem. The governor of the People's Bank was fired and replaced by Zhu Rongji, then senior vice premier. Amazingly, the banks reported by August 15 that they had recalled 70 percent of the loans made through the interbank market and by the end of 1993, 80 percent. These funds were then placed in payment and settlement reserves, and the payments problem was resolved.

Chinese authorities cited institutional flaws as the source of the banking crisis, and in November 1993, the Third Plenum of the Fourteenth Party Central Committee decided to increase the autonomy of the People's Bank and make it responsible for monetary policy and supervision of the banking system; separate policy lending from commercial lending; gradually transform the specialized banks into commercial banks; separate banking from securities firms and trust and investment companies; control development of nonbank financial institutions and capital markets; and modernize financial infrastructure.

In December 1993, the State Council issued its *Decision on Reform of the Financial System,* which spelled out how these objectives were to be achieved. A key element was establishing the legal foundation to support reform, and central banking and commercial banking legislation, as well as laws governing insurance, guarantees, and negotiable bills were subsequently enacted by the National People's Congress. The appointment of Zhu Rongji as president of the People's Bank indicated that the government had finally become serious about the need for a strong central bank. In 1994, Zhu refused to provide funds to the Ministry of Finance to cover the budget deficit, and this principle was subsequently affirmed under the People's Bank of China Law, which was promulgated by the National People's Congress in 1995. The law defined the People's Bank's most important tasks: maintaining currency stability and supervising financial institutions. The bank's independence from local governments was increased, but power to set monetary policy was still centralized in the executive branch. A new Monetary Policy Committee appointed by China's premier would develop policy recommendations. Real power over monetary policy still lay with the State Council, which would provide the leadership the People's Bank would require in its function of implementing monetary policy. The People's Bank was not allowed to make loans to enterprises, local governments, government departments, nonbank financial institutions, or individuals; and the credit-granting function was taken away entirely from its branches. This step was essential for limiting the influence of local governments, because they still controlled appointments of the senior managers of the People's Bank's provincial branches.

Breaking the financial link between the People's Bank and the Ministry of Finance had an unintended impact on the development of the capital market. The Ministry of Finance had to increase bond sales so substantially that it had to market them widely, which required increasing interest rates and creating a secondary market for the bonds. When banks subsequently introduced inflation indexing on time deposits, the ministry had to follow suit and index its bonds in order to compete.

Since 1988, the standards produced by the Basle Committee on Banking Regulations and Supervisory Practices have provided the international standard for banking regulation. In 1994 the People's Bank began to adopt the committee's recommendations, beginning with a capital-adequacy standard. These standards require that the paid-in equity capital of a bank be equal to at least 4 percent of the bank's risk-adjusted assets (the concept is that capital should be increased as assets are associated with greater risk), and that its net worth (paid-in capital plus reserves and retained earnings) be equal to 8 percent of risk-adjusted assets.

According to the Basle standards, investments made in nonbank financial institutions should be deducted from the bank's capital prior to determining capital adequacy, but in China they are not.

The Commercial Bank Law of 1995 stipulated that total outstanding loans could not exceed 75 percent of total deposits. To further safeguard the banks, the law provided that their exposure in any single borrower be limited to 10 percent of the bank's capital. Minimum amounts of paid-in capital were prescribed for commercial banks (RMB 1 billion), urban cooperative banks (RMB 100 million), and rural cooperative banks (RMB 50 million). It was further stipulated that the capital adequacy ratio of all banks must be no less than 8 percent of total loans outstanding, as established by the Basle Committee.

Three policy banks were created in 1994 to finance priority investment projects selected by the government. These were the Export-Import Bank of China to finance foreign trade, the State Development Bank of China to finance infrastructure or industrial projects, and the Agricultural Development Bank of China to finance rural development. These banks were established especially to finance projects that had a high social value but were not commercially viable because they had a long gestation period, were subject to high risk, or had low financial returns. The policy banks raised capital by the sale of bonds to the banking system and received loans from the People's Bank. However, lending interest rates charged by the policy banks were less than the interest cost of the bonds they issued, and mismatching liabilities expense with asset income resulted in operational losses. In fact, their bonds were sold only because the People's Bank compelled the specialized banks to buy them. Moreover, they were subject to interference and feuding among the powerful government entities that could claim jurisdiction over their activities. Most disturbing, despite the existence of the policy banks, which were supposed to take over policy lending from the specialized banks, the latter were not allowed to become fully commercial, because under government pressure they continued to make policy loans. So long as the specialized banks continue to make policy loans, they retain the character of policy banks.

The policy banks exemplify the ambiguity that still underlies the government's policy of financing economic development. On the one hand, the policy banks are simply the financing arm of the State Council and its agencies. On the other hand, every project has to be presented to the policy bank's loan committee for approval. But even if a project is not approved by the bank's loan committee, the government can insist that it is in the national interest to finance the project, and the bank is helpless to oppose it further. Moreover, although the policy banks cannot apply commercial criteria in making their lending decisions, the government still expects them to operate profitably. This has led the policy banks to obtain third-party guarantees for their loans, often from state enterprises or banks. The policy banks were also expected to assume the liability for the policy loans made by the specialized banks, but this has not happened.

One of the reformers' major goals was regulation of the interbank markets which was drastically reduced in size. From 1994 onward, tightened regulation reduced the volume of the market considerably. Only nineteen banks and thirty-five regional financing centers were licensed and connected with a single electronic currency trading system, which began operations in 1996. On June 1, 1996, interest rates on the interbank market were completely freed, the first instance of decontrol of interest rates in China.

Under the Commercial Bank Law of 1995, banks had to divest themselves of any interest in securities firms and in trust and investment companies. By the end of 1996, the banks reported that this had been accomplished. Yet in early 1997 there was a large inflow of funds into the stock markets from the banks, and in June, 1997, the People's Bank ordered the banks to liquidate their positions in securities companies within ten days. The chief executives of four large brokerage companies and of the Shenzhen Development Bank were dismissed, as were the Shanghai branch managers of Industrial and Commercial Bank and Everbright Bank.

The interest paid on demand deposits was 2.88 percent throughout the 1980s. By the mid-1990s the rate had risen to just 3.15 percent. One-year deposit rates rose from around 5 percent in the early 1980s to about 11 percent in the mid-1990s, and three-, five-, and eight-year rates climbed even higher. But most households still needed to keep substantial portions of their savings as demand deposits to pay bills. In 1995, the government eliminated preferential interest rates for thirteen sectors of the economy, yet it still had 200 rates under its control, most of them at preferential rates. Lending rates were also under strict control, and until the mid-1990s, the margin between the two was negligible or even negative. When inflation spiraled out of control in 1989 and 1993, negative real interest rates for financing industrial inputs and machinery were just under 8 percent and 13 percent, respectively, providing a substantial subsidy to the borrowing enterprises. During times of high inflation, as savings rates became more and more unattractive, the inflow of new savings deposits was severely curtailed. In order to stimulate more deposits, the government in 1994 tied three-, five-, and eight-year deposit rates to the rate of inflation while keeping lending rates under strict control. The result was that deposit rates quickly rose to *double* the lending rates. This wide negative margin between long-term deposit and lending rates coincided with the first operating losses reported by the specialized banks in 1995.[12]

Because the government controlled both borrowing and lending rates and kept the margins between the two artificially narrow or even negative for loans made with medium- and long-term time deposits after 1994, the banks were never able to adequately cover their own cost of doing business. The experience of the Bank of China, the best performer among the four specialized banks, is revealing. During 1989, the Bank of China's average cost of funds on its domestic lending was 14.8 percent, while its average lending rate was 11.6 percent, resulting in an average negative lending margin of 3.2 percent. Since the Bank of China's operating costs for the year were equivalent to 1.6 percent of its total domestic lending, the total negative return on its lending operations was 4.8 percent. Yet the bank reported a pre-tax profit of RMB 5.1 billion. How could this be possible? Lardy points out that RMB 3.9 billion was noninterest income from other sources and that the bank apparently made an additional profit on its foreign-exchange operations.[13] Also, overestimation of interest income undoubtedly accounted for some of the difference. The bottom line is that other financing activities are subsidizing the bank's domestic lending and that income is also being inflated.

Reserves for bad debt, which are part of the bank's capital, were established according to requirements set by the Ministry of Finance rather than the People's Bank. This reserve was initially established at 0.6 percent of loans outstanding in 1991 and subsequently was raised to 1.0 percent at the end of 1997. Loan loss reserves of the specialized banks have not met even this very low standard. The Industrial and Commercial Bank of China reported reserves of just 0.5 percent of total loan portfolios in 1994. In 1996, the Agricultural Bank of China reported somewhat less than 0.5 percent, and the People's Construction Bank of China, just under 0.6 percent.[14] Given their level of nonperforming loans (see below), the reserves allocated to protect the capital of the four banks were hopelessly inadequate.

Like state enterprises, state banks have excessive staff at all levels and thus are burdened with social welfare costs. They established extensive branch systems based on political considerations rather than on any cost–benefit analysis of branch locations. The key to reducing costs is to start with reducing staff, but shedding redundant staff is subject to government control. Similarly sized foreign banks operating in China have a ratio of assets per employee that is five times that of the specialized banks. This is reflected in the results of a 1997 survey made by the *Banker* magazine,[15] which shows that Chinese state banks have the highest ratio of operating costs relative to income of all countries surveyed. No wonder Chinese state banks find themselves in a financial straitjacket: They have an inflexible structure of high fixed costs, which is quite vulnerable to fluctuations in income.

Before 1995, when the People's Bank adopted a loan classification system, it had actually prohibited the banks from classifying their loans beyond very low ceilings regardless of the actual quality of a bank's portfolio. Now, nonperforming loans are to be classified according to three kinds of situations: loans past due (not repaid by the due date); doubtful loans (past due two years or more, or the borrower has suspended production); and bad debt (loans due from borrowers in bankruptcy). This system is still more lenient than what was intended by the Basle Committee, because loans remain on the books of Chinese banks as performing for much longer periods than acceptable by international standards. According to accepted international practice, when either a principal or an interest payment is overdue more than 180 days, the *entire* loan should be classified as nonperforming. Chinese banks generally classify loans only when the principal is overdue, and the banks often take steps to prevent this from happening by making loans in which the principal is paid in a balloon payment at the end of the loan maturity and by routinely rolling over short-term loans by extending the maturity date and adding the interest due to the principal amount. From the perspective of the Basle Committee, the amount of loans actually reported by Chinese banks as nonperforming is just the tip of a very dangerous iceberg.

How much of these loans is actually uncollectable? At the end of 1997, nonperforming loans amounted to 25 percent of the combined value of the loan portfolios of the four specialized banks.[16] Assuming that all bad debt, which is about 2 percent of total nonperforming debt, will have to be written off and that one-fourth of the remaining nonperforming debt is actually repaid, total write-offs would exceed the combined net worth of the banks. At the end of 1998, the government's official estimate of total nonperforming loans for the specialized banks was RMB 1 trillion (US$121 billion).[17]

When it comes to actually writing off a nonperforming loan by reducing net worth and assets on the balance sheet, the government has been very reluctant to take action. Before a bankruptcy law was promulgated in 1988, the State Council had to approve the write-off of every bad loan. After 1988, the People's Bank could authorize write-offs of up to RMB 100,000, but the banks themselves could not. In 1992, this limit was raised to RMB 500,000. Reliable data for actual write-offs are hard to find, and what are available indicate that amounts are minuscule and bear no clear relation to the amount of bad debts.

Enterprise bankruptcy will not provide the banks with any real compensation. Many bank loans to state enterprises are unsecured, but under the Civil Procedure Law of 1991, state banks have first claim on assets, even if their loans are unsecured. In practice, however, the banks have received very little compensation from bankruptcy liquidation proceedings. The bankruptcy process is not clear-cut in China. The government is always in the background making sure that the workers and their families are taken care of, and in 1996, the State Council decreed that the proceeds of liquidations should first be used to meet the enterprise's pension and social welfare obligations.

All this is having a negative effect on state bank profitability, as reflected in the amount of net profit before taxes compared to the bank's total assets. Net profit as a percentage of assets has declined for the four specialized banks from an average of 1.4 percent from 1985 to 1987 to under 0.3 percent from 1995 to 1997.[18] Since loans made by the four banks expanded rapidly during this period while profits grew much more slowly, this points to nonpayment of interest charges and low interest rates as probable causes. When the banks lent the money to a borrower to meet interest payments, the amount was recorded by the banks as interest income on the banks' income statements and as a new loan on their balance sheets. Or unpaid interest was just added to the principal amount without extending a new loan. In effect, this practice of capitalization of interest overstated interest income.

Banking regulations are at the root of the problem because banks are required to carry unpaid interest on their balance sheets for three years, and this is reported as income. According to Lardy, "[A] very large share of the interest income reported by banks is accrued interest or originates with the capitalization of interest when loans are rolled over."[19] In addition, provisions against bad debt should be deducted from income, but since the banks' provisioning is wholly inadequate, income is again overstated. Also, banks do not report their subsidiaries' income or loss, and this further limits understanding of actual profitability. Banks often withhold interest payments on time deposits until the final maturity date, thus shifting their interest costs to the future. The net effect of recognizing unearned income and deferring costs is to inflate profitability significantly, and to the degree that their subsidiaries are doing poorly, the banks are subject to further losses.

Banking Reform Flounders, While Government Insists It Will Be Completed by 2000

The failure of the 1993 reforms to go far enough was clearly evident in the financial status of China's state banks, which were far weaker than official data suggested. They were sustaining real operating losses that were not reflected on their financial statements. Their capital was substantially overstated because the amount of bad debt and other nonperforming debt that would eventually have to be written off exceed the banks' net worth (the combined value of their paid-in capital, capital reserves, and retained earnings). In fact, they were insolvent according to most experts.

Finally, the highest levels of government seemed to have understood that the credit quota system had not worked, had been circumvented by the banks, and was incompatible with real reform of the financial sector. Although mandatory lending quotas were terminated effective January 1, 1998, the banks were still subject to "guidance quotas" established by the People's Bank—after consultation, no doubt, with the State Council. In 1998, the People's Bank replaced the quota with the asset–liability ratio as a ceiling for limiting the amount of lending to what is appropriate for individual banks. This was a major improvement, because the ceiling was a reflection of the bank's own balance sheet rather than an arbitrary limit imposed by the government.

At the Ninth National People's Congress in March 1998, new premier Zhu Rongji announced that banking reform would be completed in three years through an accelerated program of mergers, acquisitions, and closures. To begin with, local branches of the People's Bank were consolidated to reduce political influence in bank lending decisions. The specialized banks were directed to continue lending to state enterprises, and in return, the four specialized banks were recapitalized to the tune of US$32 billion. Central government financing of the write-offs of state enterprise debt, which was tied to restructuring and mergers within group companies, was specifically targeted in March 1998 to textiles, which the government had made its number one industrial reform priority (see chapter 1). Part of the government's bargain with the group companies was that the price of government financial support in debt restructuring includes acceptance into the group of weaker enterprises that were not performing well and needed group support.

Tax reform must accompany recapitalization in Lardy's view, because excessive taxation is a major drain on state bank profitability. The Ministry of Finance has resisted any tax reduction because the specialized banks account for one-sixth of central government revenues. They have to pay not only income taxes on net earnings of 33 percent but also business taxes on gross earnings of 8 percent. The net impact on profit retention is dramatic. In 1995, for example, the effective tax rates as a percentage of earnings for the four specialized banks ranged from 72.8 to 83.8 of net income.[20] Since the earnings of the state banks are substantially overstated, they are paying those high taxes on income that was not really earned. The government should eliminate the tax on gross income.

By 1998, the inadequately regulated international trust and investment companies had become the most visible weakness in China's financial system. Many of them had built up huge unhedged foreign currency exposures. In October 1998, over the objections of the Guangdong provincial government, the central government forced the closure of Guangdong International Trust and Investment Company (GITIC). The company was unable to meet a foreign debt payment of US$700 million. It had sunk much of its foreign borrowing into real estate speculation, and there was apparently no likelihood that it could generate revenues to pay this or the rest of its foreign debt, which totaled US$2.55 billion. GITIC had also extended guarantees equal to five times its own capital, which did not appear on its balance sheet since a guarantee is accounted for as a contingent (below the line) liability.

The government was clearly trying to send a message to both domestic and foreign banks that the government was not going to support insolvent "ITICs." The response of foreign banks was to stop making new loans to ITICs and cease rolling over existing loans. Many ITICs had been borrowing from one bank to pay another, and this action placed them in a very difficult liquidity position. In Guangdong, the fallout was considerable: Two other ITICs defaulted on foreign loan payments, and a major conglomerate, Guangdong Enterprises, suffered the same fate. In early January 1999, GITIC filed for bankruptcy, showing debts of US$4.7 billion—almost double the amount originally announced—and total assets of only US$2.6 billion. After more than two years of nego-tiations, the creditors agreed on a plan for repaying 3.4 percent of the debt, and the company declared its intention to recover up to one-third of the debt.[21] In 2000, the Dalian International Trust and Investment Corporation, which had also closed its doors about the same time as GITIC, agreed to pay its Japanese creditors 60 percent of the total amount they were owed. The total outstanding foreign debt of China's 239 other ITICs was said to be US$50 billion.

In 1999, the government announced with great fanfare a shift from its industry-specific debt forgiveness exercise to a national program of debt–equity swaps involving swapping nonperforming loans for an equivalent value of the enterprise's capital. The government had be-come convinced that debt–equity swaps were the solution to the prob-lems of the banks and the state enterprises (see also chapter 1). Four asset management corporations (AMCs) were created—one for each of the specialized banks. In 1999–2000, US$169 billion in nonperforming loans were transferred from the specialized banks to the balance sheets of the AMCs in exchange for cash and bonds. Given the extremely dif-ficult task of repackaging and reselling these assets, there is consider-able doubt in the financial community whether the AMCs will eventually be able to redeem these bonds. Moody's Investor Service raised its rat-ings for the specialized banks for the first time since it had lowered them in 1998, citing their "unprecedented efforts which herald a new beginning in China's long struggle to reform its beleaguered financial system."[22] This was in spite of the fact that 20 percent of loans outstand-ing at the end of 2000 were still classified as nonperforming.[23]

The second half of the 1990s saw the establishment of China's first private bank, the consolidation of credit cooperatives into banks, and the arrival of foreign banks in large numbers. China's first private bank, China Minsheng Bank, received its charter in 1995. It was sponsored by a trade association for nonstate enterprises, the All-China Federation of Industry and Commerce. All of its fifty-nine shareholders are associa-tion members. Minsheng is distinguished by the fact that it is the only bank in China that has hired a firm with international stature to audit its accounts. It was also a time of rapid growth of shareholding commercial banks, established in the 1980s and early 1990s, and the market share of the four specialized banks declined from 71.2 percent of total financial assets in 1986 to 61.0 percent in 1996.[24] Loans outstanding grew from 50 percent of China's gross domestic product in 1978 to 100 percent in 1997. This amounted to RMB 190 billion at the end of 1978 and RMB 7.4 trillion at the end of 1997. In comparison to the annual national budget, loans granted in 1978 were just 16 percent of the total, while in 1997 they had reached 136 percent of the budget.[25]

The Financial System at the New Millennium

At the end of 1999, there were eleven shareholder banks: Bank of Communications, China Everbright Bank, China Merchants Bank, Huaxia Bank, CITIC Industrial Bank, Shanghai Pudong Development Bank, Shenzhen Development Bank, Guangdong Development Bank, Minsheng Bank, Hainan Development Bank and Fujian Xingye Bank. China Investment Bank was absorbed by Everbright Bank in 1999. Shanghai Pudong Development Bank and Shenzhen Development Bank both were successfully listed on their respective domestic stock exchanges in 1999. In December 2000, Minsheng Bank raised US$494 million in an initial public offering. Demand for its shares was 100 times the amount of shares issued.[26] This disparate group included banks that operate nationally, development banks that are limited geographically, and China's only private bank. There were also eighty-eight new city cooperative banks, which had been created out of mergers of urban credit cooperatives. This left 3,240 urban credit cooperatives and 41,500 rural credit cooperatives serving small enterprises and individuals throughout China.

By year-end 1999, the number of foreign banks had reached 182, including 163 with branch or representative offices, seven joint-venture banks, six wholly foreign-owned banks, and six financial companies. Twenty-five banks had been granted permission to conduct *renminbi* business for foreign clients in Shanghai and Shenzhen.[27] The insurance business is still in its infancy with twelve Chinese companies, six joint ventures and thirteen foreign firms, whose premiums totaled US$118 billion and claims US$37 billion at the end of 2000.[28] Life insurance accounted for 60 percent, and property and casualty insurance (mostly motor vehicle), for 40 percent. A single state enterprise dominates in each area.

In the late 1990s, the government began vigorously promoting listing on stock exchanges as the primary source of new capital for its core large enterprise group companies. Most enterprises were listed on the Shanghai and Shenzhen exchanges. High-tech companies and leading pillar industries (which are dominated by state enterprises and receive substantial government support) sought the prestige and large financial rewards of listing on the Hong Kong, New York, and NASDAQ exchanges. Underwriting became big business for both Chinese and foreign investment banks. The government controls which firm gets the underwriting mandate and requires that a Chinese investment bank be part of each consortium.

The newest financial vehicle for raising funds from savers has been closed-end funds, which have a fixed amount of shares that can only be bought from other shareholders, and are traded on a stock exchange. In China, there are ten fund-management companies operating twenty-five funds. Closed-end funds really took off in 1999, when total fund portfolio increased 400 percent over 1998, to reach US$6 billion (6 percent of the total traded volume on both of China's exchanges). The China Securities Regulatory Commission, which regulates this activity, has also prepared regulations governing mutual (open-end) funds, which have been approved by the government. Unlike closed-end funds, they can issue new shares, and shares are redeemable on demand and therefore much more liquid. Foreign investment advisors, such as Jardine Asset Management and Schroder Investment Management, have signed agreements with Chinese fund-management companies to help them establish open-end funds. This move to expand the market substantially for fund investing comes on the heels of a report prepared by the supervision department of the Shanghai Stock Exchange, which surveyed the twenty-two closed-end funds and found that market manipulation among fund managers was widely practiced. Common practices included insider trading and fund managers' purchasing one another's securities at inflated prices in return for kickbacks.[29]

For twenty years, Chinese banks engaged in a rapid build-up of debt, significantly exceeding the rate of economic growth, which was accompanied by an equally rapid deterioration of their loan portfolio. Chinese bank credit has increased by an average of 21 percent annually since 1978, almost triple the real rate of economic growth for the period. That this trend cannot be sustained and will inevitably end in crisis is borne out by the experience of other East Asian countries such as Thailand and Japan in the late 1990s, where the growth of bank lending far exceeded economic growth rates and much of this excess lending was channeled into speculative investments in real estate and higher risk financial assets. When prices collapsed, the loans could not be repaid.

China did not catch the Asian "contagion" because it resisted the lure of globalization of capital flows, and Chinese currency is convertible into other currencies only for costs incurred by foreign trade transactions, tourism, foreign loan repayment, and repatriation of profits. Chinese currency cannot be used to purchase foreign financial assets, and foreigners' ability to purchase Chinese currency financial assets is circumscribed. Foreign joint-venture agreements involve investments in assets that cannot be readily converted into cash. In any case, repatriation of such funds is carefully controlled. Foreigners are also barred from purchasing Chinese currency denominated *A* shares on the Shenzhen and Shanghai stock exchanges; they must buy foreign-currency denominated *B* shares. Although the government has permitted ITICs to borrow from abroad with no real oversight as to extent of the foreign debt involved, the lack of capital account convertibility and consequent inability of foreign speculators and lenders to precipitate the kind of crisis that has occurred elsewhere in East Asia has given the Chinese government breathing space.

The Challenge of World Trade Organization Membership

As in other sectors, the government has been preparing the financial sector for its accession to the WTO under the guiding principle that the banking market should first be opened to domestic banks before it is opened to international rivals. This has led the government to take a behind-the-scenes role in supporting the establishment of privately owned Chinese banks. A group of experts is presently carrying out feasibility studies of proposals to establish up to ten Chinese private banks. Studies for four of the banks were said to have been completed by the end of 2000. One unanswered question, which is key to determining if there is real government support behind these banks, is whether they would have access to the domestic capital market. The government is also grooming one of its own banks, China Everbright Bank, to be competitive in the global market. The Ministry of Finance has relieved it of US$846 million in nonperforming loans, and it has received clearance to list its shares on one of the domestic exchanges within the next year.[30]

China has joined the world trading community without a real central bank. The People's Bank of China has no role in determining monetary policy or in establishing regulations for the banking system. It simply carries out decisions taken by the State Council and the Communist Party's Central Financial Work Committee. The only time the People's Bank exercised any independent decision-making, was when it was headed by Premier Zhu Rongji in 1993–1994. After that, Zhu still called the shots as head of the party's Central Financial and Economic Leading Group. In 1998, the party created the Central Financial Works Committee to assume leadership in monetary and banking policy making. Clearly, the party wants to remain in direct control of financial and monetary policy, and the role of the People's Bank will continue to be limited to implementing party decisions promulgated by the State Council.

Bank of China, generally considered the soundest of the specialized banks, has listed 15 percent of its domestic loans as nonperforming, which exceeds its net worth and makes the bank technically insolvent. Like the other specialized banks, it is able to continue to operate with negative net worth because the government implicitly guarantees its deposits. While its management has acknowledged shortcomings in its risk-management and information disclosure, it nevertheless is going forward with plans to consolidate its holdings in Hong Kong into a new merchant bank with global ambitions. This is part of a pattern that is becoming increasingly common among core government-supported state banks and enterprises. They establish an offshore subsidiary with a clean balance sheet and new identity in, say, Hong Kong to represent them in the global market. This enables them to become more independent from Beijing and to keep good and bad assets separate. These subsidiaries can also help the parent look good. Bank of China's Hong Kong subsidiaries have been quite profitable and have had a significant positive impact on the consolidated profitability of the Bank of China group.

China's largest bank, Industrial and Commercial Bank of China, concluded an agreement with China's largest insurance company, People's Insurance Company of China, that the former would have access to insurance premiums for lending purposes and the latter would be able to use thousands of local bank branches to market insurance products. The government is also allowing insurance companies to invest in the securities market and permitting securities dealers and investment funds to raise funds in the interbank market. The blurring of boundaries between banking, insurance, and securities dealing is all the rage in the West. But in China it can have very serious consequences for entities that have not yet grasped the essentials of their principal line of business. In the rush to be ready for global competition, China is taking enormous risks with its financial institutions. The specialized banks, for example, have yet to demonstrate their technical competence, managerial expertise, or financial viability but are allowed to use bank deposits from individual savers to purchase stocks of questionable merit and to use insurance premiums to make high-risk loans.

Recapitalization will not prevent the banks from repeating past mistakes. Behavior will not change unless it is tied to an incentive structure that rewards managers for basing their decisions on commercial criteria. While Lardy believes that increasing competition is the most effective way to impose commercial discipline on the banking system, he nevertheless cautions that premature liberalization of the financial markets, especially in response to foreign pressure, could trigger a crisis.[31] The World Bank is also cautious about allowing unrestricted competition between domestic and foreign banks. It has concluded that state banks should be given greater flexibility in setting lending rates (not deposit rates) only when satisfactory progress has been made in the commercialization of their lending. Similarly, foreign banks should be allowed to compete with Chinese banks "only after the domestic banking system is competitive and working well."[32] Nevertheless, in 2000, the government initiated a plan to deregulate interest rates in three years, and since then it has widened the bands, or ranges, within which banks can change rates on their own authority.

It is not simply that the Chinese banks are ill equipped to deal with competition. With competition has come a much greater emphasis on making profits. In fact, the government has become so profit conscious that it has threatened to fire bank general managers if they do not produce profits. At first glance, this may seem to be a step in the right direction. It is actually the reverse because it forces managers to do whatever it takes to make profits and will lead general managers of unprofitable banks, which are most in need of prudent management, to take greater and greater risks to try to improve returns. Open competition with foreign and private banks dedicated to bottom-line profitability is likely to produce a similar response, and the government should be concerned about allowing opening up the banking sector to full competition.

The incentive structure must be changed to establish a careful balance between risk taking and prudent management, and regulation must be improved so that bank managers will know they are being supervised. This means that independent outside audits must become the norm, bank inspectors must make regular visits to head offices and branches, adequate international standards for classifying loans as nonperforming should be adopted, detailed risk analysis must become a part of every lending decision, banks must be held accountable for maintaining capital adequacy ratios and asset-liability ratios, and the provisions of the banking laws that make political interference in lending decisions must be strictly enforced. As long as the government maintains control of the decision making of the state banks, this scenario is not likely to happen.

The government is able to continue to support state banks and state enterprises and to finance the massive public works programs that keep economic growth at rates of 7 to 8 percent because of its substantial borrowing capacity. This is why government debt became an important source of revenue beginning in 1994. The level of government debt to GDP was only 14 percent at the end of 1998.[33] This is quite low in comparison to Japan, for example, where government debt is almost 100 percent of GDP and severely constrains the Japanese government's ability to rescue the banking system. In China, however, the real problem is with the government's capacity to service the debt. In 1993, interest payments on government debt amounted to just 5 percent of the annual budget, but by 1998, they had ballooned to 23 percent.

Continued government support of state enterprises is requiring continued financing from the specialized banks because the policy banks are unable to bear the burden alone. This raises the specter of additional bail-outs of the banking system in the future. Even if the government is willing to bear this cost as an added burden to the fiscal system, it may be unable to do so and also keep inflationary pressures in check. In this circumstance, will the government be able to keep the confidence of depositors?

So far, most depositors seem to believe that the government will stand behind the banks, and they are undoubtedly correct. The government feels strongly that it cannot afford to let state enterprises fail for fear of labor unrest, nor can it avoid compensating the banks for their nonperforming portfolio for fear of a massive flight of depositors. Such is the government's cruel dilemma.

The financial sector epitomizes the conflicts and contradictions that have arisen in the reform process. The long-term goal of making the banking system both responsible and accountable for the efficient allocation of resources as the only way to reverse continued resource misallocation is in sharp conflict with the government's short-term goal of maximizing economic growth. So far, the short-term view prevails, and the state banks are again and again called upon to fund the government's annual investment program. Ultimately, there is but one solution to the problem. The government must stop requiring the banking system to support state enterprises that have proven themselves to be inefficient and unprofitable beyond the power of reform and government projects designed to meet government policy objectives.

Chapter Three

The Good Earth

Growing corn in Sichuan.

China has 22 percent of the world's population but only 7 percent of its arable land. The best cropland lies along its great river valleys and deltas, where most cities are located. Expanding cities are absorbing farmland, which, according to the government, is disappearing at a rate of 1.5 percent annually. The question of whether or not China can feed itself was hotly debated in the mid-1990s after Lester Brown presented his apocalyptic vision of a China incapable of feeding itself by the year 2030. Brown's argument was based on the rapid conversion of croplands into urban space, so much so, he said, that it will not be possible for China to improve yields on the diminishing land fast enough to counteract land losses. The government responded that China was capable of feeding itself and by the year 2030 would be producing 640 million tons of grain per year, enough to feed its expected population of 1.6 billion.

China's rugged topography favored small-scale, intensive agriculture, which began some 4,000 years ago in the Yellow River valley. Labor-intensive agriculture has characterized China's rural economy ever since. One China scholar aptly describes the farmer as China's principal agricultural resource, because "good muscles are more plentiful than good earth."[1] The Chinese farmer adapted to the lack of land and capital with intensive hand planting and harvesting, and a dense population has provided both the incentive and the means for intensive agricultural development. Farmers were bound to feudal landlords until Emperor Huang Di unified China in 221 B.C. and abolished serfdom. He gave the farmer independence but required him to pay taxes to the state, provide the state with his labor when required, and serve in the emperor's armies. The financial and service obligations were so onerous that the farmer was often not much better off than he had been as a serf. Local officials formed a class of landed gentry, but China continued to be a nation of small landholders because the Chinese system of land inheritance was based on equal distribution among all the sons of the deceased, which limited the growth of great estates. Labor was so cheap there was no incentive to pay for new technology or use more costly animal labor (which had to be fed and housed when not working).

Except for the mid-seventeenth and mid-to-late nineteenth centuries, the last 600 years has been a time of relative stability in Chinese history, during which China's population increased about eight times. The food required to support this population increase came from new land under cultivation and increased yields—mostly from the use of manure as fertilizer and more hand labor to produce double crops. Most agricultural techniques in use in the early twentieth century had been in use in 1400. For the individual farmer, conditions in the countryside had scarcely improved in the 300 years since the Ming dynasty ended.

The Communist Revolution brought farm families into producers' cooperatives and grouped villages in communes. The farmer, tied to the land, had no ownership rights except for the output of a small private plot. Mao Zedong's Great Leap Forward resulted in the worst famine in Chinese history. Thirty million people died, and millions more were nutritionally crippled for life. The commune system of agricultural production never recovered from this setback.

The "household responsibility" and land-contracting system introduced under Deng Xiaoping's reforms released farmers from the virtual serfdom of the commune system and converted them into long-term tenant farmers. A minimum portion of the land was held by the farmer for the length of tenure, but the rest could be reallocated by the village government, so the contracts provided no commitment that those who invested to improve the land would end up being the ultimate beneficiaries of these investments.[2] The state's move to increase contracts from fifteen to thirty years in 1993 still did not address the fundamental problem: The farmer and his family have no long-lasting physical tie to the land. With other opportunities arising, many of China's peasants have already left the farm. By 1996, 23 million rural enterprises were employing 135 million people.[3] Between 100 million and 120 million more have gone to live in urban areas in search of employment, but their status is tenuous at best, and they are treated as second-class citizens by the state (see chapter 4).

Water availability is the single largest constraint to improving the productivity of Chinese agriculture. Many Chinese farmers depend upon irrigation to keep yields and output high, but China has pronounced wet and dry seasons, and from the farmer's point of view, when water is most needed it is often not available. Almost one-half of China's cities face water shortages, which exacerbate the urban–rural competition for this scarce resource. A persistent drought in north China has reached the crisis stage, and the government is moving ahead with three massive water-transfer projects to transport water from the Yangtze River to the Yellow River. Even when the supply is sufficient, water is priced so low that each locality tries to maximize its water use, and much water is wasted. Yet, the government is so concerned with the effect of rising input costs such as water, seeds, fertilizers and pesticides, and on farm incomes that it is reluctant to raise costs sufficiently even to cover the water providers' operating costs.

China's desire to maintain direct government control over its staple grain supply has left the iron rice bowl largely intact in rural China. The government sets urban grain prices that are below cost to benefit consuming state enterprises, and it controls market prices to maintain price stability in the grain market and support farm income. When market prices fall, as they did after bountiful harvests from 1995 to 1998, the government maintained a floor price that cost it dearly. Meanwhile, production costs were steadily increasing—about 15 percent per annum between 1984 and 1996.

In spite of large subsidies, however, the deficits of state grain bureaus keep rising. Much of this is due to high bank debt repayments generated when the grain bureaus began borrowing from state banks in the early 1980s to pay for grain purchases, and by 1994, such loans had risen to US$27.3 billion.[4] In 1998, the government resumed monopoly control over the grain market. The World Bank's recommendation that the government commercialize grain marketing, eliminate large grain reserves held by both national and provincial governments, and introduce a much smaller buffer stock system linking reserve size with price triggers for open market purchases, fell on deaf ears.[5] The reintroduction of a central government monopoly over grain commercialization at government-determined prices, in the name of self-sufficiency and income stability, is requiring the government to hold immense amounts of grain at a very high cost. Since over 800 million Chinese depend upon agriculture for their livelihood, the government's concern about controlling grain commercialization and pricing is understandable. But other Asian countries with large agricultural populations, like India and Indonesia, are able to stabilize grain prices by purchasing only 20 to 25 percent of grain production as buffer stocks. That China should be perfectly capable of doing the same seems reasonable.

Good Muscles and Good Earth

China's agricultural origins go back some six thousand years to the Yangshao culture in the Yellow River valley, where proximity to water was essential for the development of large-scale grain production. China's rugged topography favored small holdings, and intensive agriculture began during the Shang dynasty (1766–1122 B.C.) when a feudal manorial system was established—farming villages grouped around walled towns ruled by a local aristocrat.

Huang Ti, the "Yellow Emperor" who founded the Qin dynasty (221–207 B.C.) and unified China, abolished serfdom and the manorial estates and replaced them with the freehold system of tax-paying, service-rendering independent farmers. The system began to break down almost as soon as it began, as some farmers became prosperous while most did not. High taxes plus forced military and labor service severely limited the surpluses the farmer could accumulate, leaving him vulnerable to natural or other disasters. At such times, the farmer had two choices: He could sell his land and become someone else's tenant; or if the situation was truly desperate, he could sell himself and his family into slavery. A large landowning class, mostly made up of officials, merchants, and money lenders, was created, and by the middle of the Han dynasty, most land was worked by indentured farmers and slaves. The Han emperor Wu Ti (141–87 B.C.) viewed large estates as economic rivals in capturing surpluses and a source of unrest because of the great poverty of the landless. He placed a maximum limit of 3,000 *mou* (about 500 acres) on individual family holdings. However, this edict was never implemented because the same officials who were supposed to enforce it at the local level were mostly large landowners.

In the fifth century A.D., the ruler of the northern Wei dynasty took the radical step of confiscating all land, abolishing land taxes, and reallocating land based on the number of males and oxen in each family. Land tenure lasted for the life of an individual, and his portion reverted to the state on his death. The idea was to perpetuate independent free-holding farmers, but officials were given inheritable tracts of land, and land revenues ended up as their salaries. The system was further compromised by successive emperors who granted large tax-exempt land holdings to their favorites.[6]

Feeding China's large cities was always a problem, and in the sixth century, the Sui emperor Wen Ti began what was to become the Grand Canal by building connecting canals to streams and rivers linking the Yellow and Yangtze rivers. His successor extended the canal system north to Beijing and south to Hangzhou in A.D. 605. For the next 1,300 years, the Grand Canal was the lifeline bringing agricultural produce to imperial capitals and other large cities of eastern and northern China. By the end of the first millennium, 30,000 miles of navigable waterways made China the world's largest trading area.[7]

The next major shift in land tenure occurred in the Tang dynasty (A.D. 617–907), a time when local market towns and regional commerce became much more important, reflecting a loss of central authority and a rapidly increasing population. The equal-field system was adopted, in which land was periodically reallocated according to population registers. But as the state lost control of the countryside, the system fell into disuse. Up to this time, population had been densest in the north, where millet and winter wheat were the staple grains. Wet rice production in the south became important during the Southern Sung dynasty (A.D. 1127–1279), and the use of human waste as fertilizer became widespread. With new quick-ripening seeds, double- and even triple-cropping rice became possible.

The Mongol conquest of China in the thirteenth century began two centuries of dynastic wars, as the Mongol Yuan dynasty and its successor, the Ming dynasty, tried to gain control over China. Agricultural production and population declined, all land was confiscated, and most peasants became serfs or slaves under Mongol overlords. Ming emperors abolished slavery but retained the great estates as state lands to be rented at a profit or given to court favorites. Once the Ming had established themselves, China began a remarkable period of six centuries of economic and population growth. Two periods of warfare interrupted the general prosperity, first during the Ming decline and Manchu conquest of China in 1644 and later when the weakened Manchus had to put down the Taiping rebels and defeat a Muslim revolt in the mid- to late 1800s.

The Chinese system of land inheritance was based on equal distribution among all the sons of the deceased, which limited the growth of great estates. Local officials formed a class of landed gentry, but most Chinese lived in villages and farmed small plots. Labor was so cheap there was no incentive to pay for new technology or use more costly animal labor. For 1,500 years after the birth of Christ, only three new crops—tea, cotton, and sorghum—entered China. Then, in the seventeenth century, after the Spanish conquest of the New World, corn, potatoes, tobacco, and peanuts were introduced. Both corn and potatoes could flourish under harsher conditions than traditional grains.

China's population rose from 65 million to 80 million in 1400 to

400 million by 1900 and 600 million by 1950. Local histories reveal that placing new land under grain cultivation and increased yields each accounted for about one-half of the rising population's need for grain. Most of the yield increase came from increased use of human and pig manure as fertilizer and from labor inputs, enabling double-cropping rice or sowing two different crops during the summer and winter. Between A.D. 1400 and 1900, grain output increased sixfold and irrigated land threefold. Fertilizer use per unit of land was twice that of 1400. By the twentieth century, however, productivity began to decline because the cost of making marginal land more productive became too high, while population increase reduced per capita land ownership.[8]

But had life really improved for the individual farmer? Studies undertaken in the 1930s showed that conditions in the countryside had scarcely improved since agriculture's decline in the late Ming dynasty 300 hundred years before and that the benefits of a growing and expanding economy had failed to reach millions of people. Many, who led brief, miserable lives were even too poor to marry. They subsisted day by day, their only asset a pair of hands or a bamboo pole for hauling heavy loads. During sowing and harvesting seasons, they lined up in the night and waited anxiously to be chosen the next day to work in the fields.[9]

Agriculture under Mao Zedong

In September 1949, Mao convened a People's Political Consultative Conference to adopt a Common Program for China. Primacy was given to developing an industrial base on the Soviet model, while agriculture was to be collectivized under government control, thus assuring that China's grain supplies would be sufficient to rebuild the economy and feed the people. Agricultural reform began with rent reduction and land redistribution. It was a gradual approach in which at first landlords were expropriated and their land was distributed to former tenants and the landless. Then, families were organized into temporary work teams, which were subsequently made permanent and expanded into producers' cooperatives or brigades in which farmers worked for wages. Families were allowed a private plot for growing vegetables to sell, which enabled them to have some disposable income.

The state first took its share of the harvest, and then a part had to be allocated to buy next year's seeds and animal fodder. The peasant's share was based on a subsistence calculation plus an additional amount for work performed. The remainder of the harvest was a "surplus," which the government purchased and allotted to the six administrative tiers above the work unit—essentially an "overhead" cost. The production team leader was responsible for selling the surplus and was thus the ultimate broker in the grain-procurement system, mediating between his team inferiors and brigade cadre superiors. This function was as old as China's history, and the team leader's patron–client relationship was where his *guanxi* connections came into play and where corruption inevitably occurred and often flourished.[10]

During the first Five Year Plan (1952–57), industrial production rose 18.7 percent, while agricultural output grew only 3.8 percent. In 1957, grain output grew only 1 percent—one-half the rate of population growth.[11] Unless something drastic was done, more grain could not be extracted to support the industrial boom. Mao wanted to harness the energy of the farmer through an ideological campaign supported by a new and more vigorous form of collective rural organization. Zhou Enlai and others felt that farmers could produce more if they were given more material incentive to do so, plus more fertilizer and better tools. Mao prevailed, and in 1958, the production brigades were grouped into people's communes. What made this work was the emergence of a new rural elite made up of cadres of energetic and ambitious younger people who sought status and power in the new organization. Villagers were tied to the land by a household registration system, and they could obtain their food supply only at the same location. The peasant was boxed in as never before, in a modern version of serfdom under party control.[12]

According to Mao, agriculture and industry were to be transformed simultaneously by "walking on two legs."[13] Water resources had been barely tapped for agricultural use, and only about 15 percent of all cultivated land was irrigated. Millions of peasants were removed from the fields to work on large projects such as irrigation, land reclamation, flood control, and rural industry. Local cadres were indoctrinated with the twin concepts of taking initiative while relying on their own resources to make a "Great Leap Forward." Soon millions were caught up in the fervor of a great crusade under the personal direction of Mao, and cadres competed in setting up wildly exaggerated output targets. The numbers are startling. Mao outdid the emperors who built the Great Wall and the Grand Canal by mobilizing 650 million Chinese who worked around the clock to build public works all over China. Many of these proved to be faulty.

One hundred million Chinese helped build 1 million "backyard" iron smelters, but the iron produced was of such low quality that it was useless.[14] Another hundred million opened up almost 8 million acres of new irrigated land. Millions more built 84,000 dams storing 470 billion cubic meters of water, 175,000 kilometers of river dikes and levees to control the flow of water, and over five million wells in the north. This was sufficient to increase crop land under irrigation from 16 million to 48 million hectares and to drain a further 17 million hectares of water-logged land. However, there was a high incidence of dam failures, siltation and waterlogging became recurring problems, earthen levees were subject to erosion, and many wells dried up or filled with silt. Poor management compounded the problem. Very little emphasis was placed on efficient water use, cost recovery was ignored, necessary maintenance did not take place, and people displaced by these projects were not properly compensated or resettled.[15]

Based on data furnished by local governments, the State Statistical Bureau claimed that food crops and cotton output had almost doubled in 1958. This figure of 375 million tons of grain was later revised downward to 250 million, and Western economists estimated that the real production was only 215 million tons.[16] Nevertheless, the Party's Central Committee set 1959 targets that were 50 percent higher than what they thought had been achieved in 1958. Mao's prophetic vision had become self-fulfilling in the minds of the cadres and bureaucrats who eagerly accepted at face value these inflated claims. Mao had his old friend, Peng Dehuai, the defense minister, sacked because he dared to raise questions about what was really happening in the countryside. Mao then used an antirightist campaign to weed out other critics of the Great Leap Forward, which was then carried out with even greater vigor in 1959. With the diversion of so many peasants into construction, there were not enough hands to harvest the crops, which were not as plentiful as those of 1958 due to bad weather. To meet the demands of the cities, the local population was forced to reduce their own allotments by as much as four-fifths in some cases. Cadres continued to report wildly exaggerated outputs, and tragedy was inevitable. From 1959 to 1962 some 20 million Chinese died of malnutrition and disease. Millions more were so malnourished they later succumbed to disease or suffered the permanent results of nutritional deprivation.[17] The famine also sparked corruption, as cadres confiscated grain to protect themselves and their friends.

In 1961, one of the party's most respected leaders, Chen Yun, wrote a report recommending strengthening private-plot agriculture, giving households responsibility for setting grain quotas and closing inefficient Great Leap industrial enterprises. Mao agreed to circulate his views, but he did not endorse them. Although the party began a policy of economic retrenchment, Mao never lost faith in his policies, and a socialist reeducation campaign was launched to reform the system by purging or reeducating cadres who no longer shared his vision. Above all, Mao needed a symbol of self-reliance and revolutionary zeal to show the way to cadres all over China. In a bleak and remote part of Shanxi Province, the commune of Dazhai was apparently achieving wonders and improving production fivefold. The commune's leader was brought to Beijing, honored, and given a private audience with Mao, who proclaimed, "in agriculture, learn from Dazhai."[18]

During the Cultural Revolution of 1966–1976, incessant indoctrination and unremitting labor were the daily round for most farmers. Sending 14 million urban youth to live in villages often resulted in conflicts among the better educated youth, the cadres, and the villagers, but for some of those sent, it was life's most formative experience. "I was sixteen years old when I was sent to a desperately poor village in Jiangsu Province," related one senior Chinese official. "The men in the village had nothing, yet anyone who was sixteen was considered a man and had to do a man's work. There, I became a man."[19] For the farmers, the rhythms of work and family continued despite the political chaos, wall slogans, and exhortations to "emulate Dazhai." In 1975, the First National Conference in Learning from Dazhai was held. It was a blatant attempt by Maoists to reinforce and reinvigorate the policies of local initiative and self-reliance within the commune-centered production structure. The attempt was short-lived, and by 1980, with reform under way, the "folly" of pursuing the spirit of Dazhai was publicly aired in the *Peoples Daily.*[20]

Agriculture under Deng Xiaoping

By the late 1970s, the amount of arable land had declined by 11 percent as urban space conquered green space, while the population had doubled. One-fourth of the rural population was illiterate and unemployable in urban areas for any but the most menial jobs. Mao's policies of providing low-cost food to support urban growth and industrialization were replaced by greater emphasis on food security and self-sufficiency and more concern for farmers' incomes.[21] In 1978, the "production responsibility system" was adopted, involving a contract between the production unit and the individual household, which was allocated a parcel of land with tenure for fifteen years if it agreed to produce a certain output at an agreed compensation. Any excess belonged to the household. With the state no longer guaranteeing a basic grain allowance, rural families needed a wage earner, and millions of men left the farm for nearby market towns or more distant cities. Women, children, and even the elderly took their place in grain production. Local officials were responsible for establishing cropping patterns and setting production goals. To stimulate output, the official grain price was raised 20 percent and the surplus grain price 50 percent. Meanwhile, the state increased its grain subsidy to urban workers to protect them from the impact of the price increase. Markets for fruits, vegetables, oilseeds, fish, and livestock were opened up to private trading from the mid-1980s, but private trading in the grain and cotton markets was allowed only after government quota requirements had been met. Agriculture was identified as one of the four priority areas under the "four modernizations," the catchphrase that became the litany justifying every new turn in the economic road.

By the mid-1980s, the system of peoples' communes had been completely dismantled. Between 1978 and 1984, grain output increased from 199 million tons to 306 million tons, a phenomenal achievement not equaled by any other major food-producing country.[22] Much of the increase came from the widespread use of fertilizer. Yields increased by 62 percent, equal to an average increase of 7.1 percent per year. For the rest of the 1980s, however, annual yields increased by only about 2 percent, and in the first half of the 1990s increases had slowed to less than 1 percent.[23] But with the whole economy still growing at 8 percent and industry at 11 percent, income surged and with it demand for grain-fed food products like pork and chicken. Meat consumption rose from 7.7 million tons in 1977 to 40 million tons in 1994.[24]

Grain production in the reform period can be divided into four distinct phases based on medium-term shifts in the pattern of output. After the phenomenal increases of 1978 through 1984, grain production stagnated from 1985 to 1989. In the first half of the 1990s, output varied, but in 1995 through 1998, bumper crops resulted in large surpluses. What does this all mean? Part of the answer lies in dramatic changes in regional outputs. Southern China's share in incremental grain output actually declined in the second half of the 1980s, as the economic boom ate up prime rice-growing land, while northern China was responsible for 58 percent of the increase. From 1990 to 1994, it was the center-east grain basket that virtually stagnated, while northern China continued to increase its share of incremental grain output to almost four-fifths of the total. The kinds of grains being produced also are part of the answer. As rice production declined in the south and center east, new rice production shifted to the northeast. The north also continued to expand production of wheat, and both regions expanded corn and soy production, which declined or stagnated in other regions. In per capita terms, the south replaced the northwest as the least important grain growing region, with per capita grain output at a lower level in 1995 than it had been in 1978. By 1994, urbanization of agricultural land was having such an impact that only the northeast region was producing a small surplus, while the densely populated center-east and southern provinces had undergone spectacular declines.[25]

The "governor's responsibility system" was adopted in 1995 to make grain markets more stable. Provincial governors were made responsible for maintaining an overall balance between grain supply and demand in their jurisdictions. Provincial self-sufficiency did result in increased grain production that helped boost the bumper crops of the late 1990s, and again it was the northeast that registered the largest increase. However, the system impeded the efficient marketing of grain to areas where the need was greatest and led to outright regional protectionism as provinces placed limits or stoppages on grain movements across provincial borders. Transaction costs were extremely high—up to four times international costs—because of obsolete grain handling and storage systems and inadequate transportation.[26] Similar program required city mayors to ensure the supply of meat, fish, vegetables, and dairy products in urban areas.

When grain supplies exceeded demand in the mid-1990s, government-quota grain prices were increased (by 60 percent in 1994 alone), and by 1997, market prices had fallen below quota prices after three consecutive years of bumper crops. At that point, the government established a support price, including a RMB 0.60 subsidy for each kilogram purchased.[27] Grain-purchasing enterprises ran up huge debts to finance grain purchases. They borrowed heavily from the Agricultural Development Bank, a government "policy" bank established to help finance agriculture.[28] The net result is that both the agencies and trading entities and the bank are in deep financial trouble. By the end of 1997, indebtedness of state grain enterprises had risen to US$65.6 million equivalent, and US$25.8 million of these loans simply could not be accounted for. These same enterprises had accumulated losses of RMB 100 billion.[29]

Disappearing farmland is one of the government's biggest worries, and it claims that China is losing arable land at the rate of 1.5 percent a year. In 1997, the State Council decreed that there would be a one-year freeze on conversion of arable land to nonagricultural purposes. The freeze has been renewed ever since, but the state exempted key projects such as low-income housing from the freeze, and 180,000 hectares were still converted to urban use in 1997.[30] Some of this land is lost completely to development. A recent survey shows that 80,000 hectares of land set aside for construction projects remain idle because the projects were never completed.[31] Land loss is said to be so serious in the south that the Guangzhou provincial government in 1998 decreed that no new cemeteries may be built. "We cannot afford to allow the dead to take land from the living," intoned a local official.[32]

Between 1978 and 1990, although the total area sown with crops in China declined from 150.1 to 148.4 million hectares, by 1996 it had risen to 152.4 million. Meanwhile, the multiple cropping index, which measures the degree to which cultivated land is used to raise more than one crop, had increased from 150 in 1978 to 160 in 1996.[33] Judged by these indicators, the state of Chinese agriculture is better than when only loss of arable land is considered. Land actually under cultivation is also a far more useful indicator than amount of arable land, as much of the land that is arable but uncultivated may be unsuited for crop cultivation because of its location, infertility, or for other reasons. Nevertheless, the rise in the multiple cropping index reflects more planting of early season rice and spring wheat, which are inferior in quality to rice and wheat grown at other seasons. The government has become increasingly concerned about the rising stocks of unsold inferior grains, and for the year 2000 it did not support prices for these grains.

After two decades of reform, farmland tenure is still unresolved. China's Organization Law of the Village Committee of 1988 provided for the direct election of village officials and gave them legal authority over land rights. Under the household-responsibility system, households were given tenure over the land for fifteen years, but village leaders could reallocate most of the land by transferring it among farm households in the village. In the absence of labor and land markets, village leaders viewed reallocation as a leveling mechanism, in which new households are provided with the land they need, government quota fulfillment is ensured, income disparities among households are reduced, and acceptable land–labor relationships are maintained.[34] In 1994, land tenure was extended to thirty years to provide farmers with a greater incentive to invest more time and money in their land. But with the threat of reallocation ever present, the impact of this change has been minimal.

Perhaps the principal achievement of agricultural reform has been its attack on poverty. Between 1978 and 1984, a Food for Work and other programs providing rural employment enabled about 171 million Chinese to escape poverty by increasing their incomes above the poverty threshold of a dollar a day—a remarkable achievement in just six years. Over the next decade about 130 million more people crossed above the poverty line. Still, some 176 million Chinese remain mired in poverty, including 50 million unfortunates who live in isolated upland areas where the land is so infertile that it cannot produce enough food even for basic subsistence. The World Bank believes that more of these unfortunates could have been reached by better targeting.[35]

Most Financial Benefits of Reform Go Elsewhere

Farmers were among the first agents of reform, because they began to dismantle the collective system on their own, and because their unwillingness to contribute to local infrastructure projects without representation in decision making helped push the government to support democratic elections at the village level.[36] Yet the urban–rural income gap remains just as wide as it was when reform began twenty years ago. The average income of a farmworker was 40 percent of that of the average urban worker in 1978, and although by 1985 farmers' incomes had risen to about 54 percent of urban incomes, rural incomes declined to just 35 percent in 1994, only to rise to 40 percent after the bumper harvests of 1995 to 1997. If the subsidies that urban dwellers receive are included in urban income, then rural income falls to 31 percent of urban income—the lowest ratio in the world.[37]

What disposable income farmers have is greatly reduced by ever more onerous local taxes. Fiscal decentralization after 1978 shifted much of the revenue burden to local governments, which have to finance about one-half of their budgetary expenditures. When communes reverted to villages in the 1980s, they inherited a collective system of salaries, subsidies, and social welfare payments, but not the resource base to pay for them. They raised money by placing levies on farm income and output, charging fees and rents, and receiving remittances from local township and village enterprises. A survey of 1,000 villages in Sichuan Province revealed that the number of levies had increased from sixty-four in 1985 to 107 in 1991.[38]

The central government mandates certain annual expenditure targets—for example, in the year 2000, that 5 percent of rural budgets be spent on health and 4 percent on education—and local officials are evaluated on how well they fulfill these mandates. They have little choice but to create new fees and assessments to finance them. Above the village level, local governments must support a vast array of bureaus and agencies, which they are unable to fund adequately. In 1994, for example, 70 percent of China's county governments had budget deficits and could not meet operating expenses. Government entities are therefore encouraged to raise revenue to cover the portion of their operating costs that cannot be met by the budget. When politically sensitive budgetary obligations, like wage bills, cannot be met, county governments regularly divert funds destined for other purposes to make sure wages are paid.[39] Such transfers amount to huge hidden deficits whose size can only be guessed at.

Corruption can be even more of a curse in the countryside than it is in the cities, and intended beneficiaries of reform often end up with little or nothing after intermediaries take more than their share. In 1998, the State Council issued a decree to curb fraudulent practices among local grain enterprises, which are refusing to buy all the grain offered by farmers or pay them the full amount due. The funds they receive are often diverted to other purposes. A typical example occurred in 1996 when the Suihua Grain Administration of Heilongjiang Province transferred 100,000 tons of grain reported to be worth US$14,500,000 to Dalian in Liaoning Province. The grain was sold for only US$11,000,000, and the money was used to construct hotels, offices, and residential buildings.[40]

To be fair, state grain enterprises are in a terrible bind. They are stuck with too much grain, and much of it is of low quality. Storage costs are very high because the grain has been purchased with bank loans bearing a high interest rate. Indeed, the cost of holding the grain is so high that it makes sense to sell the grain as quickly as possible, even at a price below its cost. Exporting the grain is not really an alternative since all grain exports are channeled through a single giant state trading corporation that sets its own export quotas based on a national export plan.

Lester Brown's Wake-up Call

Lester Brown published *Who Will Feed China? Wake-up Call for a Small Planet* in 1995. In it, he argued that, like Japan, Korea, and Taiwan—all countries with dense populations and limited agricultural land—China will become a major importer of grain by the time its population reaches its projected peak of 1.6 billion by 2030. Like these three countries, which lost between 42 and 52 percent of their land planted in grain, China's loss of arable land to urban growth and industrialization will exceed its ability to improve agricultural yields and output.[41] Brown predicted that by the year 2030, grain acreage will be only four-fifths of what it was in 1990, while China's population not only will be one-third larger but will be consuming more grain per person (400 kilograms a year). The rest of the world will have to provide China with enough grain—a staggering 369 million tons annually—to feed its people. This is almost double present world grain exports, and with world production, which has been declining, expected to continue to decline, this could lead to global food scarcity.[42]

Brown supported his contention by chronicling China's changing food consumption patterns as more disposable income allowed people to "move up the food chain" and more grain was required as animal feed to support meat consumption. A century ago, Japan had a similar problem and turned to the sea for its protein. Fish and rice have characterized the Japanese diet ever since. With ocean fisheries pushed to their biological limits, China would have to turn to fish farming, which not only would use up agricultural land but would require two kilograms of grain for each kilogram of fish produced.[43]

The other side of the food equation is shrinking cropland, and from 1990 to 1994, land devoted to growing grain declined 5.6 percent while China's population increased 4.9 percent, resulting in a per capita grain loss of 10.5 percent. Can China avoid the drastic loss of cropland that occurred among its Asian neighbors during the 1960s and 1970s? Brown believes there is a remarkable consistency in the effect of industrialization on the cropland base of China's neighbors. Conversion of farmland to factories, houses and roads; decline in multiple cropping and abandonment of marginal land due to exodus of rural workers; and a shift from grain to more profitable crops occurred in all three countries and is occurring in China as well.

For China, Brown speaks of the need for 1 million new factories, 98 million more housing units, and more roads to support 22 million auto-mobiles.[44] The result is that per person land under grain will shrink from 0.08 hectares in 1990 to 0.03 hectares by 2030.[45] Brown identifies the central question as whether productivity can be raised to offset the loss of land. Again, he looks at China's neighbors. Although the support price Japan pays its farmers is six times the world market price for rice, rice yields hit a ceiling in 1984 of 4.7 tons per hectare, and except for an unusual year in 1994, yields have not risen since then.[46] China's phe-nomenal rise in productivity during the late 1970s to the mid-1980s, was due to improved irrigation and fertilization, but with the highest fertilizer use in the world and a declining water supply, Brown sees little room for further gains from either for China. Barring some dramatic breakthrough in technology, Brown concludes that "with the cropland base shrinking and with water shortages spreading, much if not all the growth in demand for food in China translates directly into imports."[47]

Although by the mid-1990s China had the world's largest irrigated land area—47 million hectares over the last twenty years—the annual increase was only one-third of 1 percent, and most of this came from tapping underground reserves rather than surface water. In the north, underground pumping was exceeding the recharge rate of aquifers, water tables began falling, and aquifers became depleted. Another se-rious problem is the diversion of irrigation water to industrial and resi-dential use.[48]

Brown looked to Japan as China's closest surrogate, because condi-tions in China seem so similar to those in Japan forty years earlier. Tak-ing a conservative stance that China's grain output of 340 million tons in 1990 would fall by about one-half of Japan's rate of decline during its own period of rapid industrialization, grain output would only be 272 million tons in 2030. If per capita grain consumption stays at the present annual level of just under 300 kilograms per person, China will have to import 207 million tons to feed its people. If, however, the increasingly affluent Chinese people continue to move up the food chain, to con-sume, say, 400 kilograms of grain a year, then China would have to import 369 million tons.[49]

Brown's book created a furor. While the Chinese government agreed with him that the world could not feed China, it disagreed that China could not feed itself. In 1996 the government produced its own "white paper," entitled "The Grain Issue in China," which concluded that China would be fully capable of meeting any grain demand and by 2030, would be producing 640 million tons per annum, enough to meet the needs of 1.6 billion people.[50] Most experts in and outside China also took exception to Brown's views.

Brown's critics questioned his comparisons with China's Asian neighbors, because Brown ignores the fact that Japan idled a significant portion of its rice-producing land due to excess production. In South Korea and Taiwan, while land cultivated with grain declined sharply, total land under cultivation did not and could easily be shifted back into grain. They also argue that Brown grossly exaggerated land scarcity in China, because official estimates of cultivated land of 95 million hectares are about 40 percent less than the amount of 132 million hectares revealed in satellite photographs. The difference is due to farmers' underreporting land for tax purposes.[51] Critics also point out that underreporting of cultivated land results in overestimating yields. Citing U.S. experience with hybrid corn, a number of critics insist that better crop management can improve yields. They also challenge Brown's assertion that increasing water scarcity will reduce cropland under irrigation. Since water is priced at 20 percent or less of its actual cost, there is no incentive to use it efficiently, and pricing at cost or above would lead to much more efficient use. Also, evaporation and seepage losses commonly amount to 50 to 60 percent, and using less water more effectively could reduce water loss considerably. More effective fertilizer application would produce higher yields, say the critics. Finally, Brown's critics say that if they use his assumptions and simply increase cultivable land by 40 percent, they arrive at an import requirement in 2030 of 131 million tons—only 36 percent of Brown's projected 368 million tons and a much more manageable amount of imports.[52]

Brown's response is to stick to his assertion that cropping efficiency and yield increases are at their limit in China, even with a 40 percent greater area, because the natural fertility of land in China is far less than that in Japan. He noted that Chinese government concern about the loss of agricultural land mirrors his own and that rising demand for fruits, vegetables, and oilseeds will continue to shift land out of grain production. He also says that too much is made of possible efficiency and management improvements in crop yields and fertilizer application, because while in the United States only marginal changes were needed to improve hybrid corn yields, in China the situation is quite different and it is not clear how current practices can be improved. Regarding better water use, he cites the difference between efficiency at the farm level and for the watershed as a whole—water misused by one farmer returns to the stream or aquifer and is used by another farmer—and the difficulty of increasing overall efficiency of water use.[53]

In its "China 2020" series, the World Bank comes out on the side of Brown's critics and argues that China can remain essentially self-sufficient in food over the next twenty to thirty years, although China will have to import at least 10 percent of its grain needs. The World Bank believes China has little choice but to be largely self-sufficient in grain production. Chinese ports have neither berths for large, deep-draft seagoing vessels, nor facilities for bulk cargo handling, transfer, and storage. China's railroads and inland river system are inadequate for bulk cargo transport and unless upgraded would raise import transport and storage costs to unacceptable levels.[54]

Brown's comparison of China with Japan also suffers from his assumption that China, with its much larger and more diverse population, will move in step with Japan in altering its food habits. In China, serious urban–rural inequalities remain wide, and while the more affluent part of the population will climb the food chain as rapidly as the Japanese, the larger, less affluent, mostly rural group will not.

Too Much or Too Little Water

China has seven large river basins that encompass one-half of its land area and are home to 86 percent of its population. Yet, the limited availability of water is the single biggest constraint to improving China's agricultural productivity. The two largest systems, the Yellow and Yangtze Rivers, dominate northern and central China and include roughly one-half of China's river basin area and population. Yet, while the Yangtze and other river basins in central and southern China account for four-fifths of the nation's rainfall and runoff, they include only about one-third of its cultivated land.[55]

Each river basin has its own river conservancy commission, which is responsible for developing a comprehensive river basin development plan. However, the commissions have neither the authority to implement the plans nor the financial resources to give them leverage over local governments, each trying to maximize its own water use. A water law was promulgated in 1988 specifying that developing and utilizing water resources should be based on unified planning at the river-basin or regional level. However, the regulations necessary to carry out the law have been slow in coming, and an administrative structure to implement river-basin plans simply does not exist. A major part of the problem is the difficulty in resolving differences between competing agricultural, industrial, navigational, and electric power objectives over water use. This is compounded by a lack of resources. In 1988, for example, the central government provided only 15 percent of the total annual cost of the operations, maintenance, and upgrading of state water projects across the nation.

During the 1980s, more authority was delegated to local governments to select water control projects, but they were also expected to finance them if located within their jurisdictions. Many agencies had to resort to bank loans to obtain the financing they needed. In 1985, the State Council issued a directive entitled "Methods for Water Charges Pricing, Collection, and Control for Water Conservancy Projects," aimed at relating water user fees to the cost of water. But water tariffs were still one-third to one-half of the cost of water, and the financial condition of water entities was worsened by difficulties in collecting charges, with actual collections only 40 percent of the amount assessed. Not only were most localities unable to make up the difference, but many had diverted funds to other more profitable projects.[56]

In practice, provincial officials ignore water management plans if it suits their interests to do so, and each community along the river bank tries to store water or use as much of it as possible. When competition for water reaches a crisis, the central government often has to intervene. The group that has the most *guanxi* usually wins. In 1996, just one month away from the summer wheat harvest, furious farmers in north China watched millions of gallons of water flow past their thirsty crops to an oil refinery downriver, while guards stood by the valves controlling the water flow to their fields. The refinery had threatened to shut down, and the government declared a state of emergency and closed a 400-mile stretch of river to water use. To make matters worse, it was the only time that spring that the river had carried enough water to reach the farmers' fields.[57]

Meanwhile, human water consumption has risen over the last forty years from 12 billion to 30 billion cubic meters every year. Lester Brown forecasts that water use will explode, with human consumption increasing 430 percent and industrial use 518 percent by 2030. Although farms still represent 85 percent of water use, a thousand tons of water are needed to produce a ton of wheat with a market value of US$200, while the same amount of water can produce US$14,000 in industrial output. As competition for the scarce commodity intensifies, farms are losing out.[58]

Water Crisis in the North

In the north, the Yellow River makes a long loop through Inner Mongolia and becomes choked with yellow sediment, so much so that one-third of its annual flow is used to flush the mud downstream. The Yellow River has fifteen times *less* volume and five times *more* silt than the Yangtze and no overall river basin system for managing this—and therein lies the source of its problem. Silt narrows the width of the river and raises the bottom, making the effects of flooding much more serious. But the big problem today is falling water quantity, due partly to increasing seasonality of water flows due to changes in weather patterns, and partly to poor management of a resource decreasing amid rapidly growing use. In 1972, the Yellow River stopped flowing for the first time in its history. By the 1990s, the river was running dry every year, and each reduction of one cubic meter of water meant one less kilogram of grain. In 1996, it was dry for 133 days and in 1997 for 226 days.[59] The government is pursuing two strategies to deal with the problem. It wants to improve water retention as well as bring additional water to the Yellow River. A dam second in scale only to the Three Gorges and said to be capable of surviving a once-in-a-thousand-year flood is being built at Xiaolangdi, and another large dam is being built at Wanjaizhai. But together they will contribute only 4 billion cubic meters of additional water annually—less than 1 percent of China's total yearly water use.[60]

Plans are also being drafted to transfer water from the Yangtze to the Yellow River at three separate locations through huge tunnels and aqueducts and along the Grand Canal, which altogether will cost far more than the Three Gorges Dam. These three schemes will provide about fourteen billion cubic meters of water per year to the north, but this is less than the current annual reduction in groundwater supplies. How will the difference be made up?

Three hundred of China's 617 cities are facing water shortages. The situation in the north is especially critical, and a Chinese survey indicates that the water table beneath the North China Plain fell by 1.5 meters annually during the first half of the 1990s. The Fen River, which ran through Taiyuan, the capital of Shanxi Province in China's northwest, has ceased to exist. Wells have been dug as deep as 2,500 feet, chasing

Taiyuan's groundwater deposits. According to a World Bank expert, the city must either move or transfer water from the Yellow River, 200 miles away.[61] But upstream transfer from the Yellow River only exacerbates the problem for downstream users.

Many experts think that China should focus on water conservation rather than on costly projects to increase the supply of water. Lester Brown again is at the forefront of conservation. He believes that the three water transfer projects now under way will provide only "a drop in the bucket" and will cost billions. As an alternative to water transfer, Brown recommends more water-efficient irrigation techniques, shifting to less-water-intensive crops, and saving and recycling water from industrial plants, where there is enormous overuse. Brown says China must shift from a supply-side to a demand-management approach but is vague about how this could be achieved. He fails to take into account that nothing will happen unless incentives make it attractive to use water more efficiently, reduce water wastage, and encourage its recycling. The key is to raise the price of water to cover its cost and provide a return on investment for local water agencies. Meanwhile, the government continues to focus on improving the supply of water as the answer to its problems. This is partly because of its faith in big projects to solve big problems and also because it is reluctant to raise the price of water since this would raise on-farm costs and have a negative impact on farmers' income. However, farmers tilling infertile land on the upper reaches of the Yellow River require twice as much water to grow the same amount of food as farmers downstream on the fertile plains. If water is sold to the highest bidder, then marginal farmers like those on the upper reaches will not be able to afford to continue farming.

Agricultural Trade and World Trade Organization Membership

A country's comparative advantage in producing agricultural products, especially land-intensive crops like grain, often declines as a result of economic growth—and this is happening in China. It is reflected in China's agricultural trade, which is far less important than industrial exports, and grew only at a rate of about 2 percent annually between 1980 and 1997. Agriculture's share in total exports has declined from about 30 percent in 1980 to about 10 percent in 1997. Grain exports have become even less important and fell from 23 percent to 11 percent of agricultural exports, while fruits, vegetables, animal and seafood exports grew rapidly and now account for four-fifths of agricultural exports. [62] Now that China is a member of the World Trade Organization, China's grain exports will likely increase, especially when the government dismantles its export-import monopoly and opens international trade to the private sector. Import quotas for grain and other agricultural commodities tied to low tariff levels became effective in 2000. They will be increased annually through the year 2004 in accordance with an agreed schedule.

China has made significant reductions in its nonagricultural tariffs in recent years. Average import tariffs were reduced from 42 percent in 1995 to 17 percent in 1997. Like most countries, China has high tariffs protecting agriculture. To meet the conditions of World Trade Organization membership, China has agreed to reduce its weighted average agricultural tariffs to 14.5 percent from the current 31 percent by the year 2004, but grain tariffs will remain high, although they will be reduced from 77 to 65 percent. [63]

In China, nontariff barriers such as import quotas and licenses, are often combined with tariffs at very different rates and thus distort the whole tariff structure. Yet, the impact of quotas is hard to judge because the quota size is not revealed. For example, China's most favored nation tariff on wheat was 114 percent in 1996, and China has agreed with the World Trade Organization to reduce the wheat tariff to 65 percent by 2004. However, quota wheat imports are subject to a mere 1 percent tariff, and the listed rate only applies to imports above the quota. [64] To the degree that most imports occur within the quota, the tariff level is meaningless.

Will the Good Earth Feed China in 2020 or 2030?

Faced with consecutive bumper grain crops and falling farm gate prices in the late 1990s, the government was forced to buy more and more grain to maintain price stability. In effect, the state price was set above the market price to protect farmer incomes. However, this level of intervention became fiscally unsustainable in 1998, and Premier Zhu Rongji announced that the government would reimpose its monopoly over the grain market to provide greater price stability. Zhu criticized state grain bureaus for diverting grain purchasing funds to other purposes, for their poor management, and for being overstaffed. He said the present marketing system was harming the farmer and failing to meet the needs of a socialist market economy, and the increasing subsidies necessary to support the system had become an unbearable burden for the government. Premier Zhu also announced a further reform of the grain marketing and storage system. Under a program given the numerological cachet of "Four Separations; One Perfection," functions related to carrying out state grain policy were to be separated from commercial functions; government-owned grain was to be separated from commercial grain stocks; provincial, prefectural, and county grain bureaus were to have separate policy and commercial entities; and "old debts" separated from "new debts," with the grain marketing enterprises responsible for the latter. The "perfection" was the requirement that bureaus could not sell grain below cost. It appears that neither the reform measures nor the trade monopoly is being enforced very effectively, although they are still official policy.[65]

The World Bank argues that much can be done to improve agricultural yields. China has 40 million hectares of unutilized land that is probably reclaimable, although the government is currently reclaiming only about 250,000 hectares a year. Fertilizer applications must be increased now that China's actual cultivated area is known to be so much larger than government statistics indicate. In addition, improving the balance between potash and other fertilizers could increase yields by 12 to 15 percent. Much more can be done to improve water use. Wastewater currently dumped into rivers and streams should be treated and recycled for agricultural use, and water prices should be raised forthwith to cover at least the cost of supplying the water and, over the longer term, to reflect marginal cost increases. As only about 30 percent of the water in irrigation canals actually reaches the crops, this inefficiency can be improved by lining the canals and using piping/hose systems to carry the water to the fields. Continued growth in China's grain output since 1984 is largely attributed to successful agricultural research, but in the 1990s the amount spent on research declined by 40 percent. Agricultural research has also suffered because research institutes have been diverted from their main purpose and encouraged to engage in commercial activities to earn income to support themselves.[66] The government should end trading monopolies and procurement at prices subsidized by government grain bureaus and enterprises. It should limit itself to price stabilization and maintenance of strategic grain reserves. If these steps are not taken, says the World Bank, China's actual grain deficit in 2020 will likely be double the 10 percent projected.[67]

Can China's farmers look forward to a better life? Rural reform has lifted millions of Chinese out of poverty and has raised incomes for millions more, but in many ways China's farmers cannot escape their own history. They cannot own the land they farm and they are tenant farmers under a reallocation system reminiscent of the one adopted in the Tang dynasty over one thousand years ago. Like their forebears, they must surrender the fruits of their labors to an onerous and unfair tax system enforced by local officials. They cannot obtain permanent residence or work permits in the cities and are treated as second-class citizens when they do relocate to the cities.

China's food policy of today is a consequence of the terrible famine that gripped the country from 1959 to 1962, when 20 million Chinese lost their lives, about 10 million more, mostly children, died shortly thereafter, and millions were nutritionally crippled. This catastrophe left a deep mark on those responsible for feeding China, and they have pursued a policy of food self-sufficiency ever since. China's goal is to maintain domestic grain production at 95 percent of demand and have to rely on importing just 5 percent of its needs, should the grim reaper reappear. However, the reintroduction of a central government monopoly over grain commercialization at government-determined prices is requiring the government to hold immense amounts of grain at a very high cost. Since over 800 million Chinese depend upon agriculture for their livelihood, the government's concern with maintaining national grain self-sufficiency and ensuring stability in the countryside by keeping on-farm costs low and insulating farm incomes from the effects of grain price fluctuations is understandable. But other Asian countries with large agricultural populations, like India and Indonesia, are able to stabilize grain prices by purchasing only 20 to 25 percent of grain production as buffer stocks. China should be perfectly capable of doing the same.

Chapter Four
Cities Without Walls

Old Beijing. Ancient roofs and walled courtyards are jammed together in a maze of alleys.

For three thousand years, massive city walls protected the inhabitants of China's cities and kept other people out. After the triumph of the Communist Revolution in 1949, almost all of the walls surrounding China's cities were torn down. Over the next twenty-seven years, policies were adopted to try to stop the flow of rural migrants to cities, to control city growth, to restrict all economic activity to agents of the state, and to relocate large numbers of urban residents in rural areas. With residency status and access to urban jobs, housing, social services, and welfare benefits, employees of the state assumed privileged positions within the cities. In fact, the government had raised invisible bureaucratic walls around China's cities by limiting outsiders' access to jobs, housing, and other essential services. By 1978, China was still a poor, mainly rural, economy, but in that year, China began to transform its centrally controlled economy by dismantling the state monopoly over production, commercialization, and distribution and opening the economy to competitive forces. The invisible walls should have come down, but have they?

For more than two decades, China's gross domestic product has grown at a phenomenal average of 8 percent a year, its industrial output at an even more amazing 11 percent per year. Its cities became the main focus of this explosive economic growth, which was fueled by economic reforms involving privatizing most farming activities, helping make state industrial enterprises more independent and efficient, and freeing prices and opening access to markets for most goods and services. A major rural-to-urban migration resulted in the population of cities rising from 20 percent of total population in 1978 to 31 percent in 2000.[1] Unofficial estimates suggest that the urban population is much higher, and accounts for 36 percent of the total population.[2] The discussion which follows indicates just how difficult it is to arrive at an accurate total. China has created hundreds of new cities which include thousands of rural counties with large agricultural populations. Urban areas also include 100 million to 120 million rural migrants who are not classified as urban residents.

Throughout its history, Chinese cities have been a source of economic opportunity and refuge. As more and more people find their way into China's already crowded cities, will they continue to view the city as a haven and a source of employment, or are cities becoming less attractive places to live? China's cities have run out of space. Agricultural land is disappearing at the rate of 1.5 percent of China's arable land every year, and the government has prohibited nonagricultural use of agricultural land without central government approval. This means that Chinese cities cannot expand. The reforms of the last twenty-three years have greatly improved the overall quality of urban life for most city residents. They have access to urban infrastructure and services, which were largely ignored under Mao Zedong. They are free to move around and change jobs, they have more income to buy consumer goods and have greater access to recreational and cultural activities, and they can communicate freely. Yet, they are subject to environmental pollution, uncertain job security, lack of housing, traffic congestion, and inadequate public transport. Worse yet, divisions have been created between those who have permanent urban status and rural migrants who live on the margin of urban society.

The Beginnings of City Life

Urban life has been a feature of Chinese civilization for some thirty-five hundred years, ever since Shang dynasty administrative centers were established along the Yellow River in the second millennium B.C. In the Warring States Period (403–221 B.C.) cities seem to have increased significantly in size, number, and complexity. Statistics are lacking, but a literary source provides a population figure of 350,000 for one of the state capitals.[3] At the beginning of the Christian era, the Han dynasty capital of Ch'ang-an (modern Xi'an) had 250,000 inhabitants, wide avenues, and a sixteen-mile-long wall encircling the city. By the seventh century A.D., Ch'ang-an, then the seat of the Tang dynasty and residence for 1 million people, had become the world's largest and most cosmopolitan city.[4] In the late Tang dynasty, central authority weakened, and political power devolved to provincial capitals, which became regional centers for administration, trade, and finance, and the bases for growing networks of market towns.

The Yangtze River valley was heavily settled between the ninth and thirteenth centuries, when a shift from dry land farming in the north to paddy rice farming in the south resulted in a doubling of the population along the middle and lower regions of the Yangtze. When Marco Polo visited China in the thirteenth century, the locus of urban life had shifted to the lower Yangtze River delta. The great cities of China were

Hangzhou, Suzhou, and Nanjing. Before the Mongol conquest in A.D. 1279, Hangzhou was the largest city in the world with a population variously estimated at between one- and two-and-a-half million.[5] Polo marveled at Hangzhou, with its commerce, industry, and dense population. Inhabitants of major European cities—none of which had more than 50,000 people—dismissed Polo's account as sheer fantasy. China's level of urbanization was 500 years ahead of Europe, and for the next 500 years, these three cities remained preeminent, but they and other Chinese cities had ceased to grow rapidly because rural population was on the rise, and new market towns spread rapidly. Yet European visitors continued to be awed by their size. A trade mission from the new Dutch Republic visited Nanjing in 1655. The Hollanders were amazed by the sheer extent of the city, noting that two horsemen leaving the main city gate at dawn and riding in opposite directions around the city wall would meet again only at the end of the day.[6]

The Dutch were rebuffed, and the British became the first Europeans to obtain limited trading privileges with the Chinese. The British wanted much more, and in 1840, they provoked China into fighting—and losing—the Opium War. The Qing emperor was forced to make concessions that had far-reaching effects on China's urbanization. A system of treaty ports—which were opened to foreign trade under the various treaties with foreign powers—was established, beginning a process of urbanization resulting from the expansion of trade in coastal and riverine cities that led Shanghai to develop from a small fishing village to a major center of commerce. Hong Kong Island was ceded to the British and became the center for British trade and finance in the Far East. This was followed by treaties with the United States in 1843 and France in 1844. As the American treaty had a clause requiring renegotiation in twelve years, the British invoked a most-favored-nation clause in their treaty and forced the Chinese to renegotiate the British treaty in 1854. They made many new demands to which the Qing emperor refused to agree. The British seized Canton (modern Guangzhou) and occupied the forts fronting Tiensin (modern Tianjin). The way to Peking was open, and the Qing emperor capitulated. The Treaty of Tianjin of 1858 established four treaty ports along the Yangtze River and six more ports along China's coast, allowed foreigners to travel anywhere in China, established standard weights and measures for all treaty ports, and stipulated that the English language was to serve as the medium of official communication. The stage was set for China's entry into international trade and the growth of its coastal and riverine trading cities. The preeminence of these cities and the treaty port system lasted until the 1930s.

Chinese cities have always been crowded, dense havens of humanity with a centripetal force of their own, particularly in bad times—drawing in unfortunates, refugees, and starving peasants. A description of turn-of-the-twentieth-century Chongqing provides a chilling sense of what it must have been like when disease and disaster struck: "Girdled by its walls, crumbling verminous huts gripping the flanks of it supporting rock, Chungking riding its jutting rock was tumultuous, cholera-ridden, and full of starving peasants selling their children, for there was a famine in the north and girls were to be bought for twenty strings of cash. . . . The city was a hive of flies, buzzing over the excrement and the corpses. The rats were cat-big, ate the cats and the corpses, and sated fought in great bands; mothers suspended their babies in wire-net cages and baskets from hooks hanging from the ceiling beams, but the rats were too clever, they climbed up the beams, then let themselves drop upon the babies and ate them."[7]

Urbanization and Economic Growth Under Mao Zedong

City government in China is a microcosm of the country's national government, which is organized in a unitary fashion with responsibilities divided among commissions and ministries at the national level and reflected in the corresponding commissions and bureaus at the provincial and municipal levels. Authority and responsibility from the center are delegated vertically, providing the respective local administrative units with a great deal of autonomy in managing their own affairs. They are therefore not very susceptible to horizontal influences from other municipal organizations. When the interests of more than one vertical structure are affected, matters have to be referred to the highest local authority, the mayor's office, for resolution. To carry out their functions, commissions have established subordinate entities such as planning and regulatory bodies, research institutes, and operating enterprises. The mixture of planning, administrative, regulatory, and operational functions all within the same organizational structure has created conflicts of interest that have hindered coordination, reduced efficiency, and greatly hampered the capacity of municipal organizations to respond to reform initiatives and adopt commercial practices.

Understanding China's urbanization patterns depends a great deal on accurate data, particularly population statistics. The almost complete blackout from the 1950s through the 1970s limited any attempts of those outside China to understand the urbanization process during Mao Zedong's regime. Although a lot of data were made available to the outside world in the 1980s, changes in urban definitions and difficulty in establishing boundaries between urban and rural areas still hindered understanding of the organization process. Only with the introduction of new urban criteria in the 1990 census has a real measure of statistical consistency been established. The calculation of urban population size depends on three factors: urban designation criteria, urban boundaries, and household registration classification. These factors have changed over the years and have been combined in different ways to produce one of the world's most complex systems of urban population definition. Statistics are presently collected at two levels: the city and its suburbs, which are divided into urban districts; and the city, its suburbs, and the rural counties it administers. The counties were attached to cities during the Maoist period to ensure the delivery of food to the cities but, being agricultural in nature, are not classified as urban. City size definitions include only the city and its suburbs and are further limited to the non-agricultural population within the city and suburbs.

The period of economic recovery after the Communist triumph was one of rapid urban population growth (7.2 percent annually from 1950 to 1957), but population flows were complex: that from rural to urban areas was composed largely of returning soldiers and other urban residents who had been driven out of the cities and towns by twelve years of war, and peasants fleeing collectivization; and flow from urban to rural areas involved huge roundups to remove undesirables (vagrants, prostitutes) and ex-Guomindang officials and soldiers from the cities. By 1958, the administrative system to control migration through household registration and work and study permits had been placed in effect.

Yet this system was almost immediately rendered ineffective when the Great Leap Forward mobilized millions to the task of industrializing China and enabling agricultural production to leap forward. Thus began six years of turmoil as three-quarters of a million peasant cooperatives were merged into 26,000 peoples' communes, 1 million backyard iron and steel furnaces were built, and hundreds of thousands of small industrial workshops were established. Mass labor was used in construction projects, particularly flood control and irrigation, and it is estimated that at one point 100 million laborers were involved in irrigation works.

Millions of farmers (many of them women) were recruited to fill the urgent need for more industrial workers.

The Great Leap Forward was a dismal failure. Local officials were afraid to report grain shortfalls below quota levels and in many cases grossly inflated output, and most small industrial establishments could not produce goods of sufficient quality or volume to justify their existence. The quality of many of the dams and water-control systems built was substandard. In rural areas, the circle became increasingly vicious—quotas were increased further, and peasants were forced to give up all their grain. Twenty million Chinese died of famine from 1959 to 1962, and 10 million more, especially children weakened by years of malnutrition, died soon after.[8] The government was so worried that China's grain production would be unable to sustain the urban population that from 1961 to 1963, it not only imported grain but returned 24 million people, who had migrated to the cities during the Great Leap Forward, back to their villages.

Forced migration and mass labor mobilization defy classification, but the net effect of this period of turmoil was that the urban population as a percent of the total population increased only slightly, from 16.2 percent in 1958 to 17.0 percent in 1963. The lessons learned from the Great Leap Forward and its aftermath have had a profound effect on subsequent urbanization policies because keeping the growth of the urban population within the bounds of the food supply became the main justification for the government's strong interventionist urban policy during the 1960s and 1970s.[9]

Mao Zedong realized that for China to become an industrialized nation, it would have to concentrate its economic resources on building up the productive capacity of China's cities. Urbanization and the growth of cities under the Maoist regime was closely linked to the Stalinist model of economic development, emphasizing centralized planning and control over the whole economy, carried out through nationalization of economic agents and managed pricing of inputs and outputs. Production was paramount, and a slogan coined then, "putting production first, standard of living second," aptly expresses the party's view at the time. Investments in activities not directly related to production, such as urban infrastructure and services, were given very low priority, and in order not to strain existing facilities, an explicit antiurban policy was followed to limit city growth. This was partly based on an ambivalent attitude toward cities, which were regarded as centers of corrupt bureaucrats, an exploitive bourgeoisie, and capitalists who extracted sur-pluses from the peasants.

Ironically, in the early Maoist years, as the old walls of many of the larger cities were torn down, new invisible administrative walls were being erected, which effectively kept out the vast majority of rural inhabitants and led to increasing disparities between the urban state sector and the rural nonstate sector.[10] Residency requirements were established to keep rural migrants out of urban areas, and compulsory state procurement of farm products at subsidized prices was instituted to enable the cities and their industries to receive a guaranteed supply of grain and other foodstuffs at artificially low prices. This led to wide urban–rural disparities, with urban per capita real income being four to five times that of real rural per capita income.[11]

Beginning in 1964, China's urbanization was again greatly affected by the attempt to create a "Third Front," or self-sufficient industrial base, in China's heartland to serve as a third line of defense if China were drawn into a war with a foreign power. The recent involvement of China in the Korean conflict, the possibility of Chinese involvement in the Vietnam War, as well as a perceived threat of invasion from Taiwan and the loss of its Soviet ally, all led Mao Zedong to believe that war was a distinct possibility. As a result, large industrial complexes and major transportation networks, again using mass labor, were constructed in the inland provinces of Sichuan, Guizhou, Yunnan, Qinghai, Gansu, and Ningxia. Over the next decade, 38 percent of total national investment was channeled to these areas.

With the inception of the Cultural Revolution in 1966, the movement of people became ever more complex and politically motivated. The forced movement of urban youth to be reeducated in the countryside and the resettling of political cadres and intellectuals in rural exile led to a massive urban exodus. Yet during the 1966 to 1977 span of the Cultural Revolution, the urban population actually increased, although at not quite the rate of the nation's population. This reflects an influx of rural temporary or contract workers into urban areas, especially because of Third Front industry and construction, as well as the return of urban youth from the countryside toward the end of the period. Most of the increase in the urban industrial labor force came about as a result of much higher urban female participation and controlled hiring of rural labor through contracting or the use of temporary residence permits.

Mao's policies simultaneously promoted industrial growth while slowing down urban population growth. Urban immigration was strictly controlled through the household registration system and through access to state-controlled jobs and rationed goods.

The net effect of the Maoists' antiurban bias, the Third Front investments, and the dislocations and vast population movements of the Great Leap Forward and the Cultural Revolution, was that China's urban population grew from 13.0 percent of the total population in 1953 to 20.6 percent in 1978. This contrasts with the next twelve years, when China's urban population grew three times as fast, reaching 31 percent of the total population by 2000.[12] Perhaps the most compelling urban statistic at the end of Mao's regime is the one indicating the extreme density of China's largest cities where humanity was packed together on a scale unimaginable in most other countries. Guangzhou had 57,142 people per square kilometer and Shanghai 39,429.[13] After three decades of neglect of urban infrastructure and services and rapidly growing environmental pollution, China's cities were extremely crowded and unhealthy places to live.

Urbanization Under Deng Xiaoping

Economic reforms initiated by Deng Xiaoping decollectivized farming and returned control of farms to the family unit, ended state monopoly of economic activity and opened the economy to private interests and foreign investment, and opened the closed command-and-control economy to market forces by means of the gradual freeing of prices and by decentralizing much decision making to local governments. These changes had an enormous impact on the process of urbanization. During Mao's regime, identity documents were used as an internal passport control to deny entry to the cities. Under Deng, the approach was more indirect: Entry into the city was not banned, but access to residency status and the benefits thus accrued were withheld. The invisible walls were beginning to crack.

China's official urban policy under Deng's reform movement was strictly to control the growth of large cities, rationally develop the medium-sized cities, and vigorously promote the growth of small cities and towns.[14] The government was concerned over the growing migration from rural areas to cities because of the cities' limited absorptive capacity. Urban infrastructure and services were so overburdened that they could barely attend to the needs of the existing population.

A major administrative reform involved putting rural counties under the administration of large cities so that agricultural output and rural labor could be geared to the needs of the cities. By 1984, one-fourth of all the counties in China were under the administration of one-half of China's cities. By 1988, 35 percent of all counties were so administered.[15] Many of China's cities, therefore, have very large agricultural populations under their administrative control. Nevertheless, the government continued to be deeply preoccupied with the problem of cities overburdened with surplus rural workers, and this gave rise to the strategy of "leaving the land but not the village," in which local governments would help local entrepreneurs promote and establish rural nonstate enterprises in townships and villages. This provided a major impetus to promoting the growth of both privately owned and collectively owned enterprises. But many private individuals who were establishing enterprises registered as collectives to avoid higher taxes and other forms of discrimination against private ownership.

From 1978 to 1990, township and village enterprises grew at double (8 percent) the annual rate of growth of state enterprises, and they grew fastest in suburban areas just outside major industrial cities. During this period, it is estimated that these enterprises hired 55 million rural workers while state enterprises hired 15 million.[16] The creation of township and village enterprises in combination with the rapidly expanding rural markets, which increased from 33,302 in 1978 to 59,473 in 1990, has been crucial in turning thousands of previously small settlements into newly designated towns by generating the required threshold of non-agricultural resident population and activities.[17] In 1978, state enterprises had accounted for 77 percent of the value of industrial output. By the mid-1990s, nonstate enterprises had surpassed state enterprises and accounted for 40 percent of the nation's total industrial output while the state's output share had fallen to 34 percent.[18]

An economic reform that is having a great impact on urbanization, especially in coastal cities, was the establishment in 1979 of four special economic zones in cities that were close to sources of foreign capital in Hong Kong, Macao, and Taiwan. Foreign investors were offered financial incentives, factory sites, and cheap labor to produce exports, but initial results were disappointing. The government found that it had to invest far more in construction and support systems than it had expected. Transfer of advanced technology did not occur to the degree anticipated, workers lacked specialized skills, and the quality of goods produced was often low. Yet in 1984, fourteen more such zones were approved for coastal cities and Hainan Island. The most successful have been zones located in Guangdong's Pearl River delta, including Shenzhen (on the mainland opposite Hong Kong), and Zhuhai (next to Macao). By 1994, 6 million workers in Guangdong were employed in export-related manufactures, producing three-quarters of the province's industrial output and exports.[19]

In 1983, many new towns and cities were designated. Based on the concept of the "town leading the development of the countryside," entire rural townships, with their overwhelmingly rural populations, were turned into towns. Similarly, many counties were reclassified as cities under a 1986 State Council directive that stipulated that counties with fewer than 500,000 people but with more than 100,000 nonagricultural residents and an annual output of RMB 300 million could be designated as a city. Therefore, most newly designated cities at the county level have huge agricultural populations.

Much of the power to grant nonagricultural household-residence status was given to local authorities in 1984. This led to widespread outright sale of residency rights. Overseas Chinese with relatives on the mainland were attracted to a scheme begun in 1988 in Guangdong Province for financing urban housing construction with foreign investment, which included granting urban-household status to the investors' relatives and allowing them to move into the properties acquired. This proved so popular that the State Council became alarmed and in 1989 stripped the provinces of their powers to make such decisions.

With the abolition of the agricultural commune and its replacement with the household-responsibility system, there began a peasant exodus that has continued to the present day. This floating population has no permanent residency status and no access to urban services. A 1990 survey carried out by the Ministry of Construction in eleven large cities indicated that the floating population amounted to 23.7 percent of the total urban population. If this is extrapolated to include the rest of the urban population, the floaters would amount to 70 million.[20] More-recent estimates put this population at one hundred million to two hundred million.[21] Informal rural-to-urban migration was much more important in terms of the human transfer involved than was formal migration, mainly of contract labor to state enterprises. Informal migrants were classified as "seeking employment in industry and businesses," and they amounted to 87 percent of work-related migration and 67 percent of total urban immigration to cities and towns in the second half of the 1980s.[22] The hiring of migrant rural temporary workers on a contract basis to fill low-skilled jobs was an attractive option for reducing an enterprise's social welfare burden. In Hangzhou, for example, contract workers in state enterprises in 1987 amounted to 36.7 percent of total employment in construction, textiles, engineering, and transportation.[23] Local governments tolerated the existence of a temporary urban population because informal migrants were not entitled to residency status or to receive grain allotments at artificially low prices. However, their status was formalized in 1984 when the State Council permitted migrants who had secured employment and housing to settle in undesignated towns as permanent residents under the classification of "households with self-supplied grains." In 1985, the Ministry of Public Security made available temporary residence permits for migrants, a tacit admission of the scope of the rural invasion, of the ministry's intention to improve their control over it, and of the ministry's concern with the threat to public order such migration represented. More recently, rural migrants have been linked to rising crime rates, and cities have been cracking down on them. Beijing police destroyed 100,000 illegally built shacks, and Shanghai sent more than 100,000 back to their own villages.[24]

Urban Growth and the Environment

Almost fifty years of industrialization and urban growth have come at a substantial environmental cost. China is currently the world's largest producer of ozone-depleting substances and the second-largest producer of greenhouse gas emissions.[25] For the first two decades of economic reform, the material well-being of many Chinese dramatically improved, especially in urban areas, but little was done to make cities more pollution free. The World Bank estimated that in 1995 damage to human health from air and water pollution amounted in monetary terms to the equivalent of 8 percent of gross domestic product, about equal to the level of economic growth. Chinese researchers estimated a much lower level of damage, 3.5 percent, because they placed a lower valuation on the economic loss attached to each premature death.[26] Whatever the cost, what was abundantly clear was that China's most immediate urban challenge for the twenty-first century was to make its cities healthy places to live because they had become among the most polluted places on earth.

China's cities were blanketed by particulate and sulfur emission levels that exceeded the World Health Organization's standards and China's own by two to five times. Where had the air pollution come from? In China, factories had been built right in the middle of cities and towns, where infrastructure was readily available, and workers' housing was built close to the factory. A growing economy also demanded more energy to power it. Coal is China's principal energy fuel, and annual coal use more than doubled from 1980 to 1995, to 1.3 billion tons and 78 percent of total energy use.[27] The government claims that since then coal use as a percentage of total energy output dropped to 67 percent by the end of 1999.[28] This was mainly because traditional coal-using industries like iron and steel, nonferrous metals, and chemicals, have not been growing and their coal use has declined and because China has begun to look for cleaner coal substitutes. Coal is a major factor in most forms of air pollution, particularly that from industrial boilers and furnaces and household stoves, which together account for about three-fourths of ground-level air pollution.[29] The balance is generated by local heating systems and commercial establishments and the energy sector. On the north China plain, dust from poorly managed agricultural land has also become a major problem. Coal particles are particularly insidious, since they account for the finest (less than ten microns) airborne particles, which are most damaging to human health. The citizens of the larger cities are especially at risk. They are exposed to 30 percent higher particulate levels and 60 percent higher sulfur dioxide levels than the residents of medium and small cities.[30] Urban pollution also affects agriculture, and a study carried out in 1993 in Chongqing municipality, where sulfur dioxide emissions were arguably the highest in the world, found that one-fourth of the vegetable and grain crops had been damaged by acid rain.[31]

The government is developing new boiler technologies to remove most sulfur from coal and also to improve coal's efficiency, and the government is being assisted in this task by the Global Environmental Facility and the World Bank. However, this is a long-term solution that requires technology transfer of foreign boiler designs, and developing marketable products and setting up manufacturing plants to produce them. The ash problem must be dealt with by capturing the ash before it escapes into the atmosphere by using electrostatic precipitators or baghouses.[32]

In the 1990s, Chinese researchers analyzed the relationship between ambient air pollution and human health in Beijing, Shenyang, and Chongqing. All three cities typified the air pollution danger in China's larger cities and far exceeded World Health Organization standards for sulfur dioxide and particulate emissions. Chongqing had the highest sulfur dioxide emissions but had the lowest particulate emissions because its subtropical climate eliminated the need for space heating. The studies were able to correlate increasing emission concentrations and rapidly rising rates of chronic respiratory illness, pulmonary heart disease, premature death, and hospital occupancy. By extrapolating the data to include other Chinese cities, the World Bank estimated that 240 million people were exposed to serious ambient air pollution, resulting in an estimated one hundred seventy-eight thousand premature deaths, three hundred forty-six thousand hospital admissions, six million eight hundred thousand emergency room visits, and four-and a-half million workdays lost per year.[33] Other pollutants had more insidious effects. Child development studies carried out in Beijing, Shanghai, Shenyang, and Fuzhou linked exposure to lead to retarded development of the brain, nervous system, and physical growth.[34]

Municipal sewage and industrial effluent each account for about one-half of wastewater discharges in cities, with pulp and paper mills the biggest industrial transgressor. Less than 10 percent of sewage is treated, and water quality is so poor in China's rivers that 40 percent of all river sections being monitored cannot meet the lowest water-quality classification (for irrigation water) and are effectively cesspools. Municipal wastewater discharges tripled from 1981 to 1995, and although data were not available on discharges from households without sewage connections, they presumably increased by similar if not larger amounts during the same period.[35] With industrial effluent added to municipal wastewater, water quality near cities is extremely poor, especially downstream of wastewater discharges. Data provided by the National Environmental Protection Agency showed that annual industrial wastewater discharges remained in the range of twenty to twenty-five billion tons during the period 1981 to 1995. This was based on reports received from 67,956 state enterprises, which did not include 100,000 small state enterprises and about two million township and village enterprises.[36] Since the output of the latter group had been growing far more rapidly than that of the larger state enterprises, it is likely that actual industrial discharges were greatly understated by government statisticians.

Water-related diseases (diarrhea, hepatitis, trachoma, and intestinal nematodes) accounted for just 1.5 percent of total deaths in 1990,[37] but sewage collection and treatment had not kept up with the explosive level of urban growth, and urban sanitation had become a much more serious problem. Other diseases, such as liver cancer, birth defects, and spontaneous abortion, believed to be caused by water-borne heavy metals and toxic chemicals, are much harder to track without long-term epidemiological studies of city populations. Nevertheless, Chinese research among farmers and fishermen showed that people dependent on pond or river water had significantly higher rates of liver cancer and spontaneous abortion than those dependent on well water.[38]

From 1991 to 1999, municipal wastewater treatment capacity in China increased by 19 percent a year. Although this resulted in an increase in wastewater treatment from 4 percent of total wastewater discharges in 1991 to 10 percent in 1999, only 70 percent of the new capacity was being utilized.[39] This is partly because sewer construction lagged behind, increasing by only 9–10 percent per annum. It is also because many treatment plants suffer from low-capacity utilization because of design deficiencies, complex or unsuitable equipment, or lack of sufficient operating funding. Some are not even connected to sewer systems. A big problem is that wastewater tariffs collected by local finance bureaus are not usually passed along to the treatment plants. The Ministry of Construction plans to build 400 new wastewater treatment plants over the next decade, yet no national strategy has been developed to ensure that this will be done in an optimal manner. What is required is a comprehensive review of wastewater collection and treatment at the national level.

The legal basis for protecting the environment was established under the Chinese Constitution of 1982. A State Environmental Protection Commission was established in 1979 to develop national environmental policy. A National Environmental Protection Agency was created in 1988 to carry it out using a national system of environmental protection bureaus at the provincial, county, and local levels. A basic Environmental Protection Law was enacted in 1989. It laid out four guiding principles: environmental protection must be integrated and coordinated with economic development; pollution prevention should receive as much emphasis as pollution control; polluters should pay for environmental degradation (the polluter-pays principle); and more effective management is required to improve environmental quality. This law prohibits new industries from locating near populated or protected areas and permits relocation or closure of industrial plants that are in violation of the law. More specific laws govern the generation and disposal of airborne particles and gases, and wastewater and solid waste; the conservation of rivers, lakes, and oceans; and the protection and management of soil, water sources, forests, grasslands, and wildlife. Underpinning these statutes are even more specific and technical regulations that are issued by the state or by provincial governments and municipal governments with provincial status. Supplementary directives are issued as required by local environmental protection bureaus for their own jurisdictions. Even with this apparatus in place and a corpus of environmental legislation, China was unable to control pollution and preserve its natural environment.

China relied on three regulatory instruments: submission of satisfactory environmental impact assessments before approving any new projects; the "three synchronizations" licensing system, which required affirmations that the project was indeed in conformity with the environmental impact assessment at the design, construction, and initiation of operations stages of each new project; and pollution levies charged against people responsible for causing air emissions and wastewater streams that have concentrations of pollutants above permitted levels.

This strategy had two basic faults. It focused on controlling pollution concentrations at the source rather than the volume of pollution being emitted into the wastewater system, and the amount of pollution levies was typically set below the marginal cost of effluent treatment. Although individual enterprises might be able to meet the source concentration requirement, overall air and water quality were adversely affected through the sheer volume of pollutants emitted. Low levies encouraged enterprises to pay the fee rather than invest in treatment facilities or cleaner production technologies. In practice, many enterprises—with local government officials looking the other way—paid only a portion of the levy, which most enterprise managers regarded as simply another cost of doing business.[40] In addition, local environmental protection bureaus were required to return 80 percent of collected fees and fines to the polluting enterprise to be used for the purchase of pollution control equipment. The bureaus did not account for how these funds were used, and there was considerable speculation about how much was actually used for the intended investments. The bureaus were allowed to keep the remaining 20 percent to cover their own costs.

Central government policy is clear that pollution must be controlled, and all the necessary legislation and bureaucratic infrastructure is in place. Yet, at the local level, where most enterprise ownership is really exercised, the conflict of interest between the state as owner of polluting enterprises and the state as regulator of pollution has often been decided in favor of the enterprise, as reflected in lack of enforcement. Local environmental bureaus' capacity to enforce the regulatory system is limited due to financial and staff constraints—which became even more of a problem as the government downsized—and the intervention of local governments to protect favored enterprises. Most bureaus understandably focus on large polluters who are monitored once or twice annually, and most small enterprises are visited infrequently or not at all.

China Launches a Nationwide Effort to Control Environmental Pollution

The government became much more serious about pollution control in the mid-1990s. In 1996, it launched a nationwide campaign to close down major polluting township and village enterprises that were polluting sensitive waterways, and over 60,000 enterprises were closed down over a two-year period. Many of these were food- and pulp-and-paper-processing plants which account for two-thirds of the industrial pollution in China's rivers and streams, but amount to only 10 percent of the gross value of industrial output.[41] After the passage of legislation governing the treatment of solid and toxic wastes in 1996, preparation began for regulation of the transport, treatment, and disposal of such wastes. Most wastes have simply been left on site, so the cleanup involved will be immense. There is no infrastructure to take care of the problem, and until landfills are established all over China, this will remain a serious problem. By the end of 1997, Beijing and Shanghai had phased out leaded gasoline and a national ban on the production and sale of leaded gasoline became effective on July 1, 2000.[42] Shortly after the government ban on unleaded gasoline went into effect, China's major automakers appealed to the government to import unleaded fuel because the quality of domestically produced unleaded fuel was so bad it could not meet emission standards. It is worth considering that the United States required ten years to remove lead completely from all gasoline and construct a parallel system for producing and distributing unleaded gasoline.

In 1998, the National Environmental Protection Agency was upgraded to a ministry and renamed the State Environmental Protection Administration. Forty-seven of China's largest cities were targeted to intensify their environmental pollution-control efforts. A primary objective was to improve environmental monitoring, and a forty-seven-city air-quality forecasting network is being established. A law was also passed requiring all industrial enterprises to meet air emission and wastewater effluent standards by 2000. Much more emphasis was placed on controlling the volume of pollution; control was to be achieved, for example, by basing water discharge permits on volume rather than on pollutant concentration. Little attention is being paid, however, to dilution and the absorptive capacity of rivers. The Yangtze River, for example, with a volume second only to the Amazon is, has the flow necessary to dilute and absorb wastewater but is regulated much more strictly than dried-up rivers in north China whose flow is mostly untreated sewage.

China's motives are a mixture of the altruistic, the practical, and the self-serving. There is genuine concern for the effect of pollution on its citizens, especially the younger and future generations. There is new awareness of the impossibility of controlling pollution at point sources that number in the millions over the entire nation. The fast-rising cost of public health and pollution control is another consideration, as is the fear that pollution will keep away foreign investors and tourists.

As the capital, Beijing is setting the example for China's other cities in cleaning up its pollution. In addition, it has been awarded the 2008 Olympic Games, which is a big spur to the city to clean up pollution. Beijing authorities realized that with a highly polluting fuel like coal, controlling pollution at the source has become difficult if not impossible. The municipal government decided to convert from coal to clean-energy sources and to strengthen enforcement of pollution controls. In 1998, a sulfur tax was imposed on emitters of sulfur dioxide gas, and coal users were required to use low-sulfur coal. A natural gas pipeline that could deliver 2 million cubic meters a day was built. One-fifth of the city was designated as "coal-free zones" where no coal-burning boilers with an output of under twenty steam tons per hour were allowed. Most boilers and furnaces with a larger capacity now have pollution-control equipment in place. A "clean air program" was begun to convert thousands of small, scattered coal stoves to cleaner fuels or integrate them into larger district heating systems—all of which was to take place by 2003. This still left about 8,000 coal-fired medium-sized boilers and furnaces, which were responsible for almost two-thirds of sulfur dioxide and coal-dust pollution in Beijing. With World Bank assistance, Beijing plans by 2005 to convert 6,000 of these boilers to natural gas or to coal gas or fuel oil when natural gas is not available. Furthermore, the rivers running through Beijing have little natural flow but large volumes of wastewater. The city is presently quadrupling its sewage treatment capability.

Beijing is also closing down, relocating, or retooling its most polluting factories, which produce metals, chemicals, and cement. Like Chongqing (see below) it has focused on its iron and steel industry, which accounts for one-seventh of the city's coal consumption. Rather than use gasoline, 60 percent of Beijing's public buses now run on compressed natural gas, and one-half of the city's taxi cabs use liquefied petroleum gas. Shanghai is also converting thousands of buses and taxis to using these fuels, but full conversion for both cities will be a long-term process. Also, 95 percent of Beijing households now use gas rather than coal for cooking. Tougher emissions standards for vehicles were said to have resulted in an 18 percent decline in carbon monoxide and 17 percent fewer nitrogen oxide emissions in Beijing between 1998 and 2000.[43]

Other large Chinese cities do not have the political clout, visibility, or resources that Beijing has, and it will take longer for them to emulate the capital. Chongqing, China's largest municipality, serves as an example of what is beginning to be achieved under the forty-seven-city program to control pollution. Growing energy use from boilers burning high-sulfur coal had created a significant air pollution problem, and sulfur dioxide concentrations in the air were perhaps the world's highest. Following Beijing's example, the municipality is converting or closing down coal-fired boilers with a capacity of ten tons of steam per hour or less and is requiring larger boilers to install desulfurization equipment. With the support of the World Bank, it developed a plan to eliminate pollution at each plant in its most air-polluting industry, iron and steel; it has achieved 90 percent of its goals and expects to reach 100 percent before the end of 2002. Chongqing also expects to close down all coal-fired electricity-generating plants below fifty megawatts by 2003 and is requiring larger plants to install desulfurization equipment. Following the lead of the State Environmental Protection Administration, the municipality has been more rigorous in enforcing industrial pollution control standards and in 2000 was able to reduce citywide sulfur dioxide emissions by 50,000 tons. It was one of the first cities to begin to deal with solid- and toxic-waste control and disposal. Although the city is located at the confluence of two rivers, municipal sewage was largely untreated. The prevailing attitude was that what went in the rivers was carried downstream. But with the construction of the Three Gorges Dam, river flows will be greatly reduced, and officials realized that something had to be done. In 1999, again with World Bank assistance, Chongqing began construction of a municipal sewage transport and treatment network covering the entire city (see chapter 5).

China's new approach to dealing with pollution is revolutionary because it involves nationwide substitution of clean-energy sources for highly polluting coal. This requires dismantling the existing coal-based heating infrastructure and replacing it with gas- or oil-fired systems. The cost will be enormous, but millions of Chinese will live longer and healthier lives because of the change. At the same time, enforcement of environmental pollution control laws and regulations has been stepped up, especially targeting chronic big polluters, who are no longer allowed to pay a fine or part of it and continue to pollute. China is making a great effort to develop new sources of clean energy, such as natural gas and liquefied petroleum gas. Xianjiang's Tarim Basin is the source of much of China's natural gas, and a new pipeline is being constructed that will deliver 12 billion cubic meters of gas annually beginning in 2005, through a 4,000–kilometer-long pipeline from the basin to the Yangtze River delta.

The government plans to spend US$12 billion over the next decade to combat sulfur dioxide and other air pollution in thirty-four cities. Desulfurization will be required for all new power plants and industrial facilities in designated sulfur dioxide and acid-rain control zones. Nevertheless, such equipment is affordable only for larger electric power and industrial boilers, and it will be a long time before users of the hundreds of thousands of smaller furnaces, boilers, kilns, and stoves in cities, towns, and villages all over China are able to control their pollution.

Just how dramatic China's turnaround is in cleaning up its air pollution is supported by a report released by the U.S. Department of Energy. The report indicates that China's annual emissions of carbon dioxide fell by 17 percent in the four-year period from 1996 to 1999. This occurred while its economy was growing by 36 percent.[44] Carbon dioxide emissions in the United States grew at about 2 percent annually during the same period. This negates a commonly held assumption that China, which is second to the United States as the world's largest emitter of carbon dioxide and other gases responsible for global warning known as greenhouse gases, will soon overtake the United States as world leader in greenhouse gas emissions. Comparisons with the United States are not altogether fair, however. China suffers from high combustion inefficiencies in its boilers and furnaces and uses highly polluting fuels and by improving in both areas, is achieving significant reductions in gaseous emissions. U.S. fuels are much cleaner, and combustion systems are much more efficient, and even with the U.S. economy growing much more slowly than China's, it would be extremely difficult for the United States to achieve net reductions in greenhouse gas emissions on the scale of China's. The problem with the United States is that it is not taking any significant action to reduce its greenhouse gas emissions.

That China's air pollution cleanup is continuing is supported by data, released by the State Environmental Protection Administration, which show that between 1999 and 2000 air quality in China's cities continued to improve. For example, the percentage of cities that achieved the minimum air quality standard for residential areas rose from 30 percent in 1999 to 36.5 percent in 2000. During the same period, the number of Chinese cities with the worst air quality declined from 40.6 percent to 33.1 percent.[45]

Hidden Unemployment Is Growing Rapidly

The urban workforce is estimated at 190 million. The government is responding to the specter of rising unemployment by limiting the number of workers officially classified as unemployed. At the end of 1997, the number of unemployed urban workers rose to about 6.5 million, equal to an unemployment rate of 3.4 percent. Although the number of workers actually becoming redundant is assuming crisis proportions, the government carefully controls the number it officially registers as unemployed. Most redundant workers stay with their work units and are classified as laid off. They receive a minimal stipend, which is augmented by the municipal government and amounts to about US$30 per month (see chapter 1). At the end of 1999 their numbers were estimated at between 15 million and 18 million.[46]

New industrial jobs or new service sector employment cannot be created fast enough to meet the needs of laid-off workers, and government has had to rely on investment in public services or public works to create jobs. The government also finally recognized that the growth of the private sector, which it had tried to circumscribe, was actually providing job opportunities for redundant state-enterprise workers, and the Chinese constitution was amended to recognize officially the importance of the private sector as part of the socialist market economy (see chapter 1).

The Most Compact Cities on Earth

Chinese cities are the densest in the world and have been for two millennia. Such densities are possible only under a system that balances a high level of administrative organization with reliance on neighborhood organizations to deliver and maintain urban services. The origins of such a system can be traced to the Qin dynasty (221–207 B.C.), when five or ten households were made mutually responsible for providing urban services to one another. This concept was perpetuated by succeeding dynasties in different forms.[47] Under Communism this system evolved into self-contained neighborhoods located adjacent to work units in which the latter assumed the leadership in providing urban services while neighborhood committees acted as watchdogs over the behavior of individuals.

The relative denseness of Chinese city cores compared with city cores in the rest of the world is reflected in extremely sharp, visible drops in population densities, not characteristic of other cities, one sees when moving out from the city center. Shanghai, for example, which has a population similar to that of Seoul and Paris, has 250 percent more people within a radius of five kilometers of the city center than the other two cities. This extreme concentration has enabled Chinese cities to function without public transport until recently and was a major reason for the great popularity of first the rickshaw and then the bicycle. With growing concern for the loss of agricultural land, this trend is being perpetuated. When Shanghai expanded by 82 percent in the 1980s, the radius of the city expanded by only eight percent—almost all the new construction took place in the city's existing core.[48] It was only when municipal officials with central government support began to visualize Shanghai as an international city that the tall buildings of the Pudong development zone across the Huangpo River sprouted up like a forest of concrete, steel, and glass in the mid-1990s to lure foreign investors and visitors and provide land for a new international airport.

The Urban Transport Bottleneck

Chinese cities are characterized by two phenomena that result in a transportation nightmare: very high population densities and very little road space per capita. On main thoroughfares of China's large cities, bicycles mingle with motorcycles, cars, and vans in a dangerous minuet of avoidance and near collision; side streets are narrow and crowded with cars, pedestrians, bicycles, and hand (or bicycle) carts. Very little of the land area in major cities is devoted to roads. In the three major cities of Beijing, Guangzhou, and Shanghai it varies from 8 to 17 percent of total area with the least amount of space in the city center. This compares with ratios of 18 percent for Seoul, 23 percent for Tokyo, and 35 percent for London.[49] International experience shows that road construction alone does not provide a solution to congestion because it induces motor vehicle traffic from other roads and shifts to motor vehicle use from other forms of transport. Therefore, transport demand tends to exceed supply no matter how efficient the road network. Local governments should therefore give the same priority to controlling and managing this demand and controlling traffic flows and volume as they do to road construction.

Most Chinese used to live grouped around tiny courtyards accessible only by alleys or one-lane streets. As cities expanded and roads were built, the courtyard style of living was maintained by building large four- to six-lane streets bordering the living areas, and access into them was still provided only by narrow lanes and alleys. Streets and roads never did keep up with the growth in population and traffic even after multistory apartment complexes began to be built on city blocks ringed with streets on four sides. Government policy was largely to blame, since transport investment was considered unproductive by Mao Zedong and was given low priority during his lifetime.

The situation has improved since Mao's death twenty-five years ago, but annual transportation investment in China during the first two decades of reform averaged only 1.5 percent of gross national product (most other large developing countries were investing 2 to 3 percent of GNP annually). Between 1980 and 1993, total urban road length increased from 29,485 kilometers to 104,897 kilometers, representing an increase from 3.3 kilometers per 10,000 of population to 6.3 kilometers. The number of buses increased two and one-half times during the period, but the average speed of the buses was reduced by congestion by 50 percent.[50] State enterprises carry three-fourths of total urban passenger volume, but fares are kept below operating costs and transport enterprises are perennial money losers that have to be subsidized by the government. By 1993, 70 percent of public transport operations were rarely on time, were losing money, and ridership, which had been declining every year, was mostly absorbed by increasing bicycle use.[51] Public transport is facing strong competition from the phenomenal growth of minicabs and taxis operating under private or collective ownership and government leasing or franchising arrangements.

Responsibility for urban transport is shared by the Ministry of Construction, which is in charge of road construction and public transport, and the Ministry of Public Security, which is concerned with traffic control. During Mao's regime, heavy central government intervention at the enterprise level led to gross inefficiencies and poor performance. After 1978, attempts were made to separate government administration from enterprise operations, but the concept of public transport as an entitlement to be provided as a public service at the lowest possible cost conflicted with economic reform objectives of maximizing efficiency and recovering costs.

In the last decade, use of motorcycles—mainly with highly polluting two-stroke engines—has increased dramatically. In fact, motorcycles are the fastest-growing form of urban transport. They are a major factor in increasing congestion. In fact, since 1992, Guangzhou, which has the largest motorcycle-using population, has imposed annual quotas on the issuing of new licenses.

In 1980, China produced 220,00 motor vehicles, of which only 5,280, or 2.4 percent, were passenger cars. In 1992, production reached 1 million vehicles, but only 8.3 percent were passenger cars.[52] In 1998, 1,628,000 vehicles were produced, of which 507,000 (31 percent) were passenger cars.[53]

In 1994, China had the fewest automobiles per capita of any Asian nation. There were only eight automobiles per 1,000 population, and although private automobile ownership was growing fast, it amounted to only two per 1,000. Nevertheless, urban ownership was much higher, with twenty-four cars per 1,000 in Beijing, twenty-one per 1,000 in Guangzhou, and fifteen per 1,000 in Shanghai. Rates of ownership growth were even more significant. From 1985 to 1995, the number of registrations of passenger vehicles grew at a rate of 18 percent annually while the number of privately owned cars increased by 45 percent per annum.[54] By 1998, China had surpassed India in the number of its automobiles, which amounted to ten per 1,000 population. The government's motor vehicle development policy is based on a 1994 study carried out by the State Planning Commission. It proposed speeding development of a domestic automobile industry to a projected annual production capacity of 3.5 million cars by 2010, of which 90 percent would be sold to the domestic market. The policy explicitly encourages private automobile ownership.

In 1994, there were 160 automobile assembly plants in China, but by 2000 their number was reduced to ninety. Thirteen manufacturers account for 90 percent of all motor vehicles produced, but 80 percent are made by three big producers: First Automotive Works in Changchun, Shanghai Automotive Industry Corporation, and Dongfeng Motor Corporation in Wuhan.[55] All three have joint ventures with major foreign motor vehicle manufacturers. In 2000, Chinese consumers were buying only one-half the number of automobiles forecast just one or two years earlier. Potential buyers are put off by high automobile prices, high gasoline prices, and high licensing fees, which can add 20 percent to the price of a car. Shanghai Automotive Industry Corporation, which has General Motors as a partner, presently makes luxury sedans, sold mostly to high-level government bureaucrats and state enterprise managers, and sales have been declining. With inventories climbing, the company is shifting to production of compact cars that would be more affordable for the consumer market.

There are 540 million bicycles in China, and bicycles still are the primary mode of transport, but as the number of motor vehicles rises, the number of bicycles has begun to fall. Cars now push into bicycle lanes, and the rate of accidents is rising rapidly. In the early 1990s, 60 percent of Beijing residents used bicycles to travel around the city. Now, the percentage is 40 percent. In Guangzhou, always at the forefront of modernization, only 20 percent of its residents rely on bicycles. In Shanghai, most major streets are off-limits to bicycles during rush hour. As long as people live within five miles of their place of work, it appears likely they will use bicycles in the absence of alternative reliable and cheap transportation. But one bicycle salesperson thinks that the faster pace of life is really behind the demise of the bicycle: "Everything is faster. You can't sit around and drink tea all day anymore. So a lot of people don't have time for a bicycle either."[56]

With traffic volumes increasing and speeds in city centers being reduced, congestion has become a vicious upward spiral, which severely raises economic and environmental costs. Slower engines burn more fuel, leading to a vast increase in emissions per kilometer driven, since fuel consumption at low speeds is twice that at normal speeds. Vehicles can accomplish fewer trips, so more of them are necessary; time is money, and the cost just keeps rising. In addition, the number of accidents has been rising steadily. Although Beijing has the best traffic-management facilities in China, traffic fatalities reached sixty per 10,000 vehicles in

1994, compared with 1.6 per 10,000 for Tokyo.[57] Many experts believe that congestion is largely created by the systematic pricing below cost of urban transport and lack of adequate traffic control. In most Chinese cities the mixture of motor vehicles and bicycles and the lack of road space are equally important factors.

Vehicular emissions standards have been in place since 1983. But they were very lax when compared to international standards. China allowed forty times more carbon monoxide than United States standards allowed, eight times as much nitrogen oxide, and six times as many hydrocarbons.[58]

In 1998, the government adopted Euro 1, the first European catalyst-based motor vehicle emission standards, for all new automobiles manufactured in China, beginning April 1, 2000. The Beijing municipal government then went even further, by requiring that all new cars sold in the city had to meet the Euro 1 standard beginning January 1, 1999. In March 1999, the Beijing Environmental Protection Bureau informed domestic automobile manufacturers that automobiles produced between 1995 and 1998 and sold in Beijing would have to be retrofitted with equipment designed to meet the Euro 1 standard. By the end of 1999, 80,000 vehicles had been retrofitted.[59]

Although programs to increase inspection and maintenance of existing motor vehicles and to scrap those that cannot meet emission standards have had some success, China's roads are dominated by vehicles with polluting carburetor-based fuel systems. In Guangzhou, for example, 70 percent of motor vehicles cannot meet the mandated emission standards. As a result, nitrogen oxide, generated mostly by motor vehicles, has become the major air pollutant in eight of China's largest cities, including Beijing, Shanghai, and Guangzhou. Effective September 1, 2001, the government banned 187 different automobile models equipped with carburetors. Such vehicles will no longer be officially registered, the ban mostly affects smaller local manufacturers that do not have the technology to produce fuel injection systems. The government's motives are not purely environmental. It is hoping this will spur consolidation among China's 100 motor vehicle producers, who have been slow to unite to face foreign competition now that China joined the World Trade organization (see chapter 7).

Can China avoid a transportation crisis like the one that neighboring capitals such as Bangkok and Jakarta are suffering? The World Bank thinks China can: "China's unusually low dependence on automobiles, the unusually high density of its cities, and the strength of its administrative capacity at both the national and municipal levels is unique among developing countries. China can take advantage of these circumstances to create a new framework for urban transport and environmental management."[60] According to the World Bank, this would necessitate new strategies to improve use of a very limited amount of land, devote more investment to transport infrastructure, upgrade traffic management, improve fuel quality, and eliminate subsidies in fuel prices. The centerpiece of this strategy would be support for public transport. But this argument misses the point that with extremely high population densities, very limited road space, and a fast-growing automobile population, there is no place in China's crowded cities for the private automobile.

The current approach for dealing with congestion in large cities is to follow Beijing's example and build a series of express ring roads circling the city. This is a very expensive solution founded, according to some experts, on the questionable notion that it is possible to build a way out of congestion. Instead, they say, existing arterial roads linked to public transport routes should be improved, combined with better traffic management to improve traffic flows. However, given China's low utilization of urban space for roads, there is a strong case for new road construction in China's cities.

China should also adopt a strategy that will keep the rising numbers of private automobiles outside of city centers, and limit automobile use of major arterial roads with high congestion during peak traffic hours by establishing high-occupancy-vehicle lanes for public transport and cars with three or more passengers. For large cities, rapid transit is the best alternative form of transport, and the government is allowing cities with more than a million inhabitants to build subway or light rail systems. Beijing, Shanghai, and Tianjin have developed metro rail systems. Shenzhen, Nanjing, Guangzhou, Shenyang, and Qingdao have either begun construction or are contemplating doing so. About a dozen other cities have applied to the State Development and Planning Commission for permission to build a subway system. The metro rail systems should be linked to park-and-ride locations for private automobiles. Still, underground or surface light rail is too expensive for China's smaller cities, and every effort therefore should be made to either privatize public bus transport or make it more available, efficient, and competitive with fast-growing private transportation in vans or automobiles. Public bus routes should follow highest-density corridors and fares should be raised to cover at least operating and maintenance costs.

Housing in Transition

In 1949, after decades of war and dislocation, housing was in a dreadful state. More than one-half of the nation's housing stock was said to have deteriorated badly. In Shanghai one-fifth of the people lived in slum conditions, packed into shacks or dilapidated structures with no water or sewage. In Changsha three-fourths of residential areas were classified as slums, and in Chengdu per capita living space in its slums averaged 1.6 square meters.[61] A 1955 survey of 166 cities revealed that one-half of all residential housing was too old or unsafe to be occupied, and in 1956, 580,000 square meters of housing collapsed in 175 cities.[62] One approach was to demolish old housing, and in some cities one-fifth of the total stock was demolished. The government soon found that for every square meter demolished, two square meters of new space were required to resettle the displaced individuals. Thus greater efforts were made to upgrade existing housing. The state assumed major responsibility for providing urban housing through central government budget allocations to municipal housing bureaus or to state enterprises for building rental units. By keeping wages low, the government collected an implicit income tax from civil servants and workers, and in return these individuals received housing, medical care, food subsidies, and other benefits through their work units. Rents were really token payments fixed at less than one percent of the recipient's annual wage.[63]

With most investment going into industrial production and very little into urban infrastructure from 1950 onward, the condition of most housing can only be imagined. After the failure of the Great Leap Forward in 1959, housing was removed as a separate item from the state planning system. Ironically, the subsequent dislocations and massive transfers of young people to the countryside during the Cultural Revolution raised average per capita living space nationally to five square meters.[64]

During the Cultural Revolution, local planning and housing bureaus were shut down, and the former farmers, who often became responsible for running urban centers, brought a strong antiurban bias from their own experience. It was not only almost impossible to obtain any materials to repair or maintain buildings, but anyone who did so would have run the risk of being labeled "bourgeois." The housing stock continued to deteriorate, although in the latter part of the Cultural Revolution new housing had to be built for returnees from the countryside, and more resources were devoted to this task. These trends are illustrated in the amount of housing built during each of China's first four five-year plans, spanning most of the Maoist period. It ranged from a low of 10.8 million square meters in the Third Plan (1966–1970) to a high of 25.2 million square meters in the Fourth Plan (1971–1975).[65]

At the end of Mao Zedong's regime, thirty-eight cities with more than 500,000 people contained the majority of the nation's medium and large industrial enterprises, accounting for two-thirds of China's industrial output. Most workers lived with their families within walking or cycling distance of their employment. The work unit was the economic, social, and political center of their lives. High-density housing in self-contained neighborhoods near the work unit reduced the per capita economic cost of urbanization and facilitated political control through neighborhood street committees.

The leadership that emerged in the late 1970s understood that the Communist Party's major constituency had become urban rather than rural and that they could continue to ignore the deterioration in housing and other aspects of urban life only at the party's peril. China's first national housing conference was held in 1978 with a stated objective of building more housing in the following seven years than had been built in the previous twenty-eight. This intention is clear in the massive shift that took place in investment priorities. Total capital investment in the national budget in nonproductive investment increased from 18.8 percent in 1976 to 45.5 percent in 1982, and one-fourth of the latter funds were dedicated to housing construction. In 1979 housing construction almost doubled over the previous year to 62.6 million square meters and rose in 1982 to 90 million square meters. By 1981, state enterprises were financing and building more than one-half of the country's new construction.[66]

The condition of housing continued to be a major issue. By 1978 between one-fourth and one-third of all housing was described as having severe problems. Deep-seated attitudes about the maintenance of buildings may have contributed to this situation. In Chinese tradition, a public edifice such as a temple or pavilion or even a dwelling could deteriorate to the point of collapse before receiving attention. In China today there are few buildings of genuine antiquity, although there are many completely rebuilt facsimiles. Because the larger cities had ejected a larger proportion of their inhabitants during the Cultural Revolution, whom they had to reaccommodate during the post-Mao influx, the housing situation in China's largest cities continued to worsen compared to that in smaller cities. By 1982, China's cities with 15 million-plus populations and two more key cities had average individual living spaces of 3.6 square meters (Chongqing and Chengdu in Sichuan Province had the lowest average of 2.5 square meters), as compared with the national urban average of 6.3 square meters.[67]

The concept of equity was lacking in the distribution of housing benefits, and entities that owned the housing took care of their own, with state enterprise employees and municipal civil servants receiving favored treatment. Those who benefited most were officials and other influential citizens who had obtained good-quality housing in the first instance and were able to qualify for the deepest discounts because of their rank and seniority. A common family strategy was to strive to have one member of the household working for either the government or a state enterprise so that the family could be assured of receiving housing. The double standard in housing extended to sales as well. As no market for public housing existed, units were priced at a fraction of the cost of new privately financed housing and sold primarily to city and state enterprise employees. Prices were related to the financial capacity of the work unit and the employees' ability to pay, and further subsidies were granted for age and seniority. Without market pricing, actual values were very difficult to determine, particularly since much public housing was so poorly maintained. But because rents had been so heavily subsidized, the ratio of annual rent to housing price was still very high and provided little incentive to purchase, especially since there had been little readiness on the part of the government to raise rents. The government's confiscation of private property in the 1950s also made some potential homeowners hesitant about acquiring property.

In the 1980s, privately financed housing construction became more important, and by 1990 it accounted for 12.6 percent of all housing built since 1949.[68] During the 1980s, the government carried out several housing commercialization experiments. Monthly rents were increased, and housing coupons redeemable for housing repair or purchase were issued to offset the rent increase. Usually 30 percent was required as down payment with ten to fifteen years to pay the balance.[69] Many local governments provided subsidies of up to 70 percent of the purchase price to renters of state housing. But this simply maintained the inequities and subsidies of the existing system and was not financially sustainable.[70] A State Council directive in 1988 banned deep discounts and encouraged alternative approaches, and two small cities were selected to experiment with raising rents and wages on a limited basis. In 1991, the directive was made applicable to all cities, and a national schedule of rent increases was adopted, with the objective of eventually having rents cover at least current operating costs and depreciation.

However, no serious attempts were made to raise rents, and demand for individual loans was not forthcoming. In effect, the program was not a success, and even its modest targets were unmet. The major difficulty was that the extremely low level of rents provided no incentive to purchase rental units, and borrowing was not an attractive option because of credit institutions' unfamiliarity with mortgage lending procedures, short lending maturities, and excessive interest and fees. In the early 1990s, the rent of a typical apartment of fifty-two square meters was RMB 18, or US$2, per month, less than 3 percent of household income and far less than would be required to meet the operational and maintenance costs of the rental unit.[71]

A real estate crisis in the early 1990s was caused by a bubble of speculation in the commercial and luxury residential property markets of major cities. An overheated economy fueled a wave of speculation leading to a massive outflow of funds from the banking system. More than 100 billion *renminbi* were channeled illegally into real estate markets and the new stock exchanges in Shanghai and Shenzhen.[72] Real estate speculation began as an attempt to get rich quickly by investing in the special development zones. The rapid appreciation of property values in the zones yielded extraordinary returns because the land leases were often sold at nominal cost by officials who received kickbacks or other favors. Real estate investment in 1992 increased by 117 percent over the previous year, and in the first half of 1993 by an additional 115 percent. Speculators raced to get into the action, and the number of real estate developers increased from 6,290 in 1991 to more than 20,000 in 1993. Prices were rising at annual rates ranging from 40 to 100 percent. The housing market could not absorb this level of construction, the bubble broke in mid-1993, prices plunged, and 50 million square meters of commercial housing space remained unsold.[73]

The State Council took action in July 1993 to sever incestuous relationships between developers and financial institutions and to introduce bidding procedures for all land and housing sales. The results of the burst housing bubble are still being felt. In Shanghai, for example, more than 1,000 skyscrapers had been built between 1990 and 1997, yet the vacancy rate in 1997 was 70 percent, real estate prices had dropped 50 percent since 1995, and although 7 million to 9 million square meters of residential property remained unsold, there was an acute housing shortage because those who were waiting for housing could not afford to purchase the unsold housing.[74]

At the end of 1997, per capita living space for the nation was at an all time high of 8.8 square meters.[75] In March 1998, Vice Premier Zhu Rongji announced a new government program for ending the welfare housing system and replacing it with a fully commercial system. As a first step, state employees were given the choice of buying their housing at an established "cost" price much lower than comparable market prices or of paying a much higher rent once the new system went into effect. Housing would be paid for through direct employee subsidies and loans either from municipal public housing funds or bank loans.

Municipal governments began selling off substantial amounts of public housing. This time, the demand was there because the government for the first time was serious about raising rents substantially in line with a cost-recovery formula for those who chose not to buy. But many state enterprises and municipal governments were hard put to come up with the cash to fund subsidized housing purchases by state employees. By 2000, only about three dozen Chinese cities had adopted the housing reform plan.[76] Some municipal governments had been granting subsidies of up to 80 percent of the unit cost for those who choose to buy so-called monetary housing. This is somewhere between welfare and commercial housing, because the price established by the municipal government was based on its capacity to pay subsidies, and builders were encouraged to lower their costs and meet this standard. In Guangzhou the standard was RMB 3,500, or US$422, per square meter in 1999. This compared to US$175 per square meter established as a standard for residential housing built by work units and sold to work unit employees at "cost."[77]

Millions of Chinese would like to buy a home, but the great cost differential between government-subsidized work unit housing and the private housing market cannot be bridged by their meager incomes, and it will be a long time before a real market for private housing develops in China. Nevertheless, growth in private housing sales has been stimulated in the last two to three years by growth in mortgage lending. By mid-2000, total outstanding mortgage lending by banks amounted to US$30 billion. China Construction Bank accounted for fully one-half of this amount, and China's largest bank, The Industrial and Commercial Bank of China, has 30 percent of the mortgage loans market.[78]

As for the millions of floating transients, they are not even being considered because in the government's eyes they have no right to housing or any other urban amenities. As the government sees things, its major challenges for the future will be to get out of the real estate business by increasing rents and selling off public housing and to provide the infrastructure necessary to develop a private urban housing market. However, the government seems uncertain about how fast to proceed in commercializing the housing market. Houses cannot be resold without local government approval—it effectively has a right of first refusal. In addition, the new owners are usually required to hold the property for five years before reselling it. Really privatizing housing will be a slow and difficult process, because of the lack of property rights law governing real estate transactions, because property markets are in their infancy, zoning regulations and enforceable building codes are lacking, and adequate financing mechanisms are only now being developed. Therefore, the objective of separating government from housing will not be met for some time.

Cities Without Walls

The economic experiments, resulting turmoil, and forced population movements of the Maoist years have been followed by over twenty years of relative stability and government policies that have favored urban growth, and the number of Chinese living in cities has risen from one-fourth to perhaps one-third of the total population. Yet the industrial heart of the cities—the state enterprises—are in decline, and although a favored class of civil servants and state enterprise employees still has privileged access to jobs, housing, and other benefits, downsizing of local governments and state enterprises threatens this privileged status. The invisible bureaucratic walls no longer keep out rural migrants, but barriers still exist that perpetuate urban–rural divisions within cities, whose populations are segmented according to residency, job status, and access to social services. Residence registrations are still required to obtain housing, and without residence cards, employment permits cannot be obtained. Although the government has become more lenient in issuing temporary residence permits and thus access to jobs, it actively discourages the movement of migrant families to the cities. Its most effective mechanism is to charge fees for children attending school. In Shanghai, after paying for temporary residency permits, public security fees, rent, food, school fees, and electricity out of their meager incomes, migrants have to pay an additional tuition of RMB 240 for a child who attends elementary school and RMB 450 for a child attending middle school.[79] In spite of these hardships, rural migrants in the cities have managed to become important economically—in 1999, for instance, remittances sent back to their families amounted to almost 6 percent of provincial gross domestic product in the provinces of Hunan and Henan.[80]

China's turnabout in dealing with environmental pollution is truly remarkable. It involves a nationwide effort to eliminate coal use by substituting clean fuels. At the national level this involves strategic planning and making available the funding to develop new natural gas and liquified petroleum gas resources and the infrastructure to transport, store, and distribute gas. At the city level, most small coal-burning furnaces and boilers are going to be closed and replaced by gas or oil burners. Larger units will be required to install pollution-control equipment—paying a fine while continuing to operate as before is no longer an option. A major shift in perception seems to have occurred, and economic growth that is not environmentally sustainable is no longer acceptable. Most of the immediate impact of this change is going to be felt in major cities. It will take far longer for it to percolate down to smaller cities, townships, and villages. Although major cities are already becoming more healthful places to live, there is no room for complacency. The fast-rising automobile population is presenting a new urban pollution threat. Pollution levies must be increased to at least the marginal cost of emission control or effluent treatment. Collection of pollution levies can be greatly improved through stronger political support from the mayor's office, and local environmental bureaus must be given the staff and resources to do the job.

Chinese cities have run out of space and will remain densely packed with human beings for the foreseeable future. Two-thirds of China's urban residents still travel to work by foot or bicycle and only one-third use public and private transport—although this is changing as the largest cities build ring roads and subway transport and automobiles crowd out bicycles. Road congestion and vehicular pollution will get even worse as the number of motor vehicles increases at 20 to 30 percent annually. Focusing on building high-cost ring roads is not enough. Private automobiles must be kept out of compacted city centers. Not only should larger cities build subways linking their central cores to urban districts, but they should deny private automobile access to the cores. Strategically located subway stations in urban districts should include park-and-ride facilities for private automobiles. For smaller cities, public or private bus transport is the most feasible and affordable way to extend travel beyond the range of the bicycle. But public bus transport has been hemorrhaging both money and riders for some time, and local governments must give high priority to privatizing public bus transport or making it competitive with private van or automobile transport.

Over the past twenty-two years, the amount of available housing has increased significantly and per capita living space has more than doubled. Yet housing is made available only to those who can obtain residency status, and this in turn is tied to obtaining a job. With the end of free public housing, even workers with permanent jobs who do not have enough seniority to qualify to buy cheaper public housing face an uncertain prospect of being able to afford commercially priced housing. The immediate challenge for the government is to foster a truly commercial housing market for low- and middle-income home buyers by separating the government from this activity and by providing the necessary legislation to establish specialized nonstate mortgage lending institutions. Instead of tearing down their shacks, city governments should provide housing sites and services to temporary residents as well as to permanent residents who cannot afford to buy housing and cannot qualify for financial assistance. This means providing a basic house foundation with water, sewage, and electrical connections. The recipient would be responsible for paying for the use of the utilities and building a simple structure on the foundation. Availability of essential services and possession of title would provide the motivation for the owner to build. In effect, a relatively small investment by the government would lead to privatized housing construction.

Can Chinese cities become cities without walls of any kind and with no artificial barriers to human ambition and achievement? When economic reform began over two decades ago, the government knew that the restrictive policies of the Maoist era, which had effectively segregated urban and rural populations, were incompatible with an open economy. Yet, China's leaders were afraid that farmers seeking opportunity in the cities would overwhelm an already strained urban infrastructure and services. So they temporized—they allowed rural migrants to have temporary status but with no chance of becoming permanent residents. China's cities are still surrounded by invisible walls—the outer wall is gone, but those who enter are prevented by other barriers from going very far. This has resulted in a segmented society that is deeply divided and shares unequally in the benefits of economic reform. The effect of the invisible walls is pernicious. The divisions they create contribute greatly to social instability and unrest. The government must open its eyes and realize that the urban floating population has become the most important source of income for the rural villages whence they came, that they provide the government with a critical safety valve to reduce rural discontent, and that rural migrants should be accepted into urban society. Only when this happens can the invisible walls come down, divisions be healed, and cities become places of opportunity for all their inhabitants.

New freeways and overpasses dominate the skyline in Shanghai municipality.

Chapter Five

The Three Gorges Dam Revisited

Approaching the Three Gorges.

When China celebrated fifty years of Communism on October 1, 1999, Premier Zhu Rongji proudly hailed the enormous achievements of the Chinese people, particularly the economic transformation undertaken during the previous twenty years. But the project that is meant to symbolize these achievements remains mired in controversy. Since it was first proposed by Sun Yatsen in 1919, the idea of damming the Three Gorges of the Yangtze River and constructing the world's largest hydroelectric generation and water-control project has fascinated China's leaders. Although the project had the personal endorsement of Mao Zedong and Deng Xiaoping, internal opposition was surprisingly strong and was silenced only during the crackdown on dissent after the 1989 Tiananmen protest. Meanwhile, international criticism—especially of the project's far-reaching environmental impacts—rose to a fever pitch. The United States and Canadian governments and the World Bank and Asian Development Bank, which had showed initial interest in the project, quickly backed away. China went ahead anyway, determined to make the Three Gorges Dam the crowning success of its drive to modernize its economy. The first earth was moved in 1993, and by the end of 1997, two giant cofferdams enclosed the Yangtze River and construction of the dam itself had begun. Even die-hard opponents realized that nothing would stop the project, and the furor died down.

Although other dams are bigger, Three Gorges will consume 27 million cubic meters of concrete, almost enough to pave over Washington, D.C. It will be capable of generating two-thirds more energy—84 billion kilowatt hours per year—than any other dam in the world. The dam will be 1.2 miles wide and 185 meters high. Behind it the water level will rise as high as 175 meters, submerging 10 percent of the Three Gorges, 13 cities, 140 towns, 360 villages, 1,300 known archaeological sites, and 62,000 acres of farms and orchards, and will create a reservoir 632 kilometers long. By its own admission, the government will have to resettle at least 1,133,800 people who presently live in the reservoir area below the 175-meter level. According to official 1997 estimates, it will cost US$24.4 billion. The dam is scheduled to enter into full operation in 2009, seventeen years after construction officially began.

China's Most Controversial Project

The project's detractors, both foreign and domestic, say that whatever the dam's benefits, they can never justify the environmental cost. They say that a series of smaller dams on the Yangtze tributaries would have the same effect with less environmental damage. They believe that uprooting so many people is simply unacceptable. They raise the specter of untreated municipal and industrial waste, coupled with deadly chemicals from drowned factories, accumulating in a vast open sewer when the river is converted into a reservoir. They believe sediment will accumulate behind the dam and eventually render it useless. They say that endangered species such as the Yangtze sturgeon and white-fin dolphin will no longer be able to swim upstream to spawn and will disappear forever and that the loss of cultural relics is irreparable. They claim that the project's cost has been greatly underestimated and could reach as high as US$72 billion. One observer believes that Chinese officials have lost sight of their historical roots. For over two thousand years the concept of *shuili,* the interplay between natural forces and human action in water conservancy, guided government officials. The Communist regime therefore needs to reaffirm *shuili* insights because the engineering approach now being followed underestimates social and environmental costs and overestimates benefits.[1]

In response, the government insists that the multiple benefits of the dam far outweigh the costs. It will control the most destructive floods in China and minimize the damage they do and it will increase shipping capacity five times and reduce shipping costs by a third by enabling 10,000-ton vessels to travel 2,000 kilometers up the Yangtze to Chongqing. It would substitute clean hydroelectric generation for the 100 million tons of carbon dioxide, 2 million tons of sulfur dioxide, 370,000 tons of nitrogen oxide, and 150,000 tons of ash that would enter the atmosphere annually if this electricity were provided by conventional coal-fired power plants. During the 1990s, the government made much of the fact that the dam would generate sufficient electricity to make up China's energy deficit. Now, however, the country has an electricity surplus, energy prices are falling, and should this trend continue, the project will lose money on its electricity generation.

The rhetorical wars between both camps did nothing to resolve the controversy. Both detractors and the government hardened their positions, listening to their own set of experts and relying on their own data.

It is no coincidence that the Yangtze was closed on the same day in 1997 that Hong Kong was returned to China. For the Chinese government, building the dam has become a test of national pride, purpose, ingenuity, and skill. In that same year, the central government lined up the critical provincial support it needed by making a huge political payoff to the city of Chongqing. But the 1998 Yangtze River flood—the worst in over forty years—raised new doubts about the government's strategy for controlling such floods and about the efficacy of Three Gorges Dam in the process. After revisiting the evidence, it seems clear Three Gorges Dam will not be able to prevent floods of this magnitude in the future, but it will be able to limit their impact. Yet emphasis on flood control involves trading off other benefits, therefore, electricity generation and navigation targets are unlikely to be achieved.

Calculating the economic costs and benefits of a large, complex project like Three Gorges is vastly complicated. While calculating financial costs, benefits, and rates of return is a relatively straightforward task, environmental and social costs are extremely difficult to quantify. Resettlement costs are the most difficult, because no one can put a dollar amount on human misery. Also, benefits tend to be recognized as soon as the project commences operating, while environmental costs, for instance, may become evident only over a very long period. When costs and benefits are compared to determine economic rates of return, this skews the results in favor of the benefits.

A Tourism Windfall

The controversy over the dam led to a tourism boom and a rush to see the Three Gorges before the river level rises. Travel agents made much of this and very little of the fact that only about one-tenth of the gorges will actually be inundated—the major impact will occur above the gorges, where the river will be turned into a large lake. Nicholas Kristoff, former *New York Times* Beijing bureau chief made the trip but was disappointed and said that in China there are plenty of sights far more captivating. Kristoff missed the point.

Really to see the upper Yangtze is to observe a kaleidoscope of Chinese river life that will disappear in the name of economic progress. Millions of Chinese have lived alongside the Yangtze for more than 4,000 years. Every bend in the river brings a new human settlement. In one place pollution pours from factory smokestacks, outlet pipes, and household chimneys. At another turn brick buildings weathered gray or brown stand out from a green hillside below a white pagoda. Small craft move about like water beetles, avoiding a larger vessel pushing its way peremptorily upriver. The weather is usually cloudy or rainy, mists swirl around the tops of the canyons, shapes lose their outline, perspective changes, colors merge and are muted. On a nighttime departure, the river has a special quality. Under the yellow harbor lights, the water has an oily cast, glistening and undulating like a coiling snake as the boat slides into the current. Clouds cover the sky. In the dark, the only sense of movement is provided by the running lights of other vessels, appearing as pinpricks of light, growing larger, moving by, and disappearing. All this adds to the river's mystery and in no way diminishes its majesty. It is a landscape in motion and must be searched out. It is not for the passive viewer.

Millions Fear the River Dragon

The main justification for building the Three Gorges dam is the containment of the disastrous floods that regularly inflict death and suffering on the inhabitants of the middle and lower Yangtze River. In Chinese mythology, the elemental forces that cause water to both help and harm humans take the shape of a dragon. When the river dragon escapes its banks, the human toll it exacts is captured in Han Suyin's chilling account of the horror of traveling on a train when she was twelve, eating lunch and looking out the window at a vast plain of brown water broken only by the upper branches of trees.

In the protruding tree-boughs, people
Perched like birds, unmoving
The train thunders by them
High on its embankment
Even screams at them
They do not raise a hand
Knowing it will not stop for them
They die the lazy death of water
And no one cares
Mile upon mile upon mile of them
Mama opens the hamper
The children eat[2]

The Yangtze transports more water than any other river except the Amazon, but unlike the latter, its basin shelters an immense population—one-fourth of China's 1.3 billion total. As more and more people crowd into the lakes and wetlands bordering the river and convert them to agricultural plots, the press of humanity on the fragile defenses raised against the river's annual floods can only have a tragic outcome. The river dragon is most feared when floodwaters rush out of the Three Gorges and meet the Jianghan Plain. The river spreads out and slows down, releasing massive amounts of sediment and carving a sinuous path while *raising the riverbed two meters above the land*. The floodwaters' main point of attack is the 182 kilometer-long Jingjiang embankment, which rises up as much as twelve meters higher than the surrounding land to contain the raised waters. In the riverbank town of Shishou, passersby walk calmly along streets while the river runs by above their heads. For 1,750 years, these levees have failed to hold the Yangtze in full flood. They failed most recently in the 1931 and 1935 floods, when nothing could hold back the terrible avalanche of elevated floodwaters. In the 1931 flood, an area the size of New York State was inundated, 145,000 people died, and 14 million became refugees.[3]

After assuming power in 1949, the Communist regime decided to divert floodwaters away from these embankments to prevent such a catastrophe from occurring again. The Jingjiang flood-diversion basin was built in 1952 and was used to divert the waters of the 1954 flood (the worst since 1935) from the city of Wuhan, when 100 billion cubic meters of floodwater exceeded the height of the embankments. Yet, flood diversion saved Wuhan but contributed to the inundation of 32,000 square kilometers, an event that left 19 million people homeless. These statistics hardly reflect the human suffering involved. Exposure to the elements, lack of food and water, and diseases such as hemorragic fever, dysentery, and schistosomiasis caused death rates to rise to fifteen per thousand in the affected population.[4]

Natural storage areas all along the Yangtze are disappearing rapidly. They have been drained and reduced by the encroachment of settlers. Dongting Lake, the largest natural reservoir above Wuhan, has been shrinking for the last century because of reclamation of 1.3 million acres of new farmland. In the past fifty years, the lake lost one-half of its surface area and storage capacity. Also, embanking of the riverbank has increased the flow of silt into the lake while reducing its flushing capacity. By 1980, flood diversion areas totaled 800,000 hectares, but because of the encroachment of settlers, they included a population of 3.6

million, which was at risk whenever floods were diverted. The subsequent raising of the embankments was said to have reduced the need for diversion, but a big concern was whether the Jingjiang embankments, which are known to be unstable, could continue to withstand the force of the flood as they are built higher and higher.

The 1998 flood was the worst since 1954. Even before the 1998 flood season began, eleven kilometers of Yangtze embankment had caved in or crumbled in sixteen places and had to be repaired—the biggest section was 4.6 kilometers long.[5] The flood season began in March, much earlier than usual, and continued through July and August, when the river peaked eight times, keeping embankments saturated for fifty days, causing cave-ins and crumbling of the mostly earthen structures. Crisis was about to turn into catastrophe, and the People's Liberation Army (PLA) was called in to make its largest deployment to the area since 1949, when it fought its last battles with the Guomindang forces. Although 6,700,000 PLA soldiers, police, militia, and civilian volunteers reinforced 5,900 kilometers of levee and repaired cave-ins and collapses at 5,350 separate locations, they could not prevent a major breach of the Yangtze embankments.[6] On August 7, 1998, a sixty-meter section of the embankment at Jiujiang City was carried away, much of the city was covered by water, and the breach was closed five days later only by massive levee reinforcement involving the work of thousands of people.[7] When the city of Wuhan, whose 6 million people live three meters below the river, was threatened by the fourth Yangtze flood crest, the river crested just five centimeters below the level requiring diversion—a very close call indeed, providing little comfort for the future. The 1998 flood killed 1,562 people and disrupted the lives of 21 million more, including 4 million that lost everything and had to be resettled. In addition, 2.0 million houses, stores, and factories were damaged and 1.3 million destroyed. The financial loss was about US$20 billion. The human cost was incalculable.[8]

Because the embankments had been raised, floodwaters did not have to be diverted, and President Jiang Zemin called it a great victory for the party and the army.[9] But the victory was a hollow one. Raising the embankments increased the risk of failure due to eroding of the embankment walls and seepage through undetected weakened sections, and when the embankments indeed began to fail, the army and millions of volunteers had to be called upon to save the day. The embankments are now so high that they are in constant danger of collapse during major floods and will continue to require mobilization of millions of people to avert catastrophe.

Since the 1998 flood official actions show that although the government may have won a battle, it is losing the war to control Yangtze River flooding. The government has already moved 1 million people from the middle and lower reaches of the river in Hubei, Hunan, Jiangsu, and Anhui provinces to higher ground. Even though more than one-half billion dollars has been budgeted to shore up the Yangtze levees over the next three years, the government intends to move an additional 2 million people away from the river, and 10 billion cubic meters of flood-water storage will be created.[10]

Government planners and engineers need to know how likely it is that floods will occur and how bad they might be. The severity of floods is commonly measured by the peak rate of flow, and the Jingjiang embankments are supposed to be capable of withstanding flows of up to 60,000 cubic meters per second, long considered the flow rate of a once-in-ten-year flood, since historical records reveal about two hundred floods of this magnitude or worse over the last 2,000 years.[11] In the last 100 years, however, floods with such flow levels have occurred on average once every five years,[12] so this standard is no longer reliable. Also, peak flow was inadequate to measure the impact of the 1954 and 1998 floods. Their peak flow was only that of a five-year flood, yet because the total volume of water was so great, the devastation was on the scale of a much greater flood measured by peak flow. The point is that the river dragon is far more to be feared now than ancient records would indicate.

During the flood season, the Three Gorges reservoir will be kept at a low, flood-prevention level of 145 meters, which will provide it with a holding capacity of 22 billion cubic meters of floodwaters. This will reduce flooding but will not prevent floodwaters like those of 1954 and 1998 from attacking the weak points of the Jingjiang embankments, and water will have to be diverted and stored if the river overflows the embankments or if the embankments are in danger of breaching. The Three Gorges Dam will have no impact on floodwaters entering the Yangtze from its tributaries below the dam. In addition to the Han River, three major rivers flow into Lake Dongting before it meets the Yangtze.

Conflicting Objectives

The Three Gorges Dam generators are expected to produce one-tenth of China's electric power, which will be directed to users in the lower Yangtze River basin. But the problem with creating a multipurpose dam is that one purpose always gets in the way of another. The installed yearly generating capacity is based on maintaining a "normal pool level" of water in the dam of 175 meters in depth. Since the "head" of water needed to turn the turbines is dependent on water height above the turbines, when the water level in the reservoir is brought down to a flood-control level of 145 meters, electricity generation will be severely affected. One expert believes that if water levels are maintained for proper flood control, electricity generation will only be 53 percent of capacity.[13] The dam is also expected to improve navigation by eliminating most one-way sections in the gorges, reducing water velocities, and permitting passage of 10,000-ton vessels through the ship locks at the dam. However, like power generation, navigation both in the reservoir and downriver from the dam is best served when the water level behind the dam is high and water is released downriver, as will be the case during the flood season. But when water is impounded during the dry season, this will impede navigation.

Some critics believe that eventually silt will build up behind the dam, clogging the turbines, and rendering them useless. However, because four-fifths of the silt carried by the Yangtze arrives with floodwaters, the government believes that its strategy of "impounding clear water, discharging turbid water" will maintain water dam storage capacity while controlling sedimentation.[14] This seems simple enough: release silt-laden water during the flood season; retain low-silt water after the floods. But critics also argue that coarser sediment will accumulate at the upper end of the reservoir and impede navigation and prolong flooding there, while released floodwaters will not be sediment free and will scour the base of some 30,000 kilometers of downstream embankments and greatly increase the risk of a major breach.[15] In practice, turbid floodwaters cannot simply be released downstream and will have to be stored until flood peaks have passed. This necessitates a sophisticated dam operation to try to move sediment just ahead of or behind the greatest flow of water. Citing the difficulties large dams in the United States have experienced in flushing sediment, one expert says it is unlikely the Chinese will do any better.[16]

Government projections based on computer modeling indicate that in about 100 years equilibrium will be reached with over 90 percent of sedimentation being flushed out of the reservoir. But, when considering the dynamics of river flows over such a long period of time, critics argue that using mathematical models to predict a century into the future is simply unrealistic and that silt is bound to accumulate behind such a large structure.[17] The problem with models is that they are only as good as the assumptions that underlie them, and the process of selecting assumptions over the very long term is fraught with ambiguity and subjectivity. Yet, to argue that silt is simply bound to accumulate to dangerous levels no matter what, is equally subjective.

The Outlook Is Grim for Displaced Persons

The government openly admits that over the last forty years, while 83,000 reservoirs and dams have been built and 10 million people have been displaced and resettled, resettlement has been largely a disaster. Most of the dispossessed were resettled in remote areas and simply given a sum of money and a handshake. Many of the new settlements were kept going only with government subsidies—even then, one-third failed and the population had to be moved yet again. A significant number moved back illegally to their original villages. In Yongjing county, the average annual income of one-third of people relocated was lower than it had been preresettlement, two-thirds had an annual per capita income below the poverty level, and 10 percent of the newly cultivated fields had to be abandoned because of erosion resulting from intensive farming on steeper slopes or a rising water table due to reservoir silting.[18] In 1989, China's leading poverty agency acknowledged that 70 percent of China's 10.2 million resettlers were living in extreme poverty.[19]

The government has said it has learned a hard lesson from this experience and has assumed responsibility for the future of the people displaced by the Three Gorges Dam. This time, it has emphasized consultation with the affected population and adequate compensation under the guiding principle of "resettlement with development." Its goal is to ensure that living standards at the new location are at least equal to previous standards. A major effort was made to keep those affected in their original jurisdictions by moving uphill of the flooded area or to adjacent jurisdictions. Resettlement will be phased over twelve years in accordance with rising water levels in the reservoir, with those affected earliest being resettled first. Local governments will manage the funds using a project approach to carry out parallel investments in housing, infrastructure, and productive facilities. China has an administrative system capable of carrying out such a program, but thoughtful analysts say many of the advantages perceived by the government are illusory. They claim that falsification of figures, official cover-ups of deficiencies and failures, endemic corruption and misuse of funds, discrimination against rural resettlers in favor of urban ones, and lack of adequate consultation have seriously disrupted the resettlement process.[20, 21]

The government has insisted there is plenty of unoccupied land available, but the question of why this land is unoccupied is never asked, although the rest of the upper Yangtze basin in Sichuan Province is densely populated. Mountainsides make up 74 percent of the land area, rolling hills 22 percent, and flatland just 4 percent. About one-half the land already sown with crops has a slope of twenty-five degrees or more and a soil thickness of less than one foot.[22] Over the past half-century, Sichuan's forest cover has been reduced from 26 percent of the total area to 17 percent by logging activity. Erosion is a huge problem, and within the thin soil layer, its effect is disastrous. Sixty-two percent of the land in the Three Gorges reservoir suffers from soil erosion.[23] Many are blaming deforestation and the accompanying erosion for the severity of the 1998 floods. Rainfall on the upper slopes is almost twice that on bottomland, yet only 3 to 4 percent is retained while the rest and much of the soil end up as runoff.

Nevertheless, throughout the 1990s, the government claimed that more than 13,000 square kilometers of this inhospitable land was adequate for the new settlers. It was betting the land could produce citrus fruit and thus provide a first-ever cash crop for most dispossessed farmers. But one-half of the occupied land is above 800 meters which is too high for citrus cultivation. Also, since it takes citrus trees three to four years to produce a crop, the farmers would need to be supported by the state in the interim. Where would these funds come from? During a 1999 visit to the area, Premier Zhu Rhongzi ruled out the possibility of turning forested mountainsides into terraced fields or of terracing any slopes steeper than twenty-five degrees.[24] Government policy was shifting away from resettling villagers on higher ground at the same location, and in 1999 the State Council announced that 125,000 people would be moved out of the reservoir area and resettled in ten mostly coastal provinces. In August 2000, the first group of 639 farmers from Yunyang county arrived in Shanghai.[25] What many of the dispossessed feared has come to pass—they will be forced to migrate after all.

Understanding what is going on is complicated by inflated statistics and misinformation. Local officials routinely exaggerate the number resettled to satisfy their superiors. In 1998, officials first reported that

200,000, and later 100,000, people had been resettled. Many observers question even the latter figure. If the government is going to meet its target of resettling 500,000 people before it fills the reservoir to the 135-meter mark in 2003, then the rate of resettlement will have to be greatly speeded up, with the hardships involved increasing accordingly. Rural resettlers will be the worse off because they receive less compensation than their urban counterparts. In Yunyang and Zigui counties, rural housing compensation is about one-half urban housing compensation.[26]

The government also knows it will not be able to absorb all the farmers in agricultural jobs and hopes to establish industrial enterprises to absorb the surplus labor. Yet the region lacks the infrastructure to support growth, and its inhabitants lack the education needed to learn industrial skills. Early experience with new enterprises established for those first resettled indicates that they lack a commercial justification and face an uncertain future.[27] China's industrial sector is in crisis as state enterprises grapple with the problems of obsolescence and inefficiency, production levels below capacity, large unsold inventories, low worker productivity coupled with high redundancy, and overdue debts and not enough cash flow to pay them. Faced with fierce competition and declining demand, these new enterprises will have difficulty surviving.

One potentially explosive issue is that of illegal migrants, who are said to make up about 30 percent of the urban population in the reservoir area. The government has stated that it will not compensate them for having to move because they do not have residency status and should not be "rewarded" for their illegal action.[28] Equally disturbing is rising corruption following central government delegation to local governments of control over resources. The resettlement budget has grown to almost US$9 billion, and with it, allegations of misuse of these funds. Officials are said to be involved in inflating claims and taking kickbacks from construction companies, placing the names of relatives or friends on the list of beneficiaries, artificially boosting the price of land and pocketing the difference, and charging illegal fees for performing their normal services.[29] Another report states that more than US$57 million has been stolen from the resettlement fund, and ninety-seven officials are being investigated for possible misuse of these funds. Another US$24 million has been diverted through over-invoicing of construction equipment.[30]

Environmental Impacts Will Be Severe

Regarding waste disposal, the attitude of those living on the banks of the Yangtze has been to leave solid waste where it is and pipe liquid waste into the river, which carries it away until it is someone else's problem. This attitude is changing very rapidly with the realization that when the river becomes a reservoir, water levels will rise, covering the solid waste which will leach out into the surrounding waters, and water flows will be so reduced that wastewater and sewage will remain where it is. Presently, only 10 percent of China's municipal sewage is treated, and cities that line the future reservoir are waking up. Chongqing, China's largest municipality, sits on a peninsula created by the juncture of the Yangtze and Jialing rivers. About six hundred outlet pipes discharge municipal sewage directly into both rivers. The World Bank is helping finance a project costing US$370 million to construct a system of interceptors on the banks of both rivers to carry away the city's total sewage discharge, calculated at 1.5 million cubic meters per day. The sewage will be treated and then discharged into the Yangtze downstream from Chongqing. Industrial enterprises are slow to follow suit. They are hampered by lack of funds for investment in treatment facilities, and low pollution fines coupled with limited follow-up from local environmental protection bureaus encourage them often to pay just part of the fine, so that polluting becomes simply another cost of doing business.

Critics make much of the fact that the Three Gorges Dam will prevent aquatic species unique to the Yangtze from going upriver to spawn and they will be doomed. Although the smaller Gezhouba Dam, built in 1988, just thirty-eight kilometers downstream from the Three Gorges, is responsible for creating this problem, the new dam will exacerbate it. The government recognizes that the project will have a major impact on the area's fauna and flora and has established a network of several hundred scientists to monitor ecological changes by utilizing seven monitoring stations established in the area.

Critics also claim that while 400 to 500 of the 1,282 identifiable archaeological sites to be inundated ought to be preserved, funds are available to save only half of them.[31] Above-ground sites include stone and wooden architecture 200 to 300 hundred years old (including an entire village) and stones with calligraphy up to 1,800 years old marking low water levels on river walls. Underground sites include dated artifacts from 50,000 B.C. to 221 B.C., as well as the remains of *Homo erectus* and

Homo sapiens sapiens. The earliest people referred to in historical sources are the Ba, whose origins in the Three Gorges region go back 4,000 years. Archaeologists postulate that southwestern China seems to have made a significant contribution to the development of human prehistory in China and the rest of Asia, but rising waters will drown any hope of unearthing sufficient evidence from the reservoir area to document this assertion. The little-known but important Ba culture will remain largely a question mark in the archaeological record. Salvage of cultural relics has been provided with too little funding too late. Also, money for this purpose is often lumped in with the resettlement budget, leaving archaeologists in the unenviable position of competing with the dispossessed for funding.

Among the most fascinating cultural remains in the Three Gorges are narrow tracks carved into the vertical canyon walls for human "pullers" who hauled all upstream traffic through the narrow canyons until they reached the head of the gorges. Getting through the rapids required precise coordination between rowers on the vessel and pullers on the cliffs, who inched along narrow paths cut into the vertical walls of the canyon. The pullers were completely naked and carried heavy ropes over their shoulders—it was easy to lose one's footing, but clothes were more valuable than their lives. When steam vessels arrived, they were able to go upriver on their own. The pullers are gone. The narrow paths upon which they made their hazardous journey will soon be covered by the Three Gorges reservoir.

Winners and Losers

The project has clear winners and losers. While the benefits of flood control and electricity generation will go mostly to the people living in the middle and lower Yangtze River basin, the vast majority of the negative impacts will be borne by the population of the upper Yangtze, which will be inundated by the creation of the reservoir. The biggest individual winner will be its most fervent advocate, former Chinese premier Li Peng, who now heads the National People's Congress and who was responsible for quelling internal opposition to the dam. His most difficult task was to sort out competing demands and develop a consensus of support for the project among the provinces bordering the Yangtze. Each province was interested in maximizing its benefits and was concerned that limited budgets would cause funds to be shifted from other provincial projects to Three Gorges. Many favored a number of smaller dams on local tributaries of the Yangtze.

Sichuan Province bore the brunt of the project's negative impacts and was responsible for resettling the people who had to be moved to make way for the reservoir. Chongqing authorities were especially unhappy because flooding would become a major concern once the reservoir was filled. At the flood-control level of 145 meters, a flood with a flow of 80,000 cubic meters per second would cause waters to rise to 200 meters at Chongqing, according to mathematical models.[32] The city is now undergoing a vast reconstruction program to raze low-lying neighborhoods and construct a massive wall to prevent the city from flooding should such an event occur. In order to get local officials behind the project, the State Council issued a decree in 1997 that more than doubled Chongqing's area (to 82,400 square kilometers) and population (to 30 million) and separated it from the rest of Sichuan Province. Although Sichuan Province lost its biggest city and a good deal of land, most of the project's impacts were shifted to Chongqing, because four-fifths of the reservoir now lies within the municipality. The political payoff for Chongqing was huge. Although still a municipality, Chongqing has the status of province, similar to Beijing, Shanghai, and Tianjin. This means that Chongqing officials now deal directly with Beijing and are no longer subordinate to the Sichuan provincial government.

Project Costs Keep Escalating

Official estimates of the project's cost have increased from US$10.6 billion in 1992 to US$24.4 billion in 1997.[33] Critics predict that greater cost overruns will increase the cost to as much as US$72 billion.[34] If establishing the physical cost of the project is hard, finding out its financial cost is even more difficult, because cost estimates do not include interest payments to be made during construction. Borrowers are generally required by lenders to repay interest, but not principal, during construction of a project. For projects with a very long construction period, such as Three Gorges, interest during construction amounts to a great deal of money. Resettling the population of the reservoir area is also likely to cost much more than anticipated. Financial and resettlement costs are unlikely to be revealed, especially if the overruns are considerable.

U.S. and European firms have already supplied millions of dollars' worth of construction equipment for the project. China also needs foreign firms to manufacture large, complex machinery such as the 26,680,000-kilowatt generators that will produce the dam's electricity. Although the U.S. government declined to allow the Export-Import Bank in 1995 to provide export financing for U.S.-manufactured equipment and machinery, in 1997 Japan's Export-Import Bank was authorized to provide export credit and trade insurance for Japanese companies bidding for contracts related to Three Gorges. Four of Japan's largest conglomerates are bidding to manufacture the first twelve hydroelectric generators for the dam.

China also requires foreign financing for underwriting securities issues that will provide funding for the project. Such assistance has been hard to come by. Private investors such as Merrill Lynch were frightened away by environmental and human rights issues. When it became public knowledge in 1997 that Morgan Stanley Dean Witter was in partnership with a Chinese securities company that was preparing an underwriting of a securities issue for the Three Gorges Project Development Corporation, a small but vociferous group of shareholders demanded that the firm adopt a policy that could preclude its financing projects with negative environmental and human-rights impacts. Soon after, Bank of America announced that it would not underwrite any securities that would finance construction of the dam.[35] When securities issues are not specifically earmarked for Three Gorges, however, major investment houses are more willing to participate. Goldman, Sachs and Company underwrote a billion-dollar bond issue in 1998 for the People's Republic of China, which reportedly channeled US$200 million to the Three Gorges project.[36]

China is providing most of the financing for the project. All revenues from the nearby Gezhouba Dam are channeled to Three Gorges. The government has levied a 2 percent tax on electricity use and has required the State Development Bank to make loans for the project. The first two sources are expected to generate a total of US$13 billion, and the third has promised to lend US$15 billion. However, the government lacks one-third of the funding required to carry out the 1997–2003 second phase of the project and is also asking commercial banks to come up with US$1.3 billion.[37] China Construction Bank, a state commercial bank that is a substantial contributor to the project, has been made responsible for settlement and supervision of all monetary transfers relating to the project. More than US$5 billion has already passed through its Three Gorges branch.[38] The government is also planning treasury bond issues to raise yet more funds. It is evident therefore that the government is seeking financing far in excess of the official budget figure of US$24.5 billion.

What Is the Verdict?

The most vocal critics oppose the project on grounds of principle and say no project is worth the human and environmental costs of the Three Gorges Dam. For them there is no middle ground. Led by environmentalists, more and more scientists, engineers, hydrologists, and bureaucrats no longer believe that superdams can meet the larger-than-life expectations they engender when public support is being rallied to justify the great expenditures required to build them. In spite of the obvious benefits of flood control and clean hydroelectric power generation over thermoelectric generation, China is bucking a worldwide shift in perception that is turning against such grandiose projects because of their profound environmental impact.

Are the critics right? The building of dams and impounding of rivers into reservoirs changes the nature of the ecosystem and the physical and chemical linkages of every living organism within it. But no matter how well designed, ecological studies can at best produce limited understanding of the effects of dam construction through time on ecosystems and people.[39] Many environmental and social costs and benefits, therefore, are not readily quantifiable and will continue to be debated on the basis of principle rather than fact.

Where does this leave Three Gorges? The project is hard to justify financially because escalating costs coupled with long-deferred returns make investing in Three Gorges a very unattractive financial proposition—especially since the hidden and growing costs of capital will probably never be known and the ability of the project to recover costs is subject to competing objectives, political influence, fluctuating energy demand, and consumer price structures that are kept artificially low. It is hard to justify on economic grounds because the real environmental costs will not become evident for decades. Chinese predictions of the dam's benefits are too optimistic, and they fail to include trade-offs among different objectives. Because the quantity of water is seasonal, there will always be competing demands between flood control and reservoir filling and the requirements of industry and commerce for more electricity and better navigation.

If resettlement of the affected population is not successful, then most of the claims for the project's success will evaporate. Every indication is that it will be a failure, because the key to successful resettlement is finding jobs for the dispossessed. The land is poorly endowed for agriculture, industrial jobs simply are not there, and although horticulture may have some success, now that the government is unwilling to allow more mountainous land to be cleared for fear of more erosion, most of these unfortunates will have to migrate, and their chances of resuming productive lives may be even more tenuous.

Uprooting so many people in the upper Yangtze might still be justifiable as the lesser of two evils if doing so relieves the suffering of a much larger group in the middle and lower reaches of the Yangtze, who themselves are uprooted whenever serious flooding overflows the Yangtze embankments. Three Gorges can have an impact if floods originate above the dam, but much less if they originate below it. When most of the waters of a great flood come through the Three Gorges, as in the 1954 flood, Three Gorges Dam will be able to hold back most, but not all of the total volume of floodwaters that exceed the holding capacity of the Jingjiang embankments. When so much flood water comes from tributaries joining the Yangtze below the Three Gorges, as was the case in the 1998 flood, the dam's role will be limited. Although the Jingjiang embankments were raised and held back a greater volume in the 1998 flood, their instability increased with height and a major disaster was averted only by the efforts of millions to shore-up and repair breaches in the embankments.

Perhaps the river dragon may eventually be contained after all. In a rare concession to the forces of nature, China has embarked on a program to restore 20,000 square kilometers of wetlands in the middle reaches of the Yangtze River. Local governments have begun working with the World Wide Fund for Nature to return wetlands which had been reclaimed as cropland, to their original state, so they are able to absorb seasonal floodwaters. This includes restoring Dongting and Poyang lakes to their former size and unblocking dikes which hold back the Yangtze River. These critical flood storage areas had been greatly reduced by centuries of dike construction and land reclamation projects—Dongting Lake lost one-half of its area in the twentieth century alone.[40]

The last word belongs to those who stand to lose the most. They are mostly farmers and elderly urbanites who are refusing to move because they will have to give up everything that makes life worthwhile. A physician in a riverside town, who has many elderly patients, describes their plight: "They have lived on the riverbanks for so long. They have built their houses here, cultivated their vegetable gardens on the slopes, and opened small shops near the docks, and they have particular teahouses for talking with their old friends. It will cost them more to move everything than the government will provide in compensation. Above all, they want to be buried in the family graveyard together with generations of ancestors. They are depressed by the economic loss they will suffer and disturbed by the inevitable breakup of the emotional ties they have had with this land."[41]

Chapter 6

Cyberspace Gatekeeper

A gate in the garden of the shrine of the Buddha in Leshan, Sichuan Province.

For millennia, China's walls and gates have enabled those in power to control access and keep undesirables out. The present government officially calls itself the cyberspace gatekeeper, controlling the information flow both into and out of China. The government says its gatekeeper role is essential to maintaining national security and domestic stability. But China's emergence as a world economic power coincides with the globalization of communications networks and the rapid development of information technology. The digitalized information superhighway is revolutionizing the way that economic actors interact with one another and exchange information, and China's leaders are faced with a dilemma: how to exploit the economic development potential of the new information technology while controlling its dissemination.

Because telecommunications was neglected under Mao Zedong and under the impetus of the wireless and Internet revolutions, the information and communications industries are growing at four times the rate of the rest of the economy. China's leaders believe that by adopting new technology, economic transformation and growth will surely follow, and that by becoming a world leader in telecommunications, China can open the door to foreign competition while keeping itself competitive in fast-changing global markets, now that China has entered the World Trade Organization (WTO).[1]

Telecommunications can be broadly defined as any activity whereby information is transmitted or received through wired or wireless electromagnetic or optical systems. In the late 1980s, China set out to become a telecommunications giant. Over a ten-year period, the Ministry of Posts and Telegraphs, through its operating company China Telecom, annually installed 15 million lines of switching capacity and 100,000 kilometers of fiberoptic cable—more than the rest of the developing world combined. By 1997—after just twelve years—China had gone from the world's seventeenth-largest telephone market to the second largest, and 99 percent of urban telephones were connected by digital rather than analog switches.[2] With the economy growing at 8 percent or more a year, the telecommunications sector was expanding at an astounding 30 to 40 percent annually.

To one astute observer, telecommunications epitomizes all that is bad and good about China's economic reform. State telecommunications enterprises are the spawn of powerful ministries and operate in a shady world where ministerial politics and business practices blend into one another. They are the perfect embodiment of the reform process: They lack clear structure, and the policy rationale behind their existence mixes socialism with market competition. They are supposed to be national companies with a state-centered agenda, yet any real energy they have comes from local initiative. Where this process will lead is almost impossible to predict.[3]

Telecommunications Comes to China

China's first telegraph line was installed in 1877. Alexander Graham Bell had invented the telephone in 1876, and in 1882 the first telephone exchange was established in China. Other exchanges were built and connected to one another by trunk cable systems. An Office of Posts and Telegraphs was created in 1906. When the Qing dynasty fell in 1911, 50,000 kilometers of telegraph wire and 8,800 telephone lines had been installed. Yet, by 1949 only 300,000 telephones were in use—one for every 1,800 Chinese. In rural areas, there was only one for every 18,000 people.[4] After the commune system was established, it required good communications, and the number of rural telephone exchanges increased at an average rate of 36 percent annually over the next decade.

The government's main preoccupation was ideological training and dissemination of propaganda through a national radio broadcasting system that linked the central government with work units all the way down to the village level. By 1964, 6 million loudspeakers located in 95 percent of China's cities, towns, and villages, made up the national radio network. Other communications media were neglected because the government controlled all flows of information and had no interest in expanding personal communications, and government restrictions on changing jobs and travel greatly reduced the need for communication.

The Ministry of Posts and Telecommunications was responsible for postal and telephone service in China. Its role was monopolistic because it not only provided services but was responsible for regulation and represented the government as owner of manufacturers of telecommunications equipment. The ministry controlled international and interprovincial communications and received all revenues from international, interprovincial, and intercity calls. The ministry was immensely profitable, and it retained most revenues before redistributing the rest to provincial post and telecommunications (P and T) bureaus. It grossly overcharged for long-distance and international calls, where demand was inelastic, and undercharged for local calls. Its profit margins were 75 percent on international traffic, 25 percent on long distance, and 2 to 3 percent on local calls.[5] Like other ministries, it was a large pyramidal entity extending downward through province, county, town, and village. Yet almost one-half of village level exchanges were owned by work units and village governments, and each level in the pyramid had varying autonomy depending on status.

Telecommunications Under Mao's Successors

After 1978, the lifting of restrictions on travel and job change and China's economic opening required vastly expanded communications as a whole array of new economic actors entered the economy. Lack of funding was a major problem, and the government allowed the Ministry of Posts and Telecommunications to retain a portion of its revenue from telecommunications services for financing development projects.

Rapid expansion of telecommunications began in the mid-1980s. Existing analog systems use signals that are exact reproductions of the sound, picture, or symbol transmitted as a continuous sound wave. Newer digital systems break up sound waves into binary digits, which are much easier to process and transmit and do not lose fidelity over distance as analog signals do. Conversion of the existing analog telephony infrastructure to digital technologies allowed greatly enhanced quality of service and system capacity. Concomitantly, coaxial cable trunk lines carrying electronic signals were replaced by fiberoptic cables in which signals were converted to a pulse of light traveling through strands of optical glass.

During the Seventh Five Year Plan (1986–1990), the Ministry of Posts and Telecommunications concentrated on digitizing and expanding trunk facilities and adding digital switching equipment to major urban networks, mostly provincial capitals and coastal cities. The number of digital telephones in China increased from 273,000 in 1986 to 5,701,000 in 1991.[6] Although telecommunications revenues increased by 30 percent annually, central government budget constraints and rapid sector growth led the Ministry of Posts and Telecommunications to transfer responsibility for financing network development to local P and T bureaus.

Central government financing was limited to national infrastructure such as transmission systems and satellite networks, while local P and Ts invested in switching capacity and telephone lines. They were allowed to retain the profits from their services and consequently raised their prices while seeking debt financing from domestic and foreign banks to fill the gap. As a result, central government financing of total telecommunications investment fell from 60 percent in 1983 to just 9 percent in 1989. In 1988, the government inaugurated the "Three 90 Percents" strategy in which the ministry was allowed to keep 90 percent of its taxable profit from operations, and foreign currency earnings from international traffic, and not repay 90 percent of loans made by the central government. By the end of 1989, China's telecommunications system had a debt load of US$900 million, 60 percent of which was financed by foreign lenders.[7]

The government's commitment to separate government administrative functions from enterprise management has been applied as inconsistently in the service sector as it has in manufacturing. In 1988, the ministry's manufacturing and construction enterprises were made separate legal entities while those providing services were not. Also in that year, more authority over network development, procurement, and financing was shifted to the municipal and county levels, which could be more responsive to local opportunities and conditions. But divestiture or privatization, which might threaten or undermine the government's control over telecommunications, was not considered. The ministry had enormous power over new entrants, since it alone could grant operating licenses and had sole authority to allocate frequencies for radio, paging, and mobile phone systems. The licensing criteria were so broad, they allowed the ministry and its local P and Ts great discretionary power.

During the Eighth Five Year Plan (1991–1995), investment in the telecommunications sector really took off, with the central government again taking a leading role. Fixed asset investment grew from US$1,650,000 in 1992 to US$8,350,000 in 1994—a 500 percent increase. By the mid-1990s, the sector was receiving so much support from the government that the Three 90 Percents rule was repealed. Telecommunications as a percentage of gross domestic product grew more than five times between 1990 and 1994.[8] The central government focused on creating a national fiberoptic network—so much for the low-capacity and electronically switched and amplified coaxial trunk lines of the past—and by the mid-1990s had created a system of twenty-two national fiberoptic trunk lines connecting all provincial capitals. Fiberoptic cable was also used in constructing inter- and intracity systems.

For the Ninth Five Year Plan (1996–2000), investment goals were even more optimistic. The Ministry of Posts and Telecommunications planned to add twelve million to fourteen million new lines of switching equipment annually—equal to the capacity of a U.S. regional Bell company—and to add 114 million lines of public network switching capacity. That this expansion was linked to the opening up of economic activity to millions of new economic agents was clearly demonstrated by the fact that one-third of telecommunications growth was taking place in Guandong Province where economic activity was growing fastest. In 1994, Guangdong had the highest provincial telephone density in the nation, 6.6 phones per 100 people, which was 60 percent greater than the density of the next highest province, Zhejiang, with 4.1 phones per 100.[9] The goal was to reach an urban density of 30 to 40 percent and a national density of 8 percent. By mid-2000, the number of wired telephone subscribers was 124 million while the number of mobile phone subscribers reached 56 million.[10] During the 1990s, China was able to roll out twice as much fiberoptic cable annually as the United States, largely because it could leapfrog older cable technology and go directly from line-and-pole to fiberoptic cable. While China's GDP was growing at one of the fastest rates in the world (8 to12 percent per year), telecommunications was increasing four times as fast, and as a percentage of GDP, telecommunications investment increased from 0.26 percent in 1989 to 1.13 percent in 1993.[11]

Excess capacity leading to cutthroat competition can be as much a problem in new, expanding industries like telecommunications, as it is in declining industries which are struggling simply to survive. China is the world's largest color television manufacturer, with a capacity of producing 50 million sets a year. But in 2000, only 30 million sets were sold. A five-year price war among China's 70-odd color TV producers has lowered the price of a 21-inch color television set an amazing 80 percent.[12]

After more than a decade of discussion, China still does not have a telecommunications law. This is in part because of the difficulty of getting all the vested interests in the government to agree on what the law ought to include. It also reflects the government's propensity to experiment in how the telecommunications sector develops, by "crossing the river by feeling for each stone," as Deng Xiaoping said, while maintaining control of the whole process through its licensing and project-approval power. Critics keep asking the government to set clear standards and then leave applicants who meet these standards alone. As long as the government insists that it must be the gatekeeper, it is unlikely that it will give up direct control over access and accept indirect control. In fact, in attempting to control Internet growth, the government has been drafting licensing criteria that are so stringent that they would rule out almost all companies operating in China.

Foreign Investors Fuel Fast Growth

The great expansion and modernization of the telecommunications sector could not have taken place without massive foreign investment and the introduction of new technologies. The government first explored cooperative arrangements with foreign firms, beginning with Hong Kong firms manufacturing Chinese-language paging equipment. Foreign investment in manufacturing was actively encouraged by allowing foreign firms to establish wholly owned enterprises, but foreign investment in distribution and wholesaling was prohibited. Foreign companies were also involved in technology trials, such as undertaking to build an integrated digital service network to link the government, state enterprises, and the public into a vast economic information network and develop a global system for mobile phones. Foreign investors also received tax benefits if they were located in the high-tech development zones established in most major cities.

The Ministry of Posts and Telecommunications' first foreign joint venture, Shanghai Bell Telephone Equipment Manufacturing Company, was with Alcatel in 1983. By 1994, the company was producing one-third of China's central office switching equipment.[13] Companies like Nortel, Motorola, and Lucent in the United States, Nokia of Finland, and Sweden's Ericsson also poured millions of dollars into manufacturing joint ventures and research centers and came to dominate the domestic telephone market. Rivalry between ministries also helped foreign investors. When mobile telephony emerged as the dominant equipment market, the Ministry of Electronic Industry was excluded because the Ministry of Posts and Telecommunications controlled the system, and the former's leading role in equipment manufacturing was seriously eroded.[14]

The creation of a fiberoptic national infrastructure brought every major foreign supplier rushing to China to provide fiberoptic transmission systems. When these backbone systems were constructed, local digital data networks spread like wildfire, with local P and Ts constructing their own networks. With competition fierce and price wars slashing profit margins, foreign suppliers began establishing local production bases with manufacturing companies affiliated with the Ministry of Posts and Telegraphs or the Ministry of Electronics Industry. By 1996, China had allowed seven foreign switching producers to manufacture locally and sell to the Ministry of Posts and Telecommunications, resulting in the lowest prices for digital switches in the world.[15] Nevertheless, because of the government's contradictory policies toward foreign investment, duties were still levied on imported inputs needed to complete the local assembly operations—while simultaneously state enterprises were allowed to import assembled equipment duty free.

Many of the world's telecommunications giants have established a large presence in China. At the end of 1999, Motorola, for example, had two wholly owned companies, six joint-venture companies, ten cooperative ventures, fourteen research-and-development centers, twenty branch offices, and over 10,000 employees.[16] Still, profits never met expectations because competition continued to drive prices down. Yet foreign companies kept counting on improving their positions by introducing new technology. Nortel, for example, is the world leader in optical systems. Its fast ten-gigabit (billion bit) system can carry 130,000 voice calls or 192 television channels simultaneously. Nortel has installed three ten-gigabit networks for China Telecom and one for China Unicom.[17] In 2000, Motorola announced a plan to invest US$1.9 billion in new facilities in China, which would make the company the largest foreign investor in China at US$3.44 billion.[18]

Although foreign investors were prevented from investing directly in network operations, it was unclear whether these regulations applied to the Internet, and many foreign firms used joint ventures to invest in Internet service and content providers. In 1999, the Minister of Information Industry declared that Internet service and content providers offered value-added services and were not open to foreign investment. Foreign investors were required to divest themselves of those investments. Also, domestic Internet service providers were compelled to separate their mainland content from the rest of their business operations. Sohu.com, one of China's premier portals, was required to take this step prior to being listed on the Nasdaq exchange in mid-2000.

Monopoly Gives Way to Competition with Chinese Characteristics

Like the industrial sector, the state monopoly of telecommunications began to erode through so-called spontaneous privatization, which occurred as various government agencies with their own networks formed telecommunication enterprises in the 1990s. Since most of the new telecom enterprises retained links to local governments, they represented a form of collective ownership and were hardly private. In 1993, in Shanghai alone there were eighty-three wireless and nine cable networks operated by the municipal government and 125 networks run by national ministries. Because of low start-up costs, the easiest business to enter was radio paging, and by mid-1995 there were 2,500 such enterprises.[19]

It was the rapid expansion of the paging market that led the other ministries to challenge the domination of the Ministry of Posts and Telecommunications. But how individual enterprises fared depended a great deal on the political influence of the governmental organization with which it was affiliated. The ministry's nationwide interconnection service provided a distinct advantage to clients who want to be national in scope, and it was able to deal with most competitive challenges through its monopoly over service licenses and the assignment of radio frequencies. Nevertheless, in 1994, the Ministry of Electronics Industry, with the participation of the Ministry of Railways, the Ministry of Electric Power, China International Trust and Investment Corporation, and twelve state enterprises, established a second national telecommunications network, China United Communications Corporation (China Unicom), to establish dedicated networks equipped and integrated by the Ministry of Electronics Industry. China Unicom also received 120,000 kilometers of telephone lines from the Ministry of Railroads. Jitong Communications Corporation was also created to establish specialized public information and data networks. Important questions were left unanswered regarding the prices of services to be performed and the cost effectiveness of projects to be undertaken. Thus began a period of officially sanctioned competition between government bureaucracies—monopoly had become duopoly.

Chinese ministries operate as independent fiefdoms and had been building their own dedicated telephone networks for thirty years or more. The danger for China Unicom was that the interests of each ministerial shareholder could easily conflict since they viewed the company as a shell within which to pursue their own interests.[20] These dedicated networks took advantage of the more sluggish growth of the less efficient national network to reach a huge backlog of newly affluent customers. Monopoly pricing and high installation costs created a very lucrative market, but China Unicom had great difficulty in competing with China Telecom, because China Telecom controlled all fixed or Internet telephony leases. In 1995, however, China Unicom was more successful in mobile telephony and forced the Ministry of Posts and Telecommunications to slash prices on cellular telephone handsets up to 50 percent, to move more quickly from analog to digital technology, and to integrate regional cellular systems into a truly national system with full roaming capability in order to enable subscribers to use phones in more than one network. China Unicom and Jitong Corporation were also aggressively seeking foreign investors (except of course as service providers) because they lacked access to financing.

By the late 1990s, China's leaders had come to realize that no single company like China Telecom could build the massive telecom infrastructure needed for China to become a global economic power and that only competition could improve the performance of state enterprises and lower service costs. The government's initial move in 1994 to improve competition by establishing China Unicom as a competitor with China Telecom had been largely ineffective, as the former had insufficient clout to challenge the latter's dominance. The government had also become concerned that the telecommunications industry would not be ready for the expected onslaught of foreign competition after China joined the WTO. This meant that the monopoly power of the Ministry of Posts and Telecommunications had to be broken.

In 1998, a massive reorganization of telecommunications organizations took place. The Ministry of Posts and Telecommunications was merged with the Ministry of Electronic Industries and parts of other ministries to become the new Ministry of Information Industry. The government decided to increase competition among state enterprises to reduce service costs and to allow carefully selected private enterprises to enter into niche markets with state support. The government spun off China Telecom from the Ministry of Information Industry and divided it into three parts: a wired telephone entity that retained the name China Telecom, a mobile telephone company called China Mobile Communications, and China Satellite Communications, which handled all satellite transmissions. Ministry officials were appointed to key management positions in all three entities, so the degree of real autonomy the separation achieved remains a matter of conjecture. The ministry also created China Netcom Communications to provide high-speed voice and data services to fifteen cities using Internet protocol technology.

China Telecom was compelled to transfer its paging operations to China Unicom. Paging is still the most affordable means of communicating in China and especially popular in rural areas. China Unicom was also licensed to provide wired long-distance domestic telephone service and local telephone service in three cities. In addition, it was authorized to construct and operate a nationwide mobile phone network using code division multiple access (CDMA) technology, which allows more efficient use of the wireless spectrum (the frequency range allocated by all governments) necessary for higher bandwidth applications such as the so-called third-generation service combining the Internet with mobile telephony. There was more to come, and China Unicom and the other four major carriers were licensed in 1999 to provide Internet data and Internet protocol telephone services and long-distance voice communications using the voice-over-Internet protocol, which gave it entry into the international and domestic direct dialing markets. Finally, Unicom was allowed to provide satellite telecom services. The shake-up put a hiatus on growth in telecommunications infrastructure for a whole year.[21]

Guangdong Province has emerged as the leader in information technology for a number of reasons—not the least of which is the open-minded attitude of the provincial government toward private investment. It has adopted a policy of encouraging Chinese entrepreneurs to link up with foreign partners rather than creating additional state enterprises. This policy has paid off, because in 1999, Guangdong Province received 30 percent of total foreign investment in China. The central government has been much more cautious and has carefully nurtured one private sector firm to become a major player. Huawei Technologies in Shenzhen fast became one of China's most important corporations and was being groomed to compete with multinationals after China joined the WTO. Huawei in the early 1990s provided equipment for the People's Liberation Army's first national telecom network and continues to have the backing of China's military. The turning point for the company came in 1996 when the government began to support domestic producers of telecom infrastructure equipment to counter the domination of foreign equipment producers. In 1998, Huawei unveiled its global system for mobile communications (GSM) network to challenge the market dominance of Ericsson and Nokia, with the government as cheerleader exhorting operating companies to "buy local" rather than from foreigners. GSM networks are more efficient because they allow more subscribers to use the same frequency. So far, the foreign-equipment makers are hanging on to their market share, partly because of reliability and product quality and partly because Ericsson and Nokia have localized their production.[22] Localizing production means producing key components and systems locally rather then importing them and using local plants only for assembly or for producing noncritical components. The implications of such a shift are huge, because once the Chinese partner is able to manufacture key components, the foreign partner will have greater difficulty protecting his property rights to the technology.

What were the secrets of Huawei's success? The company's connections were sufficient to propel it ahead of other domestic equipment suppliers, and with strong central-government support, the Shenzhen government declared the company one of the city's twenty-six key development projects that would be supported by the provincial government. Huawei also received credit from the Shenzhen Development Bank and the local branch of China Construction Bank, and these entities began to extend credit to the company's clients as well. Then, Vice Premier Wu Banguo visited Huawei and promised it a RMB 50 million loan to develop GSM mobile phone technology. Huawei won contracts to install telecom systems for the national railway system as well as in major cities like Beijing and Guangdong. Success bred success, and the Construction Bank and Bank of China extended more credit to the company. It now has priority status when applying for licenses, and a new factory has been declared a key construction project eligible for more special bank loans.[23] Huawei is also a beneficiary of government policies favoring domestic industry, such as "buy local," and providing bank loans to purchasers who buy Huawei's products.

In 2000, Huawei was the biggest manufacturer of switching systems in China and had 10,000 employees and sales of US$2.66 billion. Huawei is a major presence in Hong Kong and has important contracts in Thailand and Pakistan. The identity of the real owner of the company has not been revealed, and Huawei maintains a very politically correct posture by having an active branch of the Communist Party in the company and by being in lock-step with the government in denouncing the Falun Gong spiritual movement. Recently, the U.S. government asked the Chinese government whether Huawei had violated United Nations sanctions against selling the Iraqi government fiberoptic cable that has been used in Iraq's antiaircraft missile defense system. The Chinese government investigated the matter and responded that it found no evidence that Huawei was involved with the government of Iraq.[24] A source that prefers to remain anonymous says that the U.S. government has solid evidence that Huawei did sell the fiberoptic cable to Iraq.

If Huawei Technologies is a private company that often seems like a state enterprise, then China Netcom Communications is a state enterprise that acts as if it were a private company. In 1998, Hou Ziqiang, a physicist with the Chinese Academy of Sciences, argued that after entering the WTO, China could become competitive with Western information technology companies only if it launched a new initiative to construct a new generation of Internet infrastructure that would equal the best systems in the world. In his opinion, none of the existing telecommunications network companies—China Telecom, China Unicom, or Jitong Corporation—was capable of carrying out such a plan. Hou recommended that the government create an independent entity modeled on one of the Silicon Valley success stories to build the network. Hou's report was supported by the Academy of Science's leaders who included President Jiang's son, Jiang Mianheng, and who found other influential supporters at the Ministry of Railways, the State Radio, Film, and Television Administration, and the Shanghai Alliance Investment Company. In 1999, Hou and his group of supporters met with Premier Zhu Rongji, who also agreed to support the idea. China Netcom Communications was established in 1999 over the objections of China Telecom. The four state entities that had helped establish the company each invested US$75 million and became 25 percent shareholders.

China Netcom is building one of the longest (20,000 kilometers), fastest (forty-plus gigabytes per second), and cheapest broadband fiberoptic networks in the world. The first phase of 8,600 kilometers, connecting China's seventeen largest cities, has been completed. In less than two months, the company rolled out services that it took Worldcom and Sprint years to build in the United States.[25] How did China Netcom do it? The company's CEO is Edward Tian, who realized that with four powerful state entities as shareholders and a fifth as regulator, making independent management decisions would be an impossibility. He agreed to take the job only if the government's shareholders agreed to give him a free hand in management. He also saw that each shareholder had something special to offer. The Academy of Science could make available many of China's best scientific minds. The railway ministry could actually build the network using its system of railroad rights-of-way throughout China. The television administration could provide access to China's 80 million cable television subscribers. The support of President Jiang's son, Jiang Mianheng, who was also a senior official at Shanghai Alliance and head of Shanghai's Information Technology Office, was also invaluable. Yet the problem of conflicting loyalties remains. The Ministry of Railways has its own operating company, China Railways Telecom, which has received a license to extend its railway-based wired telecommunications system over the entire nation. It already has the country's largest dedicated network, extending 120,000 kilometers, including 40,000 kilometers of fiberoptic cable.[26]

Pagers and Mobile Phones

When pagers were introduced into China in 1985, demand for them was even greater than for cellular phones. Paging technology is relatively simple, and local suppliers designed their own systems or licensed foreign technology. By 1992, more than a half-million Chinese were using pagers. Guangdong Province was again the leader, with 100,000 subscribers spread across thirty-seven systems.[27] Although the Ministry of Posts and Telecommunications had a monopoly, hundreds of operators were selling pagers illegally, and in 1993, paging, mobile radio, and very small aperture terminal networks for transmitting data by satellite were opened to nonministry operators. By 1996, over 1,700 licensed paging operators were competing with the ministry, and the total number of subscribers had risen to over 26 million.[28]

China's most important and fastest growing telecommunications market is mobile phones—also known as cellular phones—because their range is restricted to the specific cell or area covered by a transmitter. The growth of cell phone telephony in China provides a case study of how determined Chinese authorities are to ensure that Chinese companies obtain the lion's share of this lucrative market. This service was first offered in China in 1987, and by mid-1992, there were 50,000 subscribers in twenty cities. At the end of 2000, there were 70 million subscribers, and by the end of 2001, China is expected to overtake the United States as the world's largest mobile phone market with 130 million subscribers.[29] The Ministry of Posts and Telecommunications controlled the allocation of radio frequencies, but provincial P and T authorities were granted wide latitude in planning, financing, and operating their own networks. Lack of communications protocol standardization hindered development of roaming systems, which enable subscribers to use phones in more than one network. Mobile networks are more profitable than wired networks, because with their shorter connection time, demand is so great that network operators charge much higher subscription fees and per-call charges, which far exceed the investment cost per subscriber yet are far cheaper than a wired connection. In 1993, it cost a mobile phone user US$1,000–3,000 to connect, while connection fees for a wired phone ranged from US$3,600–4,500.[30]

Foreign joint ventures dominate the market for mobile telephone equipment. Ericsson and Nanjing Radio Factory established China's first cellular network in Guangdong in 1988. Motorola joined with Hangzhou Telecommunications Factory in 1991. The biggest cellular markets are in coastal cities, and Guangdong, in which Ericsson had established five networks, had 40 percent of China's total cellular capacity in 1992.[31] Motorola gained ground by localizing production under licensing agreements and established networks in Fujian, Heilongjiang, and Shandong. Nokia set up seven joint ventures, two of which produce mobile phones. In mobile telephony, Nokia has steadily improved its market share and now accounts for one-third of mobile phones sold. Motorola, Ericsson, and Nokia all established joint ventures with China National Posts and Telecommunications Appliance Corporation to develop marketing strategies, establish national distribution channels, and provide after-sales service. In 2000, these three multinationals accounted for 82 percent of the mobile phone market in China.[32] This has not deterred Chinese entrepreneurs from developing their own models and engaging in price wars to try to capture market shares.

In the early 1990s, public cellular services used an analog system for which Ericsson and Motorola were the only approved suppliers, and in 1996, the networks of the two companies were connected to allow nationwide roaming. By the mid-1990s, however, digital GSM cellular technology was gaining wide acceptance because it allowed more subscribers to use the same frequency. China Unicom's great opportunity was in mobile telephony, since the company was not tied to fixed-line technologies. It was China Unicom's decision in 1995 to invest in GSM technology provided by Ericsson and Nokia that spurred the Ministry of Posts and Telecommunications to enter the digital market. All major suppliers of analog equipment began actively pursuing digital GSM contracts as well as offering alternative technologies. As mentioned above, in 1998, Huawei Technologies unveiled a GSM network to rival that of market leaders Ericsson and Nokia.

Motorola built China's first code division multiple access (CDMA) network in Hangzhou. This technology requires fewer cell sites to achieve the same coverage and has far greater capacity than GSM, because it allows multiple users to share the same part of the frequency spectrum by allocating a code to each user. In order to circumvent the government prohibition on foreign equity participation in telecommunications service companies, China Unicom established with forty-six foreign companies joint ventures that included equity investments from both foreign and Chinese partners and then set up a separate service entity with no equity from the foreign partner (known as the Chinese-Chinese-foreign formula).

In 1998, when China Telecom was forced to spin off China Mobile, China Unicom became the only full-service telecom operating entity. This was not the end of the turf wars between these entities. China Telecom subsequently reached an agreement with UTStarcom of the United States to use its personal access system, through which mobile handsets can function as extensions of wired networks. UTStarcom's Little Smart handsets sell for one-half the price of cell phones, their per-call charges are lower, and their data transmissions are faster. Yet, in mid-2000 the Ministry of Information Industry prevented China Telecom from deploying the system. Meanwhile, China Mobile announced that Vodaphone of Great Britain, the world's largest mobile phone manufacturer, had made an equity investment of US$2.5 billion in China Mobile. The deal was to help the latter acquire seven cellular networks, making China Mobile the second-largest cellular phone company in the world with 39.3 million subscribers.[33]

China Unicom encapsulates most of the real or imagined dangers of investing in China. Its business plan is untested and its debt payments overwhelm its fragile cash flow. Its rival, China Mobile, has more favorable geographic coverage, greater financial resources, and better brand recognition. China Unicom will require five years to recover the costs of building out its mobile network, compared with two years for China Mobile. Yet in 2000, China Unicom raised almost US$5 billion in capital with public offerings of its shares on the New York and Hong Kong stock exchanges. In the first six months of 2000, its earnings increased 63 percent over the equivalent period in 1999. When all the major service providers were licensed to provide Internet telephony, Unicom acted quickly and announced plans to build a data and computer network to serve over 100 cities. Nevertheless, its cash flow plus its revenues from its successful public offering are not going to be sufficient to finance its ambitious plan for investing RMB 100 billion by 2003.[34] Because of the involvement of three different ministries as China Unicom's major shareholders, it was never effectively managed, and in its first six years of operation, senior management changed three times. In 1999, a vice minister of the Ministry of Information Industry became China Unicom's fourth chairman and president. The new boss was believed to be close to Wu Jichuan, minister of information industry, and China Unicom's fortunes have improved since then.

The government ruled that China Unicom's Chinese-Chinese-foreign joint ventures were illegal because they enabled foreign firms to circumvent the ban on foreign investment in telecom service companies and obtain revenues from installation fees, which is prohibited. China Unicom's foreign partners were compelled to divest themselves of their investments. They were bought out by China Unicom with cash, stock warrants, and promises of preferential treatment in the future. In 2000, the company took a one-time charge against income of US$143 million to cover cash compensation paid to its foreign partners.[35] The partners had learned a bitter lesson, and China Unicom had gotten rid of a patchwork of regional mobile entities that were difficult to manage and emerged in control of about 15 percent of the mobile phone market. In 2000, the ministry allowed China Unicom to undercut China Mobile's prices by 10 to 20 percent because its mobile phone business was not profitable. This was due in part to the fact that its subscribers on average spend 22 percent less than China Mobile's subscribers, so its earnings per subscriber are about one-half China Mobile's. Worse yet, many of its subscribers are not paying, and its accounts receivable tripled from 1997 to 1999.[36] Meanwhile, China Unicom is forging so-called strategic alliances with global giants such as Cisco Systems and Lucent Technologies and, in 1999, had reached agreement with Qualcom of the United States to build a nationwide broadband CDMA network. But in 2000, the government intervened and stopped the project. The potential Chinese market is so huge that the government may take the route of adopting a domestic technology that is not necessarily compatible with other countries' standards, and is developing its own third-generation standard called TDS-CDMA with the help of the German firm Siemens.[37]

The China Unicom-China Mobile relationship typifies a pattern that emerged in the industrial sector, where large group companies are the "wards" of provincial governments. In the telecom sector the government also established state enterprises as separate corporate entities and encouraged them to compete, yet they are extensions of powerful ministries and other state agencies, and the party, acting through the State Council, freely intervenes in their affairs whenever some broader government policy or interest seems threatened.

Meanwhile, China Mobile is pursuing a third-generation technology known as Wideband CDMA, which has already proven itself. In the United States, Qualcom has developed a third-generation standard known as CDMA2000, which is broadly compatible with Wideband CDMA. To complicate matters further, the off-again-on-again deal between China Unicom and Qualcomm to build a 15-million-user CDMA network was on again by the end of 2000, and in a major turnabout, the government authorized China Unicom to resume construction of the CDMA network. The government also approved its purchase from the military of Great Wall Telecom, a narrowband CDMA network covering Beijing, Shanghai, Guangzhou, and Xian. In 2001, China Unicom signed an agreement with fourteen other national telecom system operators that would allow global roaming in North and South America and the Asia Pacific region, covering 60 percent of the world's CDMA users. It is evident that China Unicom and China Mobile are both intent on building national CDMA networks. It is likely that the government will wait and see how effective these are before it decides which system to support—or to go ahead with its own system. The battle for the third-generation mobile telephone market, which will enable cell phone users to access the Internet at very high speeds, has begun.

In the United States, CDMA digital technology is the standard, while Europe and most of Asia use GSM. For the systems to become compatible, dual-mode phones that can communicate over two different systems need to be developed. Europe is adopting an intermediate two-and-a-half generation technology called general packet radio service, and both Europe and Asia as a next step want to adopt a broadband CDMA. Japan planned to establish the world's first third-generation broadband CDMA-based system in spring 2001, but South Korea accomplished this feat in late 2000.[38]

Many purveyors of technology are betting that the cell phone's future lies with turning it into a mobile data terminal. At the end of 2000, China Mobil introduced its new wireless data service, called Monternet, which utilizes text-messaging capabilities built into existing handsets. It is trying to tap a huge potential market hoping that consumers with mobile phones will start using high profit-margin data services. Six months later, China Unicom introduced its own service, called Uni-Info. Both systems allow content suppliers to access consumer mobile phones directly and offer data services like news and entertainment as downloads. The system operator then bills the consumer and includes a commission for his service, which for Monternet is 15 percent. China Unicom designed its system to offer a cheaper product and take advantage of some of the teething problems of China Mobile. China Mobile is made up of thirty-one provincial and regional affiliates, which often have incompatible software and hardware—so it had to roll out its system, one province/region at a time. Monternet also used about 180 content providers with widely varying capabilities, and many could not meet their commitments. Uni-Info was quickly available nationwide and used only eleven content providers with proven reliability. It only charged a 12 percent commission. Monternet still has the advantage that it is able to offer content providers access to 78 percent of the mobile phone market, compared to Uni-Info's 22 percent.[39]

Wireless application protocol allows mobile phone users who have the correct handset to access the Internet. This could be especially attractive in China, where there are twenty Chinese with a mobile phone for each one with a computer. In Hong Kong, 60 percent of the population have a cell phone. Also almost one-half of cell phone users are women, who account for only 15 percent of computer users, and the new technology is expected to appeal to them.[40] However, subscription rates for combining Internet service with cell phone operation have so far been dismal due to lack of standardization among handsets, slow download speeds, tiny screens, and difficulty in entering Chinese characters—all problems that need to be solved for cell phones to receive really wide acceptance as a source of Internet services in China. Many also believe the next marketing challenge will be providing local content. Because each cell's position is fixed, it can be used to pinpoint the location of phones that are connected to it. System operators hope that local pinpointing coupled with more efficient and faster transmissions will enable Internet content providers to furnish a whole menu of local news, events, and services to cell phone users.

The Internet

China's computer data networks first arose in the education field. Most academic networks have been consolidated into either China Public Computer Network (ChinaNet), created by the Ministry of Posts and Telecommunications, or China Education Network (CERNET), established by the State Education Commission. When economic reform began in earnest, computer networking followed in the path of paging —rapid development through spontaneous privatization. As in other countries, China's Internet infrastructure includes registrars for domain names (the series of letters and numbers that route Internet users to Web sites) and network organizations. ChinaNet is the registrar for national (.cn) domains, and another government entity, China-Channel, offers commercial (.com) domain names. The government considers control over Chinese character domain names to be a matter of national sovereignty, and an official agency, China Internet Networking Information Center, has been set up as the sole authority to issue such names.[41] When the U.S. firm Verisign announced it would accept the registration of Chinese character Internet domain names, the Chinese government immediately struck back by announcing a rival, incompatible system. Later, the government agreed to defer the matter until the U.S.-based Internet Engineering Task Force is able to set standards for international domain names.

Six networks—ChinaNet, CERNET, China Unicom's UNINET, Jitong's China Golden Bridge, ChinaNetcom, and Chinese Science and Technology Network—form China's Internet backbone and are authorized to operate internationally. ChinaNet, China Golden Bridge, UNINET, and ChinaNetcom have also received permits to act as national business networks providing commercial connection to the Internet and to begin trial use of Internet protocol telephony—the system used for moving data from place to place in packets when voice is turned into digital data by packet switching. A packet-switching data network makes more efficient use of network capacity because it carries data bundled together in packets, which are transmitted separately along the most direct route available, then reassembled at their destination. Foreign investment in any of these organizations is prohibited. The Ministry of Information Industry approves all domestic Internet service and content providers, who are licensed to provide either national, or, more commonly, province-wide services. They are liable for any content that appears on their sites. There are even separate licenses for news and other content and an additional license to post foreign news on a web site.

The government's position regarding how the Internet should develop as a commercial vehicle has been that it should serve the national economy and that the government should strictly manage its development and ensure that national security is safeguarded. To that end, national regulations have been issued by the State Council, the Ministry of Public Security, the Ministry of Information Industry, the Ministry of Culture, the Ministry of Education, the State Corruption Management Commission, the Securities Regulatory Commission and Copyright Administration, and the State Secrets Bureau. Local governments have issued their own regulations, and provincial authorities have been allowed to experiment in areas that are unregulated and, in some cases, where such activity it prohibited. For example, officially, cable television companies are not allowed to offer Internet access, yet provincial P and Ts in Qingdao, Guangzhou, and Shenzhen are doing just that. Contradictions abound, and it is difficult for any entity, foreign or domestic, to find a clear path through the gaps and tangles of regulations.

Government use of the Internet has been increasing, and by 1998, 20 percent of local government agencies had their own Web sites. A year later, the percentage rose to 60, and by the end of 2000, 80 percent of local governments had become Internet users.[42] Overall, however, Internet use has grown relatively slowly compared to other telecommunications media. A major factor has been limited network transmission capacity. Increasing bandwidth is essential to improving speed of access as the number of subscribers rapidly increases. Although China's combined international bandwidth was a healthy 351 million bits per second (Mbps) at the end of 1999, large urban networks had capacities ranging from only 256 thousand bits per second (Kbps) to 8Mbps, and most other service providers use modems with just 56 Kbps.[43] Although broadband technology is twenty times faster in connecting to the Internet than standard dial-up service, broadband costs are double, and not many Internet users have been enticed into using it. In Hong Kong, for example, Cable and Wireless HKT has 400,000 dial-up subscribers and just 35,000 broadband subscribers although the service has been available for two years.[44]

Because of bandwidth limitations most Chinese dial-up Internet users have to spend a great deal of time and money just to get on-line. The high cost of computers combined with logging-on costs (estimated at 10 percent of the average user's income), slow speeds, and difficulty in accessing a wired telephone system have kept many Chinese off the Internet. Traditional attitudes about the cultivation of business relationships also limit Internet use in developing a wider clientele. For most Chinese, face-to-face contacts culminating in expensive banquets are still viewed as the best way of cementing business and other relationships.[45]

Although China Telecom still requires detailed personal information from subscribers, its Beijing subsidiary in 1997 allowed users to dial a simple number code with no paperwork. In 1998, the Public Multimedia Telecom Network was established, enabling users simply to dial the number 169 without registering or paying fees, and charges simply showed up on their monthly telephone bills. Additionally, the Ministry of Internal Trade established Beijing Civilink in 1996 to help firms get established on the Internet. By the end of 2000, the company claimed to have registered 10,000 domain names.[46]

The government fears the Internet because it can deliver rapid, low-cost messaging and has point-and-click access to information. By 1996, the government had become concerned about the spread of Internet access—although at that time there were only about 20,000 users—and the State Council announced a registration scheme designed to monitor and control users in an attempt to reassert the authority of national ministries over the Internet. All international traffic had to go through ministerial channels; all networks had to be legal entities conforming to State Council regulations; they had to reregister with the appropriate state entity and the police, and were prohibited from producing, obtaining, or disseminating obscene and pornographic materials or information that might hinder public order. This complex registration scheme proved to be unenforceable. The government also began intermittent blocking of foreign Web sites.

This is how it works. When Internet users in China type the foreign address on their browsers, the computer sends the request by telephone line to China's International Connection Bureau, which is operated by China Telecom. Software is programmed to reject requests to banned sites. However, blocking can be done only intermittently, because the software does not have enough computing power to block all banned sites all of the time. Also, as soon as a site is banned, another springs up to replace it, and users are e-mailed the new address. And so the process continues with the government always playing catch-up.

In 1997, the government tried to introduce a nationwide intranet to prevent Chinese from accessing overseas Web sites. That too failed. The government also used censors, derisively referred to as cleaning ladies by Internet surfers—to come on-line and erase offending material, but there are never enough cleaning ladies or funds to deal with the spread of information, except selectively. The government especially fears organized protest, and when the banned Falun Gong movement used the Internet to rally its members, the government became more determined than ever to control the web. The government tried to restrict licensing along geographic lines, which necessitated a further set of approvals should the licensee wish to move beyond the limits of the license.[47] In 2000, the government banned the release of state secrets (which covers anything not otherwise defined) and made the providers themselves responsible for enforcement.

Typical of the government's gatekeeper approach is China Internet Corporation, established by the Xinhua News Agency. It describes itself as the "cyberspace gateway into China." Since it restricts access to information services that it controls and monitors, the gatekeeper metaphor is very appropriate. This move was preceded by a State Council directive prohibiting Chinese businesses from buying information directly from foreign news sources. Instead, they were required to go through Xinhua, which would receive a share of the revenues. As Xinhua already controlled distribution of foreign news wire services in China, this was a clear attempt to give it the same power over Internet news. It also was meant to accomplish two main government goals: to continue to control access to foreign news and obtain revenues from its dissemination and to impose controls over economic and financial news, which had been exempted from the prohibition. This move reflected the government's increasing concern over the spillover effect of economic news into the political arena. Nevertheless, it will continue to be difficult for the government to exert control over Internet services because of the large number of local networks.

Also typical is China's handling of the U.S. spy plane incident on April 1, 2001. The government controlled coverage and blocked access to foreign news sites, thus ensuring that its version of events was the only one most Chinese heard. Ironically, the government ended up censoring chat rooms to tone down the anti-American rhetoric its coverage had inspired. It is not just Chinese companies that fall in line when the government commands. U.S. firms operating in China have been unwilling to speak out, and most censor themselves.[48] They are caught in the same trap as Chinese firms. They know that to offend or oppose the government may mean the end of their stay in China.

The government issued encryption regulations in 1999 and established the State Encryption Management Commission as the regulator. These controls are yet another example of the government's obsession with security. China is one of the few countries in the world to control the use of encrypted matter on the Internet—which it does by requiring authorization for its use. The problem is that the definition of what comprises encryption is broad, as it states that all hardware and software for which encryption is a "core" function must be regulated. Internet users have argued—apparently successfully—that this definition should not apply to PIN numbers, log-on passwords, and word-processing and browser software.[49] Whether these regulations will apply to encrypted inputs is also doubtful, as such software has been available on the Internet since 1991. Perhaps most important from a business point of view is that encryption is essential for safeguarding property rights, and the government's obsession with national security concerns will inevitably clash with individual rights, whether governing property or other private matters.

The Internet reflects the cultures that use it, and it is inevitable that it will become increasingly localized along cultural, linguistic, and geographic lines. In China, perhaps the greatest technological challenge has been to develop a Chinese-language software and computer keyboard or mobile phone keypad. Chinese characters are based on pictographic symbols, of which about 7,000 are used for daily communication. Initially, Chinese-language word-processing software was developed that converted *pinyin*—the system that translates Chinese characters into the Roman alphabet—into characters on the screen. Inputers had to confirm manually that the correct character was being used, and the computer's error-checking system slowed processing to twenty to thirty characters a minute (comparable to ten to fifteen English words a minute). In the late 1990s, research based on the specific sequence of brushstrokes that are used in writing each Chinese character enabled the development of a system using the eight brushstrokes most commonly used in teaching schoolchildren. Each character is entered using a series of coded brushstrokes.[50] Some experienced users of this system can type up to 100 words per minute. Still, none of these systems can match the efficiency of alphabet-based systems. Microsoft Research China, established in Beijing in 1998, is spending US$80 million over a six-year period to develop an electronic tablet that will recognize the brushstrokes of a stylus drawing Chinese characters.[51]

Castles in the Air: The Fall of the Dot.coms

In the late 1990s, Chinese entrepreneurs joined the rest of the world in rushing to set up Internet companies, although by the end of 1999, there were only 3.5 million computer owners; 8.5 million computer users; 15,000 web sites; and 49,000 registered domain names. When the NASDAQ stock exchange tumbled in March and April 2000, the shock waves reached China, and the share prices of the three leading Internet companies—Sina.com, Netease.com, and Sohu.com—fell sharply. Six months later, their share value had fallen 67 percent, 75 percent, and 85 percent, respectively.[52] Nevertheless, big firms like these have the cash resources to tide them over the next year or two, but many other firms were destined to fail. Chinese Internet companies were especially hard hit by the Nasdaq-led decline, because most of them had not been in existence for very long and had neither the experience nor the client base to carry them through the crisis. In the United States, the most successful Internet companies have a strong technological and product base, while in China most dot.com entrepreneurs had financial backgrounds with nothing to fall back on when the financing turned sour. One scientist at the Chinese Academy of Sciences described Chinese dot.coms as "merely castles in the air— they have no fundamental support."[53]

Venture capitalists have sunk hundreds of millions of dollars into Chinese Internet start-ups, with small chance of recovering their investment, let alone making a profit. Much of this initial investment was meant to finance the start-up to a level where it could seek large-scale investment through listing on the Hong Kong or international stock exchanges. By the summer of 2000, the initial public offering market for Chinese Internet companies had effectively closed down. At present, Chinese stock exchanges are not an alternative source of funding, because they require three years of profitability as a prerequisite for listing. International Data Group, a U.S. venture capital firm with the largest exposure in China, has US$120 million invested in seventy companies. Only one of its investments managed a Nasdaq listing before the market turned sour. Still, venture capitalists were pinning their hopes on a new high-tech stock exchange, which was due to open in 2001 in Shenzhen but had been postponed.

All Chinese Internet firms are sharply cutting staff and other costs, but that is not enough. Only firms with a plausible business plan and a viable concept are able to find partners to help them through the crisis. Some turned to off-line business that could help improve their profitability.[54]

Even the official media predicted that 80 to 90 percent of all Internet start-up companies would be bankrupt by the end of 2000.[55] As in the United States, business-to-consumer web sites have been the hardest hit. E-consumer business is particularly fragile in China because of consumers' unwillingness to pay for goods sight unseen coupled with the lack of a credit card network and uncertain delivery times. Although Chinese banks have issued 150 million bank cards, most are debit cards limited to purchases from web sites that have individual agreements with a particular bank. One solution has been to create intermediaries such as Chinapay.com in Shanghai, that provide a citywide payment system and save the web from the hassle of negotiating with each bank. Meanwhile, the central bank is going forward with a project to build regional switching centers to link payment systems of different banks between regions. Still, one expert describes the present efforts as a patchwork solution whose pieces must come together if significant progress is to be made in developing an efficient payments system.[56]

E-consumer leader 8848.net, which pioneered on-line retail sales in China, sold its retail business in late 2000. It is restricting itself to business-to-business operations, which account for 80 percent of its revenue. Only a year before, its founder was extolling its virtues: "We are going directly from mom-and-pop stores to us. The margins are huge (20 percent of gross sales)." The company was extremely creative in adapting to the Chinese market. To improve distribution, which is a nationwide problem, it convinced the postal service to handle cut-rate express deliveries and accept cash payments. It adapted to local conditions and used combinations of its own network of trucks, motorcycles, and bicycles; local delivery services; manufacturers' delivery systems; and chain-store interstore delivery systems. It was also able to line up most major banks to accept payments on-line. But revenues went into more and more advertising, and the company was dependent on new financing to keep up the momentum. When the money ran out, so did the business.[57]

In the short term, the e-consumer market is constrained by its small size and lack of infrastructure, which makes it extremely difficult for any company to make money with purely on-line revenues. Over the long term, the growth of e-consumer business is constrained by major bottlenecks in on-line payments and goods deliveries and resistance to buying sight unseen. Companies that provide Internet infrastructure, such as data networks or data management centers, seem to have a brighter future because they serve not only Internet retailing and information companies but also any company that generates and transmits large amounts of data, which includes most of the old economy. To survive, e-consumer firms will have to link up with old-economy enterprises that have the advantage of brand names, sales forces, delivery systems, and relationships with banks.[58] Many are also shifting from the uncertainties of on-line retail to the business-to-business market, where marketing goals can be more clearly defined and achievable and can capitalize on Internet efficiencies.[59]

If China is to become competitive internationally, the Internet has to become a major part of business practice because it is shortening the cycles that govern the pace of business. It is shortening market research, product development, manufacturing, and sales and delivery times. At giant chip-maker Intel, when paper governed transactions, customer service departments spent 90 percent of their time on administrative tasks. With the Internet, they spend 90 percent of their time meeting customer needs. Internet business has also had a big impact on inventories. The total inventory of the world's personal computer industry, for instance, has been reduced from three to four months' supply a year ago to a couple of weeks' supply at present.[60]

The Future Is Convergence and the World Trade Organization

The future shape of telecommunications networking will resemble the Internet model rather than wired telephony, and wired systems are already moving toward Internet technology in switching and network structure. This process is called convergence because it entails the coming together of information flows through digital technology, which is likely to end the traditional separation between different forms of telecommunicating. However, it could be some time before voice quality over the Internet will be able to match that provided by the telephone. When voice is digitalized and bundled together with video, e-mail, audio, graphics, and text, telephone companies will find themselves competing with cable television and Internet service providers. The other side of the coin is getting the bandwidth necessary to handle bundled services as well as rapidly increasing volume. The key to success is the use of broadband technology, which increases bandwidth and thus the capacity of lines to handle increasing volume without losing speed of transmission.

China, with the help of foreign partners, is at the forefront of this revolution in an attempt to keep a step ahead of the rest of the world as China joins the WTO. In 2000, the government published the Tenth Five Year Plan (2001–2005), which called for "promoting the convergence of telecom, television and computer networks."[61] This reversed a State Council edict of 1998 that barred telephone and cable television service providers from competing in the same markets. Competition between the two had become so fierce that it resulted in riots and even deaths in Hunan Province. Local cable television operators are already offering Internet access through customers' television sets; eighty million Chinese families watch cable television. Most cable operators are local companies that rely on local financing and are largely independent of the central telecom bureaucracy. Meanwhile, the government is hastening to try to link up local networks into a national system that it can control.[62]

In 2000, the government authorized China's four state telecom giants to begin using Internet protocol (IP) telephony. Although they moved rapidly to link up with foreign IP providers, for the immediate future these unions will have to combine both old and new technology. For instance, when an Internet protocol prefix for an international number is dialed in China, the voice is carried as an analog signal from a local exchange and converted to a digital signal at an international exchange. It is then packet-switched to its destination and converted back to an analog signal for the receiver of the call. China Telecom has a joint venture with Clarent of the United States to install Internet protocol international and domestic services in sixteen major cities. China Unicom and a foreign partner, iBasis, claimed to carry more than 10 percent of all telephone traffic between China and the United States in 2000. In fact, China telecom has lost so many customers to its four competitors that it had to cut its IP rates drastically. For Chinese consumers, long-distance rates to the United States fell from US$2.20 per minute in 1998 to US$0.60 in 2000.[63] The most serious challenge has come from China Netcom in 2001, when it introduced a discounted pre-paid IP card, and reduced its rates to 3.6 U.S. cents a minute for domestic long-distance calls, and 28 U.S. cents a minute for overseas calls. The other IP providers had no choice but to follow suit.[64]

In late 2000, the State Council approved new telecommunications regulations that provide for two types of operations: basic services covering every aspect of telecommunications offered by the operator of a network, and value-added services which enhance the form, content, storage, or retrieval of basic services offered by a provider that is not a network operator. Basic telephone service includes wired and mobile telephony as well as paging, Internet, data transmission, and satellite communications. All network operators and providers must be licensed by the state. The new regulations also establish ground rules for interconnection and service charges, quality of service, and security requirements. Basic services must be 51 percent state owned. Value-added service includes Internet content and Internet service providers, Internet data centers, and application service providers. The U.S.–China Bilateral Agreement is more specific than the new regulations about foreign investment. It provides that upon China's entry into the WTO, foreigners may purchase a 30 percent interest in a value-added service company doing business in Beijing, Shanghai, and Guangdong. This can be increased to 49 percent in the following year and to 50 percent anywhere in China in the second year after entry. Under the European Union–China Agreement, foreign investment in basic services would be phased in over six years and could not exceed 49 percent.[65] The omissions and ambiguities surrounding foreign investment in the new regulations and WTO Bilateral Agreements will need to be clarified when the telecommunications law is finally promulgated.

Cyberspace Gatekeeper

The government's view that new technology enables the productive process to modernize and that this in turn provides the seeds for renewed economic growth and more output is rooted in the materialism of the past, which held up increased output as the ultimate test of economic performance. China has learned the hard way that output unrelated to the desire of a consumer to purchase that output can spell disaster. It has also learned that monopolies—especially in the telecommunications sector—can make a lot of money for the government, but they are inherently inefficient, and somewhere somebody is going to provide a service at a lower cost or make a cheaper product and sell it illegally. It has also learned that if it wants to sell its products elsewhere, it will have to let the rest of the world into the Chinese market. Or has it? On the eve of WTO membership, the government took the extraordinary step of establishing a new cabinet level committee headed by Premier Zhu Rongji to preside over further telecommunications reform. The root of the problem is that the Ministry of Information Industry is dragging its feet over further reform of China Telecom, which still controls 99 percent of wired telephony and 90 percent of data transmissions over the Internet. China Telecom's fixed-line network gives it "last mile" connection to millions of consumers, and it has been refusing to interconnect with competing service providers, thus preventing them from direct access to consumers. The ministry is also unwilling to give ground in the battle over the convergence of telephone and television networks, which will decide who controls voice, data and video transmissions. The State Administration of Radio, Film and Television, which controls the broadcast system and wishes television to become the predominant mode for such transmissions, has been equally adamant in relinquishing power. All this points to serious turf battles within the government over relinquishing control and allowing more competition.[66]

Can Chinese companies compete with multinational corporations that encircle the world? In the telecommunications sector, it all depends on whether China really opens up its service sectors to foreign competition, and whether the Chinese regime will be willing to relax control over information content. The government continues to regard itself as China's cyberspace gatekeeper. It is still deeply concerned about unrestricted access to international information sources and networks and justifies its gatekeeper role by invoking the necessity of maintaining national security and domestic stability. Its obsession with control is reflected in the fact that national regulations governing Internet use have been issued by China's highest governing body (the State Council), four ministries, two commissions, and the State Secrets Bureau. Although China has only about 75 million Internet users, they are among the more affluent and well educated—a potential source of political opposition if they are exposed to the wrong influences as government thinking goes. Can China control proliferation of international Internet access? The real value of the Internet comes from the freedom to be able to search anywhere for information, and the economic cost of a restrictive policy will be incalculable and very probably unsuccessful.

The telecommunications sector epitomizes how politics and economics are intertwined as China tries to deal with the dilemmas and contradictions that have arisen in trying to create a socialist market economy with Chinese characteristics. The government has come to realize that allowing millions of new economic actors to take to the stage and compete with one another is profoundly affecting the way that information is handled and disseminated and poses huge problems in coordination and control. The government's dilemma is how to exploit the economic development potential of the new information technology while controlling how information is disseminated. China's leaders are hoping that the "knowledge economy" will open the door to foreign competition while keeping China competitive and enabling it to keep up in fast-changing global markets now that China has entered the WTO. But the government's concerns about maintaining social stability and controlling the direction of the economy have created unresolved tensions over how information is obtained and used.

Can China really achieve the free exchange of information necessary for lasting economic progress? As information flows faster, more cheaply, and over more media, the government will have greater and greater difficulty in maintaining control over content and its distribution. The gatekeeper will simply be overwhelmed and will rely more and more on requiring information users to regulate themselves under the threat of severe penalties for noncompliance. Self-regulation is an admission that the government is losing control and is self-defeating over the long term. The situation is mindful of trying to keep out Yangtze River floodwaters by building the levees higher and higher (see chapter 5). As levees increase in height, they become more and more unstable and subject to any new weakness, such as undermining from below. Eventually, they come crashing down and the floodwaters rush in.

Chapter Seven

From Dragon Robe
To Business Suit

Old houses juxtaposed against modern high-rise buildings,
Chongqing Municipality.

No other country has undergone such vast changes as China has in the last century: from dynastic empire to nascent republic, the horrors of foreign invasion, the triumph of the Communist revolution, the social convulsions of the failed experiments of the Mao Zedong era, the challenges posed by the reforms of the post-Mao era, and the opening of China to the world. Nothing is more symbolic of how China has changed than the contrast between the ornate silk dragon robe worn by Qing dynasty imperial officials in the early 1900s and the business suit worn by today's Chinese leaders. The dragon robe defined the place of imperial officials in a Chinese-centered cosmos. Western business suits make China's leaders look like those in the rest of the world, but many of the attitudes of the Qing dynasty autocrat are still in place.

Deng Xiaoping and his reformers took an enormous risk when they opened up China's economy twenty-four years ago because the actions they took were irreversible. The reformers felt they had no choice if China was to shed the shackles of thirty years of Mao's disastrous economic policies. Once millions of Chinese became economic actors in their own right, there was no going back. But increasing competition revealed the weaknesses of state enterprises, and many of them are losing the battle to compete. China's "socialist market economy" represents a volatile mixture of traditional networks exploiting new commercial opportunities, civil servants appropriating state assets, wide-open competition involving all enterprises regardless of ownership, the persistence of regional trade barriers, and government micromanagement, especially of the state-dominated part of the economy. Defiance of the law and corrupt trading practices are a corrosive force undermining the whole system. Corruption can be expected to continue to flourish despite draconian penalties and show trials.

President Jiang Zemin and Premier Zhu Rongji have continued to follow the path laid out by Deng, and by pursuing World Trade Organization (WTO) membership, have shown they are as great risk takers as their mentor. Opening up the economy to meet conditions for membership is putting enormous pressure on the still shaky reform effort and complicates the difficult economic policy choices facing China. Competition will become even fiercer, and many Chinese firms that are now barely surviving will probably fail. The government is relying on a core of reformed state enterprises and an expanding private sector to step in and take advantage of the export opportunities that will arise, and on an influx of foreign firms to provide new employment opportunities.

Although the changes of the past two decades have greatly increased personal freedom, they have not developed the means to protect society from individual misbehavior. The Chinese speak metaphorically of being thrown in the sea of competition, and individuals who take the plunge inevitably rely on traditional relationships in navigating these unknown waters, and with few constraints to deter them, will seek their own advantage. Although corruption is as old as China, economic freedom has turned civil servants and state employees into "businessmen" who are busily acquiring state assets and using them for personal benefit. The tradition of *guanxi*—exchange of favors and reciprocal obligations—is rapidly being adapted to new circumstances. By freeing economic activity without adequate controls, the government has inadvertently fostered corruption and pillaging of state assets on a grand scale.

Economic reforms have also created deep divisions in Chinese society because they have favored urban places over rural and have led to sharply rising inequities in income, housing, and access to urban services. The state continues to subsidize its employees, most of whom live in urban areas, while limiting opportunity of impoverished rural migrants to participate in the economic boom taking place in the cities. Income and other disparities between rural villagers and city dwellers are widening. As discontent among those left behind rises, dissent has become more vocal and organized, but the government's response is to contain individual incidents and crush organized opposition in the name of social stability. Those who have benefited from economic opening are also worried about the future. Economic growth rates are being maintained through massive fiscal stimulus, and the problems of unemployment and overcapacity continue to loom large.

Is the Communist Party really capable of governing modern China? For more than two thousand years, Chinese society depended upon a moral code based on precise gradations of authority, respect, duty, and obligation to ensure its survival. The basic unit in this system was the family, which was responsible for the behavior of its members. A legal system was established to enforce the code, and inequities were accepted as the price that had to paid for maintaining social stability and order. The party has taken the place of the family and has adopted its values.

Like the family, it has suppressed individual initiative and personal responsibility and views the development of other value systems as a threat to social order. In imperial China, the bureaucracy made and interpreted laws whose primary purpose was to maintain the existing social and political order. In Communist China, officials appointed by the party do the same. The party views the legal system as an instrument of control rather than as a means of protecting the rights of individuals. The government believes its function is to protect the rights of all the Chinese people, and that the rights of the individual must be subordinated to the greater good of society as determined by the government. The government does not want an independent judiciary making such a determination on its own.

In trying to adapt to rapid changes, the party's capacity to govern has been weakened. The party needs to look inward and realize that its best chance for survival lies in changing from autocrat to servant of the people. To serve the people best, the constitution must be changed to recognize the rule of law as paramount, guarantee individual rights, and create an independent judiciary and a strong regulatory system. The hardest part will be to let go of beliefs that tie China's leaders to the past. This is China's challenge for the future.

A Socialist Market Economy with Chinese Characteristics

When a new Chinese constitution was adopted in 1992, and a planned economy under public ownership was dropped in favor of a "socialist market economy with Chinese characteristics," the world waited to see what shape this new economic entity would assume. It did not take long for many of those writing about China's economic reforms to become convinced that the socialist market economy is a failure. In the words of one observer, it has become "market Leninism," characterized by an explosion of wealth as millions of Chinese became economic actors in their own right while a moribund Communist Party clings to an outdated ideology and shows all the signs of a collapsing dynasty.[1] Another says that it is neither a market nor a Leninist system and that traditional *guanxi* contacts aided and abetted by economic decentralization and transfer of authority to local governments have led to fragmented authoritarianism in which economic decision making is characterized by negotiation and consensus building between economic agents brought together in a complex network of relationships.[2] Yet another says that

China has adopted capitalism wholeheartedly and that the reign of un-
fettered market forces has created a capitalistic Wild West that threatens
sustained economic growth.[3]

There is truth in all these theories, but what is happening is more
complicated. China's far-reaching economic reforms became irreversible (short of revolution) once controls over prices and the exchange of
goods were removed and individuals could act as economic agents free
to pursue their own ends. Economic freedom first stimulated the "spontaneous privatization" of state assets by civil servants. Millions of private citizens also entered the economic arena, resulting in a vast
expansion of traditional *guanxi* networks and the corruption that often
accompanies them. Opportunities for theft are so great that financial
frauds are now occurring at a rate of more than 10,000 a year, compared
to just 100 annually a decade ago.[4]

Economic freedom has also stimulated competition, and once let loose,
competitive forces could not be contained. State enterprises became
subject to bottom-line considerations, and in order to survive, they sought
the best prices for inputs and outputs, and profitability replaced output
as the primary criteria for judging performance. The government and its
alter ego, the Chinese Communist Party, are always behind the scenes
because the party, through the government, wants to remain in control
of the state-dominated part of the economy and ensure its survival. The
government's involvement ranges from macropolicy pronouncements
to direct intervention in state enterprise affairs. In agriculture, it controls the supply of grain and establishes grain support prices to keep
farm incomes from falling. It still uses the five-year plan to screen all
major state enterprise investments and closely monitors the situation in
every industrial activity—intervening most commonly, by establishing
price floors for industrial products when price wars drive prices below
production cost and thus threaten the survival of state enterprises.[5]

The 1992 constitution adopted the principle of separation of government administration from the day-to-day operations of state enterprises,
and the company law of 1995 established the basis for separating government ownership from state enterprise management. In practice, the
government intervenes in state enterprise affairs whenever it decides
that it is in its interest to do so. The role of central government is further
complicated by provincial governments, which maintain trade barriers
to protect state enterprises under their jurisdictions from the impact of
competition.

The private sector has become a force to be reckoned with. The government has realized that it needs the private sector because it is a source of jobs for redundant state enterprise workers, it provides the government with tax revenues, and is the obvious purchaser when state enterprises are up for sale. Not only is the number of private enterprises growing rapidly, but their number has been underestimated because thousands of them registered as collective enterprises to avoid discrimination by local governments, and the private sector (excluding agriculture) now accounts for about one-fourth of China's gross domestic product. In 1999, a constitutional amendment recognized the private sector as an important part of the socialist market economy, and in 2000 the Communist Party's Central Committee went even further and declared that the private sector should be supported, encouraged, and guided.[6]

Foreign investment has also become an important part of China's socialist market economy. About three-fourths of total direct foreign investment in China comes from ethnic Chinese living overseas. Taiwan is a huge investor in China in spite of its political problems with the mainland. Hundreds of Western firms are investing in China with world-famous multinational corporations at the forefront. In some industries, like motor vehicles and telecommunications, they play a leading manufacturing role. A surprising number of these sophisticated enterprises have badly misjudged the Chinese market and the degree of competition they would face, and some have left China for good. Competition has become so cutthroat that well-known multinationals like Caterpillar, Whirlpool, Peugeot, Daimler-Chrysler, Carlsberg, and Bass have pulled out of their Chinese joint ventures because they felt that shrinking markets and decimated profits gave them no alternative.[7]

State Enterprises Are Ill Equipped to Survive

In the industrial sector, fierce competition fostered by declining demand, large inventories, and low-priced imports has forced enterprises to slash prices and costs, lay off workers, and shift their product mix to more value-added production. State enterprises are fighting desperately just to survive because they are losing clients to more efficient producers. In short, state enterprises are behaving like their nonstate brethren. Although large, important state enterprises receive direct assistance from the central government, they are cutting costs just as drastically as their smaller siblings in the struggle for survival. Yet, changing from a centrally planned to a corporate culture is greatly hindered by the nature of state enterprises, which are highly structured, hierarchical organizations with deeply ingrained ways of doing things. This makes it very difficult for them to adapt to rapid changes in the business environment. Even when state enterprises sell shares to the public, the government as majority shareholder has little incentive to bring in new ideas by providing minority shareholders with board representation.

State enterprises are ill equipped to win any competition because they lack management skills, have little understanding of how markets work, are slow to adapt to rapidly changing market conditions, and lack capital to import new technologies and modernize existing facilities. Regional protectionism, in which provinces act as regional economies with their own barriers to entry of nonprovincial firms, runs deep in China, fostered by traditional locally based business relationships and local government's takeover of private businesses under Mao Zedong. Moreover, protectionist tendencies and reliance on local *guanxi* connections were fostered by the increased authority given to local governments during the economic reforms. When excess capacity in many industries intensified competition for shrinking markets, provincial governments simply redoubled their efforts to protect their own enterprises.

For collectively or privately owned industries, *guanxi* was essential for getting established, and the rapid growth of nonstate enterprises was due in large part to alliances with local governments that were key to resolving their start-up problems. But in today's economy, *guanxi* relationships are useful for both sides only if they can contribute to an enterprise's competitive edge. State enterprises are in debt to their own suppliers and sell on credit to their clients, and these debtor–creditor relationships are also a powerful bond. Yet, enterprises supplying inputs to perennial loss makers run the risk of going down with them.

The telecommunications sector (see chapter 6) serves as a foreshadowing of what competition in the socialist market economy will be like now that China has joined the WTO. This is because China's leaders understood that the information superhighway was revolutionizing the way economic actors interact and exchange information, and they saw the "knowledge economy" as the key to Chinese enterprises' competing with multinational corporations. They also came to realize that competition was essential to lowering industry service costs and improving the performance of state enterprises, and if state enterprises were going to be able to compete with foreign enterprises, they first had to learn to compete among themselves. They also intended to remain firmly in control of the modernization process and of the further growth of the sector. In addition, they wanted to ensure that state enterprises retain control over highly lucrative telecommunications services.

What followed best illustrates the dilemma China faces as it allows market forces to open up its economy while it tries to remain in control of the process. It combined two competing ministries and parts of others to create a super ministry, the Ministry of Information Industry. Then it split the ministry's operating company, China Telecom, into three separate operating companies and created new state operating companies to compete with them. It allowed a private Chinese firm to take a leading role in the sector and provided it with financing and lucrative contracts. It allowed foreign investors and their partners to dominate mobile phone manufacture, the country's fastest-growing market, while pressuring them to increase local content (to manufacture critical new technology in their Chinese plants rather than import it as components). When foreign investors interpreted ill-defined foreign investment regulations as allowing them to form joint ventures that obtained revenues from telecommunications services, which were off-limits to foreign investors, the government required forty-six of them to divest themselves of their investments. The Ministry of Information Industry has enormous power as owner, operator, and regulator of telephonic systems on which the entire nation depends, and is dragging its feet on further reform. This has prompted the government to take the unusual step of establishing a cabinet-level committee chaired by Premier Zhu Rongji to preside over further sectoral reform. This indicates that serious disagreements exist within the government over how much control to give up.

The government also realized that the millions of new economic agents were affecting the way that information was disseminated and used, and this posed huge problems in coordination and control. This was government's dilemma: how to exploit the economic development potential of the new information technology while controlling its dissemination. The government is unyielding in its determination to control information content and regards itself as China's cyberspace gatekeeper, invoking the mantra of maintaining national security and domestic stability. As information flows faster and faster and over more media, the government is having difficulty in controlling access to information and is requiring information users to regulate themselves or face the consequences—which in itself is an admission that the gatekeeper can no longer do its job.

Is China Ready to Join the World Trading Community?

U.S. secretary of state Colin Powell has said that "free markets promote free societies," while discussing how exposure to a rules-based international marketplace is forcing China to see that it needs to adapt to the rest of the world.[8] Powell's statement reflects a widely held belief that by exposure to other nations, China will become more like them. Two years after the U.S.–China accord on trade was signed in Beijing on November 15, 1999, China became a member of the WTO. This signifies China's commitment to modify its economic behavior in accordance with WTO requirements. But when behavioral change conflicts with fundamental values, there can be enormous resistance. Values have to change before fundamental changes in behavior can take place. Just because China joins the WTO does not mean that it will quickly fit in with its trading partners. On the contrary, China's relationship with them is likely to be stormy. What this means is that implementation of the WTO agreement is only the beginning of a long process of elimination of persistent anticompetitive trade barriers and practices.

Tariffs and other barriers to trade such as quotas and subsidies will largely be eliminated. Average tariffs on agricultural imports, for example, will be reduced from the current 31 percent to 14.5 percent by 2004. But WTO regulations do not cover bureaucratic requirements such as operating licenses. These and other administrative controls are likely to be used by provincial and local governments as protective barriers to keep out competition. Other remaining trade barriers include discriminatory fees assessed on goods from other cities and inspections to ensure they meet local "standards," as well as extremely high road tolls for interprovincial commerce and prohibition by local governments of the transiting of commercial vehicles from other jurisdictions. The State Council recently issued an edict banning most of these practices, but implementation will be a lengthy and difficult process.

Nonetheless, competition will become much more widespread and intense with WTO membership, and thousands of government officials and enterprise managers are undergoing accelerated training in familiarization with WTO requirements and trade-related subjects. A cottage industry has sprung up with would-be experts offering advice on WTO-related services. Government-imposed mergers in aviation, power, and automobiles, designed to protect smaller state enterprises that would not survive alone, are going more slowly than expected. Most state enterprises are simply not ready to compete, and getting them up to speed is proving a Herculean task.

Membership in the WTO will initiate another irreversible process affecting China's whole economy. Expanding foreign competition is expected to result in the loss of millions of industrial and agricultural jobs over the next decade. The reformers, led by Premier Zhu Rongji, are hoping the boost to China's economy—especially the private sector, which for the first time will have access to foreign investment and technology—which will more than compensate for the unemployment. The World Bank estimates that China's share of global trade could more than triple, making China the world's second-largest trading nation.[9]

Economic Opportunity Is for City Dwellers

What is most alarming about the new freedoms is that so many Chinese cannot take advantage of them. Invisible bureaucratic walls limit access of China's impoverished rural millions to the benefits of urban life, because the government is afraid they will overwhelm urban services. Yet, rural migrants form a floating population of 100 million to 120 million who have moved to urban areas in quest of opportunity. They live in a twilight zone without permanent access to housing, jobs, and other perquisites of legitimate urban dwellers. Some receive temporary residence and work permits, but most are tolerated simply because the government does not know what to do about them. When they are seen as a potential source of social unrest, as they were during the celebration of the fiftieth anniversary of the Communist regime, the most visible are rounded up and sent back to the countryside. Nevertheless, the income stream remitted by floating workers to their home villages has become a very significant factor in rural income and is expected to be the main source of rural income growth in the years to come.[10] The government needs to understand that it is in their interest to support these unfortunates, and to recognize that they are part of the urban community.

The government is facing a terrible dilemma for which there is no easy resolution. It should close down hundreds of obsolete state enterprises that have no chance of surviving the increased competition that will result from WTO entry. However, there are already far too many redundant urban workers and rural migrants searching for too few urban jobs. From the government's viewpoint, closing down enterprises and putting workers on the street would simply create a far bigger problem for which there is no immediate solution. So the government continues to protect state enterprises from competition by subsidizing core state enterprises that absorb weaker enterprises to keep them afloat. The government really has no other choice. It would be political suicide for it simply to close down failing state enterprises without alternative employment opportunities. But its policy of keeping the iron rice bowl intact while only partially filled is not working. Workers' protests are multiplying because state enterprises are failing to meet pension, salary, and laid-off subsistence payments.

Almost one-third of all China's citizens live in its cities, which are bursting at the seams. The central cores of China's major cities remain among the most densely populated places on the planet. Such densities characterize a system in which housing and commerce are located near the workplace, and so pollution is right next door. The government has taken a giant step in adopting a national policy to replace coal with clean energy sources and in putting more teeth into enforcement of pollution control legislation. China's major cities are already becoming more healthful places to live. The test of the government's resolve will be to make all of China's cities, towns, and villages healthful places to live. China has the lowest per capita automobile population in Asia, but motorized traffic is growing fast and has led to massive congestion and increasing air pollution. The government is busy building new highways and establishing new cities to provide other destinations for rural-to-urban migration. But this is not enough. There is no place on the crowded streets and roads of China's cities for thousands—and eventually millions—of private automobiles. The government needs to take action to severely limit the number of motor vehicles in dense city centers, and to build rapid transit systems to link the city cores to park-and-ride hubs in the suburbs. Municipal governments and state enterprises are subsidizing their employees in privatizing existing publicly owned housing, and local governments are encouraging new housing construction by guaranteeing occupancy to developers who can construct a building at a government-set price. But city dwellers who do not have access to subsidized purchase of public housing cannot afford commercial housing, and inequity still rules housing markets.

Can China's farmers look forward to a better life? Rural reform has lifted 250 million Chinese out of poverty and has raised incomes for millions more, but in many ways China's farmers cannot escape their own history. They cannot own the land they farm and are tenant farmers under a reallocation system reminiscent of the one adopted in the Tang dynasty over a thousand years ago. Like their forebears, they must surrender the fruits of their labors to an onerous and unfair tax system enforced by local officials. They cannot obtain permanent residence or work permits in the cities and are treated as second-class citizens when they do relocate there. Not only is the disparity between rural and urban incomes increasing, but Premier Zhu Rongji recently admitted that contrary to official statistics which show that rural income grew in 2000, it actually declined.[11]

With reform came the household responsibility system, which made the farmer responsible for the crops he grew. With reform also came huge subsidies, because the government was concerned with maintaining national grain self-sufficiency and ensuring stability in the countryside by keeping on-farm costs low and insulating farm incomes from the effects of grain price fluctuations. This policy is a consequence of the terrible famine that gripped the country during 1959–1962, when 20 million Chinese lost their lives and millions more led short lives or were nutritionally crippled. The catastrophe left a deep mark on those responsible for feeding China, and they have pursued a policy of food self-sufficiency ever since. The government controls the marketing and distribution of grain and maintains large stocks in reserve in case the grim reaper should reappear. The government can no longer afford the massive subsidies needed to monopolize grain commerce in the name of price stability and ought to shift to a buffer stock system, which would require it to hold only a relatively small proportion of grain output in reserve. An equally grave problem is that even if government policy is able to ensure the farmer some disposable income, most local governments are insolvent, and local tax authorities are busy collecting numerous taxes that leave farmers impoverished, despairing, and outraged.

Rule of Law or Rule of Party?

China has a legal tradition going back over twenty-five hundred years. The state and the judicial system were inextricably intertwined, and the law's chief purpose was to maintain the existing political and social order. The legal code specified the penalty for each crime, leaving the magistrate handling the case almost no discretion, but making him account-able for any mistakes he might make. Only high-ranking state legal officials established precedent; judges simply ruled on guilt or innocence, lawyers were unnecessary, and the idea of a trial's outcome being decided by a panel of randomly selected citizens would have been inconceivable.

After assuming power in 1949, the communist regime dismantled the legal system of the defeated Guomindang government, and the People's Republic did not have a legal code until the reforms began over twenty years ago. The Communist Party determined what was counterrevolutionary and therefore illegal, and judgment was rendered in most instances by administrative order. During the Cultural Revolution, even this minimal system broke down, and the Red Guards and their "revolutionary masses" were allowed to establish what constituted counterrevolutionary behavior, make arrests, bring suspects to trial, and carry out sentences.

Historically, commerce was not regulated by law. It depended upon mutually binding obligations, either verbal or based on simple written contracts endorsed by trustworthy guarantors. The system worked because most businesses were family run, relationships were all-important, and correct behavior was regulated by family, guarantors, guilds, and other associations. Disputes were dealt with outside the court system. Although this is changing, economic disputes are still mainly dealt with mainly through administrative action, negotiation, or mediation.

Since 1979, China has passed hundreds of laws, many to improve the functioning of the economy as it opened up. But many laws lack the supporting structure of administrative regulations needed to implement them. China has been revising its entire corpus of trade legislation to satisfy WTO requirements. Out of 1,413 trade laws, regulations, and ministerial rulings, 573 have been abolished and 120 amended.[12] Laws governing telecommunications, foreign investment, and trade, which have been stalled for years, are being pushed ahead, and key legislation such as the commercial bank, insurance, and securities laws are being overhauled. Yet these laws lack a sound supporting structure to enforce them, because legal institutions and regulatory agencies are neither independent nor effective. The regime's harsh approach to dealing with serious economic crimes by capital punishment and long prison terms is a reflection of the underlying failure of the present system and cannot substitute for the absence of the rule of law as ultimate arbiter backed by an effective regulatory system. As observed earlier, the underlying problem is again one of control; the government does not want a strong, independent judiciary holding *it* accountable for its actions.

As mentioned before, in imperial China, the bureaucracy made and interpreted laws whose primary purpose was to maintain the existing social and political order. In Communist China, officials appointed by the government do the same, and China's leaders still hold cultural values that characterized Qing dynasty autocrats. If China is to successfully integrate itself in the world trading community, the government needs to part with these beliefs and recognize the rule of law as paramount, guarantee individual rights under the law, and create an independent judiciary and regulatory system to enforce the laws.

Economic Growth Rates Are Not the Real Test of Economic Performance

For over twenty years the world has been mesmerized by China's economic growth rate. Per capita gross domestic product increased at a phenomenal 8 percent annually during the period, and industrial output grew on average 11 percent annually. Growth in efficiency and productivity did not receive nearly the same attention; many of the products made were of inferior quality and, as economic controls were lifted, could not be sold. Increased output did not translate therefore into significant increases in value-added jobs and incomes, and while output capacity increased threefold over the last fifteen years, incomes did not even double.[13]

China's economic growth strategy is ruled by numbers and is closely tailored to the growing numbers of workers entering the job market and being laid off. One observer has noted that the reformers are like Buster Keaton on the railway tracks: No matter how fast they run, the population keeps gaining on them, and just to keep up with the demand for new jobs the economy has to grow by 6 percent annually.[14] Economic planning is also governed by shifts in age and sex. Falling birth rates resulting from the government's stringent birth-control policy are rapidly transforming the age structure of the population and will cause the number of elderly to double as a percentage of the total population over the next twenty years. This is placing enormous pressure on China's ineffective pay-as-you-go pension system. The system suffers from mismanagement of funds, limited coverage of the entire workforce, insufficient pooling between enterprises and government, payment exemptions and noncompliance, and varying contribution rates. As a result, unfounded pensions have reached crisis proportions. Efforts to move to a nationally based fully funded system have not been successful, as only a few large cities are able to generate the resources necessary for a fully funded system to work.

The government is afraid to smash the iron rice bowl for state enterprises because it is having difficulties divesting itself of weaker enterprises, and cannot run the political risk of closing them down. Massive debt–equity swaps have relieved enterprises and banks from financial obligations and have given state enterprises breathing space. Cleaning up state enterprise balance sheets will not solve their fundamental viability problems, however. They will have to borrow further to carry out the modernization they desperately need, and if operating losses continue, new debt payments will again erode whatever liquidity they have. Many observers see debt–equity swaps as a gambit by the government that enabled it to declare victory by claiming that by improving state enterprise profitability, it met its promise to reform the majority of state enterprises by the year 2000.

With competition increasing and excess capacity still a major problem, it became more and more difficult to unload stockpiled output, and with declining demand pushing prices down in the late 1990s, the government tried to stimulate consumption by cutting deposit rates and taxing interest income to make saving less attractive, by giving raises to state employees, and by increasing investment and providing new jobs in infrastructure. Reflation was finally successful in 2000, and consumer spending became the main engine for growth as export growth began to fall. Economic growth reached 8 percent of gross domestic product in 2000. In the first 6 months of 2001, China's economy grew 7.9 percent, even though global economic growth was declining. China's economy is proving more resilient than the world economy, as rising consumer spending has taken the place of lost exports, with urban retail sales growing by 12.7 percent and rural sales by 8.5 percent. As in previous years, substantial government investment in infrastructure was needed to keep growth around the 8 percent level. Government investment in 2000–2001 has been directed to narrowing the gap between China's booming coastal region and its poorer western provinces, which have become the government's number one development priority. Agricultural subsidies continued, with the government paying farmers grain prices that were higher than the world price. The nice surprise was that fiscal revenues in

2000 were up to 14 percent of gross domestic product. Joblessness and high inventories from overproduction are structural problems that are not going away, however.

Human Rights, Social Stability, and Moral Order

Before demonizing China for its human rights record, it is important to understand what is behind the set of beliefs that seems so reprehensible. As pointed out earlier, since Confucian times, the survival of Chinese society depended upon maintaining social stability and moral order through correct behavior based on precise gradations of authority, respect, duty, and obligation. The Chinese family was responsible for the behavior of all of its members and was more important than any individual in it. The family was a rigidly hierarchical patriarchy, and the obligations among the family members kept the unit intact. Individual human rights, which could conflict with familial obligations, were a threat to the system. Rights and obligations were held collectively, which meant that if one member of a family committed a crime, all members would be punished. Laws were created to support and defend this system, and any inequities were accepted as a necessary evil for maintaining stability and order.[15]

Under the Communist system, the party has assumed many of the functions of the family as well as its value system. The party, like the dynastic family, sees individual rights as a threat to the system and has suppressed individual initiative and personal responsibility. This continues to inhibit the development of other value systems. Both the party and the family are closed units, and these obligations do not extend outside the unit. This is why the party is opposed to individual involvement in public affairs outside the government hierarchy. If an accident occurs on a Chinese street, a crowd will form, but it is motivated by curiosity rather than a desire to help. The prevailing attitude is that one should not get involved in what is somebody else's business. This concept extends to the community as a whole, and civic-mindedness is not a virtue.[16]

Although China's laws no longer permit criminal prosecution based on collective guilt, collective responsibility is still embedded in society and the socialist system. If a party official is found guilty of a crime or even demoted or out of favor, the entire family not only suffers from the shame and humiliation, but their future prospects often become circumscribed. The current regime's attitude toward punishment is also deeply traditional. Capital punishment and long sentences are penalties for a long list of crimes, and harsh sentences are meted out to the worst offenders in show trials to deter wrongdoing. Most minor offenses are dealt with through administrative action by the work unit or local officials.

The party's concept of social stability is predicated on the notion that what is best for all members of society (as determined by the party) supersedes any individual rights. What is good for the individual must therefore be subordinated to the collective good of society as a whole as represented by the party. This concept has deep roots in Marxist ideology and, according to President Jiang Zemin, provides the rationale for the existence of the party. Without the Communist Party, says Jiang, there can be no stability, and without stability there can be no reform.[17]

Ironically, as the Communist Party opens up the economy and allows much greater personal freedom, it is losing moral authority and must rely more and more on repressive policies to keep itself in power. The party is afraid of Falun Gong because, for the first time since its triumph in 1949, it is facing organized civil disobedience. Although the movement has no political agenda, the party fears it because it supplants the party as a spiritual and moral force.

China has a long history of spiritual mass movements, and in the nineteenth century the Boxer and Taiping religious cults developed into full-scale rebellions that helped overturn the Qing dynasty. This lesson is not lost on the leaders of the Communist Party. What is particularly frightening to the party is Falun Gong's broad appeal to people ranging from disillusioned party members to dispossessed rural migrants and others who have been left behind by economic reforms. The party declares the movement a threat to social stability and says it has no option but to suppress the movement. However, this tactic is likely to backfire in the long term because the party's reliance on force and long prison terms to deal with organized opposition and dissent is further weakening its moral authority.

Does the Communist Party Have a Future?

People are losing confidence in the government and the party, and the real question is whether the party will survive China's economic transformation. The strength of the party has rested on its organization—its vertical hierarchy that extends from the party secretary-general in Beijing to the party secretary in the smallest village. This structure is replicated in the government bureaucracy and, during the first thirty years of the Communist regime, provided an enormously stable base upon which to govern such a vast country. Yet, delegation of authority to local governments coupled with declining tax revenues led to massive abuses. State entities providing public services, such as the gamut of law enforcement agencies ranging from public security departments to environmental protection agencies, routinely charge fees. The heart of the problem is that government appropriations meet only part of their expenses, and public service organizations are expected to raise a substantial portion of their operating budgets. They have little alternative but to charge for their services.

There are many scenarios about China's future. Some say that it is a question of improving the present system by making government more efficient and by developing a truly federal system through evolution of representative government—at the national level through the National People's Congress and at the village level through the village committee and assembly system.[18] Others say the party will continue to adapt and evolve to changing circumstances and, if necessary, will gradually jettison socialism in favor of nationalism if that is required for it to maintain control.[19] Some look beyond China for other models such as the Industrial Revolution and the accompanying social and political revolutions that have rocked Europe during the past two centuries. Once let loose, they say, rampant capitalism and liberal democracy will overcome any regime that clings to the past.[20]

The present system certainly needs a lot of improvement. Decay of government institutions has become rampant, and the party itself has rated the performance of 40 percent of provincial, prefecture, and county governments as poor and 75 percent of party branches as mediocre or poor.[21] The worsening fiscal situation during the first two decades of reform led to a decline in the level and quality of public services as well. Education and health suffered the most from this decline, and rural areas have been the hardest hit. The decline in law enforcement is also alarming: Crime rates have risen sharply, and banditry in the countryside and drug trafficking have emerged as serious problems. There is some reason to hope, however, because a parallel process of renewal is taking place in the countryside, with real democracy arising at the village level as elected village committees and assemblies replace officials chosen by the party and local governments. Like economic liberalization, this political opening is irreversible short of a major upheaval in the countryside. Yet, it is a far cry from directly electing officials at the township, city, county, and provincial levels, where most of the local power really resides. A basic problem is that candidates are nominated as individuals rather than representing a group. This works fine at the village level where everyone knows everyone else. At the township, city, or county level, voters in other countries vote based on party affiliation, since they usually do not have a personal relationship with and may lack personal knowledge about the individual who is running. As yet, the party does not allow the existence of political organizations it does not control, and without political organization, Chinese democracy cannot be effectively extended beyond the village level. China has been trying to improve the present system since 1978, but as discussed above, further substantive improvement is limited by patterns of behavior, perceptions, and attitudes that are tied to the past. The idea that an economic revolution will inevitably lead to social and political revolution is something that intrigues many China watchers. However, Europe in the eighteenth and nineteenth centuries provides a poor comparison, because in China's case it is the authoritarian government itself that began the economic revolution. A much better comparison would be the recent demise of the Soviet Union. China's leaders certainly seem to think so. Like many other party members, Jiang Zemin was shocked by the fall of the Soviet Union. He became convinced that it collapsed because it failed to change with the times and apparently feels that if the Chinese Communist Party fails to respond to change, it could suffer the same fate as the Communist Party of the Soviet Union.

In 2000 in Guangdong Province, Jiang made a speech in which he unveiled his idea that the party must learn from the mistakes of others and change accordingly. Jiang's hope is that if the party could represent "the development needs of advanced forces of production," "the forward direction of advanced culture," and "the fundamental interests of the broad masses," it would be "forever undefeatable."[22] Jiang's formulation, now known as the "Three Represents," is a significant departure for the party, which heretofore has represented only workers, peasants, and soldiers. Jiang was clearly reaching out for support to other elements of society and preparing the ground for widening the party's membership, which now includes the private sector. With a more diverse membership, the need for a binding ideology would be much less, and the party would begin to look more like a modern political party, which is often a loose coalition of different groups who can agree on a few fundamental principles. But even with more diverse membership, the party is unlikely to democratize at the top.

But the party may not be able to change fast enough, as discontent with its stewardship seems to be growing faster than has heretofore been reported. On June 1, 2001, the Organization Research Group of the Party Central Committee made available a report that describes a spreading pattern of collective protests and group incidents arising from economic, ethnic, and religious conflicts, fueled by public anger over inequality, corruption, and official indifference. The report warns that entry into the WTO may bring growing dangers and pressures, and it predicts that the number of incidents may rise, severely harming social stability. It cites two main sources of discontent: official corruption, which is described as "the main fuse exacerbating conflicts between officials and the masses," and fast-rising income inequality among urban and rural and coastal and interior populations as well as within urban areas. The report goes on to prescribe no specific remedies but only general palliatives such as reducing the income gap, improving social security, and building socialist democracy to give people more control over their affairs—all within the principle of one-party rule.[23]

Before economic reform, all aspects of people's lives were regulated by their work unit and neighborhood committee. Economic activity was circumscribed, and individual desires were subordinated to a collective ethic. The structure that constrained individual behavior disappeared with the reforms. Without a work unit to impose order and discipline, it is up to the individual to abide by the laws and regulations that now govern economic activity. The collective ethic, still being mouthed by party officials, seems a hollow remnant of the past, and many individuals feel no sense of accountability. Most critics believe that it is necessary to strengthen enforcement of the new laws, but this is not enough. What is really required is a new ethic to guide Chinese society. In the absence of that, a first step would be to subordinate the party to the rule of law and to an independent judiciary. This would provide individual Chinese with the means to obtain redress for their grievances against the government.

Since 1978, 250 million Chinese peasants have been lifted out of absolute poverty in one of the great achievements in human history. Yet, the disparity between rural and urban incomes continues to widen, and those who are being left behind by economic reforms are starting to withdraw their support. Because no organizations exist through which they can channel their discontent, collective grievances can be expressed only in violent protest. So far, these protests have been spontaneous and localized, but they are becoming more frequent and violent. The danger that they could lead to a major political crisis is limited by several factors. First is the lack of any organized opposition to the Communist Party. Second, even with its huge population and geographic diversity, it is unlikely that China would be susceptible to regional separatism, barring a total breakdown of central government control such as occurred during the warlordism that characterized China in the early decades of the twentieth century. China's great strength is that the vast majority of its people are tied together by a strong cultural identity spanning more than two millennia, and these ties are cemented by a written history that is almost equally long. China's growing nationalist sentiment—now being exploited by the party—is centered on this unifying central core of cultural beliefs, and China is unlikely therefore to experience the political fragmentation that occurred in the former Soviet Union, for example. Whether the Communist Party can survive in its present form is another matter altogether.

The widening gap between those who are benefiting from China's economic revolution and those who are being left behind and, worse yet, between those who are enriching themselves by violating the law at the expense of those who are obeying the law, has created a political climate of mistrust and hopelessness that is growing like a cancer in Chinese society. Since Mao's death in 1976, the party has changed in ways unimaginable at that time, as it tried to meet the challenges of economic reform. But adaptation and slow evolution over the past twenty-four years have weakened the party's authority, and a faster response to change and a widening of party membership are not enough to regain the support of the Chinese people. To deal with this growing crisis of confidence, the party must shed attitudes and behavior that keep it a prisoner of the past. It must take the giant step of changing itself from autocrat to servant of the people.

Notes

Chapter One

1. Jonathan D. Spence, *The Search for Modern China*, p. 219.
2. Ibid., p. 326.
3. Ibid., p. 583.
4. Barry Naughton, "The Third Front: Defence Industrialization in the Chinese Interior," pp. 351–386.
5. World Bank, *Updating Economic Memorandum: Managing Rapid Growth and Transition*, p. 30.
6. *China Daily*, January 11, 2000.
7. *China Daily*, September 23, 1997.
8. *Far Eastern Economic Review*, October 16, 1997, p. 62.
9. *China Daily*, January 12, 1998.
10. *China Daily*, July 3, 2000.
11. *China Daily*, February 19, 2001.
12. *China Business Review*, July–August, 2000, p. 22.
13. *China Daily*, January 21, 2000.
14. *China Daily*, January 10, 2000.
15. *The Economist*, September 30, 2000, p. 72.
16. The Economist Intelligence Unit, *Country Report: China.* August 2001, p. 34.
17. Albert Nyberg and Scott Rozelle, *Accelerating China's Rural Transformation*, p. 87.
18. World Bank, *Chongqing Industrial Pollution Control and Reform Project*, p. 4.
19. World Bank, *China's Management of Enterprise Assets: The State as Shareholder*, p. 1.
20. Nyberg and Rozelle, *Rural Transformation*, p. 87.
21. World Bank, *China 2020, Development Challenges in the New Century*, p. 32.
22. Nyberg and Rozelle, *Rural Transformation*, p. 91.

23. Maurice Meisner, "The Other China," p. 265.

24. Nyberg and Rozelle, *Rural Transformation*, p. 87.

25. Neil Gregory, Stoyan Tenev, and Dileep Wagle, *China's Emerging Private Enterprises*, p. 18.

26. *China Daily*, September 21, 1998.

27. Estelle James, "How Can China Solve It's Old Age Security Problem?"

28. *China Daily*, June 18, 2000.

29. World Bank, *China 2020, Pension Reform in China*, pp. 7–8.

30. Estelle James, "How Can China Solve Its Old Age Security Problem?"

31. Pieter Bottelier, "Killing Two Birds with One Stone," pp. 5–6.

32. World Bank, *China's Management of Enterprise Assets*, p. x.

33. Global Environmental Facility, *China: Efficient Industrial Boilers*, pp. 1–2.

34. World Bank, *China 2020, Development Challenges in the New Century*, p. 28.

35. Cheng Li, *Rediscovering China: Dynamics and Dilemmas of Reform*, p. 232.

36. Yang Zhong, *Studying Chinese Local Government: Searching for a Paradigm*.

37. World Bank, *China 2020, Development Challenges in the New Century*, p. 24.

38. Ibid., p. 24.

39. Michael Johnson, "The Vices—and Virtues—of Corruption," pp. 270–271.

40. *Far Eastern Economic Review*, November 30, 2000, pp. 15–18.

41. Edward S. Steinfeld, *Forging Reform in China, the Fate of State-Owned Industry*, p. 38.

42. Ibid., p. 47.

43. *Asian Wall Street Journal*, August 14–20, 2000.

44. *China Daily*, January 12, 1998.

45. Lester R. Brown, *Who Will Feed China? Wake-up Call for a Small Planet*, p. 50.

46. *Far Eastern Economic Review*, December 25, 2000–January 4, 2001, p. 106.

47. *Far Eastern Economic Review*, October 5, 2000, p. 46.

48. Ibid., p. 50.

49. World Bank, *China's Management*, p. 1.

50. *China Business Review*, January–February, 2000, p. 40.

51. The Economist Intelligence Unit, *Country Report: China*, p. 29.

52. *Far Eastern Economic Review*, April 27, 2000, p. 26.

Chapter Two

1. Nicholas R. Lardy, "China and the Asian Contagion," p. 86.

2. Ibid., pp. 79–82.

3. Charles O. Hucker, *China's Imperial Past, An Introduction to Chinese History and Culture*, p. 354.

4. Spence, *Search for Modern China*, p. 149.

5. Ibid., p. 329.

6. Minxin Pei, "The Political Economy of Banking Reforms in China, 1993–1997," p. 328.

7. Ibid., p. 330.

8. World Bank, *The Chinese Economy: Fighting Inflation, Deepening Reforms*, vol. 1, p. 34.

9. Minxin Pei, "Political Economy," p. 331.

10. Only the cities of Beijing, Shanghai, Tianjin, and Chongqing are allowed to be called municipalities because by definition, municipalities have the same status, rights, and responsibilities as provinces and, like them, deal directly with the central government.

11. Nicholas R. Lardy, *China's Unfinished Economic Revolution*, p. 90.

12. World Bank, *Chinese Economy*, vol. 1, p. 27.

13. Lardy, *China's Unfinished Economic Revolution*, p. 112.

14. Ibid., p. 99.

15. *Banker*, July 1997, p. 140.

16. Nicholas R. Lardy, "The Challenge of Bank Restructuring in China," p. 26.

17. *China Business Review*, November–December, 2000, p. 19.

18. Lardy, "Bank Restructuring," p. 23.

19. Lardy, *China's Unfinished Economic Revolution*, p. 103.

20. *Almanac of China's Finance and Banking 1995*, pp. 482–484.

21. *Asian Wall Street Journal*, November 6–12, 2000.

22. *Asian Wall Street Journal*, October 2–8, 2000.

23. *China Business Review*, (May–June 2001), p. 13.

24. Lardy, *China's Unfinished Economic Revolution*, p. 80.

25. Ibid., p. 76.

26. *Asian Wall Street Journal*, December 18–24, 2000.

27. *China Daily*, October 31, 2000.

28. *China Business Review*, (May–June 2001), p. 15.

29. *Far Eastern Economic Review*, December 14, 2000, p. 14.

30. *Asian Wall Street Journal*, December 18–24, 2000.

31. Lardy, "China and the Asian Contagion," p. 88.

32. World Bank, *Chinese Economy*, vol. 1, p. 32.

33. Lardy, "Bank Restructuring," p. 35.

Chapter Three

1. John King Fairbank, *China, a New History*, p. 16.

2. Oi, Jean. C., "Two Decades of Rural Reform in China," p. 7.

3. World Bank, *Rural China: Transition and Development*, p. 81.

4. *China Daily*, April 16, 1998.

5. World Bank, *Rural China*, p. 38.

6. Hucker, *China's Imperial Past*, p. 184.

7. Fairbank, *China, a New History*, p. 89.

8. Ibid., pp. 170–171.

9. Spence, *Search for Modern China*, p. 431.

10. Fairbank, *China, a New History*, p. 356.

11. Spence, *Search for Modern China*, p. 574.

12. Fairbank, *China, a New History*, p. 354.

13. Ibid., p. 370.

14. Ibid., p. 371.

15. Peter Sun, ed., *Multipurpose River Basin Development in China*, pp. 17–18.

16. Spence, *Search for Modern China*, p. 580.

17. Ibid., p. 583.

18. Ibid., p. 594.

19. Chinese government official. Conversation with the author. Chongqing, China: 1995.

20. Spence, *Search for Modern China*, p. 697.

21. Francis C. Tuan and Ke Bingshen, "A Review of China's Agricultural Policy: Past and Present Developments," p. 16.

22. Brown, *Who Will Feed China?* pp. 27–28.

23. Ibid., pp. 80–81.

24. Ibid., p. 46.

25. Robert F. Ash, "The Performance of China's Grain Sector: A Regional Perspective," p. 38.

26. Tuan and Ke, "Review of China's Agricultural Policy," p. 21.

27. Ibid., p. 26.

28. *China Daily*, July 16, 1998.

29. Frederick W. Crook, "An Analysis of China's Food Grain Security Policy," pp. 65–66.

30. *China Daily*, April 15, 1998.

31. *China Daily*, June 11, 1998.

32. *China Daily*, April 7, 1998.

33. Robert F. Ash and R.L. Edmonds, "China's Land Resources, Environment and Agricultural Production," pp. 855–856.

34. World Bank, *Rural China*, pp. 55–56.

35. Ibid., p. 88.

36. David Zweig, "Rural People, the Politicians, and Power," p. 154.

37. World Bank, *Rural China*, pp. 10–11.

38. Zweig, "Rural People, the Politicians, and Power," p. 165.

39. World Bank, *Rural China*, p. 89.

40. *China Daily*, July 20, 1998.

41. Brown, *Who Will Feed China?* p. 25.

42. Ibid., pp. 96–97.

43. Ibid., p. 50.

44. Ibid., pp. 57–58.

45. Ibid., p. 63.

46. Ibid., p. 77.

47. Ibid., p. 53.

48. Ibid., pp. 67–72.

49. Ibid., p. 96.

50. Tuan and Ke, "A Review of China's Agricultural Policy," pp. 17–18.

51. World Bank, *China 2020, Food Security Options: At China's Table*, p. 18.

52. Pierre Crosson, *Perspectives on the Long–Term Global Food Situation*, no. 2, pp. 4–5.

53. Ibid., p. 6.

54. World Bank, *China 2020, Food Security Options: At China's Table*, p. 3.

55. World Bank, *Rural China*, p. 60.

56. Sun, *Multipurpose River Basin Development in China*, p. 26.

57. *New York Times*, May 23, 1996.

58. Lester R. Brown and Bryan Halweil, "The Drying of China," p. 13.

59. Ibid., p. 11.

60. World Bank, *Rural China*, p. 63.

61. Brown and Halweil, "The Drying of China," p. 11.

62. World Bank, *Rural China*, pp. 41–42.

63. Embassy of the United States, the People's Republic of China, *Agreement on Market Access Between the People's Republic of China and the United States of America*, p. 11.

64. World Bank, *Rural China*, p. 43.

65. Crook, "Analysis of China's Food Grain Security Policy," pp. 65–67.

66. World Bank, *China 2020, Food Security Options: At China's Table*, p. 15.

67. Ibid., p. 36.

Chapter Four

1. *China Daily*, September 29, 2000.

2. World Bank, *China: Air, Land, and Water*, p. 5.

3. D. Twitchet and J.K. Fairbank, eds., *The Cambridge History of Modern China*, vol. 1, p. 24.

4. Hucker, *China's Imperial Past*, p. 139

5. Fairbank, *China, A New History*, p. 92.

6. John Ogilvy, *Embassy from the East-India Company of the United Provinces, to the Grand Tartar Cham, Emperor of China*.

7. Han Suyin, *The Crippled Tree*, p. 149.

8. Spence, *Search for Modern China*, p. 583.

9. Chan Kam Wing, *Cities With Invisible Walls*, p. 39.

10. Ibid., p. 147.

11. Nicholas Lardy, *Agriculture in China's Modern Economic Development*, pp. 157–164.

12. *China Daily*, September 29, 2000.

13. Laurence J.C. Ma, ed., *Urban Development in Modern China*, p. 253.

14. Megacities are those with more than one million in population; large cities have populations between 500,000 and 1 million; medium cities have populations of 200,000 to 500,000; and small cities have fewer than 200,000.

15. Chan, *Cities With Invisible Walls*, p. 105.

16. Ibid., p. 111.

17. Ibid., p. 129.

18. World Bank, *Chongqing Industrial Pollution Control*, p. 4.

19. Shahid Yusuf and Wu Weiping, *The Dynamics of Urban Growth in Three Chinese Cities*, pp. 125, 127.

20. Chan, *Cities with Invisible Walls*, p. 45.

21. Orville Schell and David Shambaugh, eds., *The China Reader: The Reform Era*, p. 362.

22. Chan, *Cities with Invisible Walls*, p. 120.

23. Ibid., p. 131.

24. *China Daily*, October 11, 1997.

25. *Far Eastern Economic Review*, March 1, 2001, p. 46.

26. World Bank, *China 2020, China's Environment in the New Century: Clear Water, Blue Skies*, p. 23.

27. Ibid., pp. 45–46.

28. *China Daily*, June 12, 2001.

29. World Bank, *China 2020, China's Environment in the New Century: Clear Water, Blue Skies*, p. 8.

30. Ibid., p. 9.

31. Ibid., p. 22.

32. Ibid., p. 50.

33. Ibid., p. 19.

34. Ibid., p. 20.

35. Ibid., p. 13.

36. Ibid., p. 12.

37. Ibid., p. 20.

38. Ibid., p. 26.

39. World Bank, *China: Air, Land, and Water*, pp. 56–57.

40. World Bank, *Chongqing Industrial Pollution Control*, p. 3.

41. World Bank, *China: Air, Land, Water*, p. 56.

42. Ibid., p. 83.

43. *Far Eastern Economic Review*, March 1, 2001, p. 50.

44. *New York Times*, June 15, 2001.

45. *China Daily*, June 9, 2001.

46. *China Business Review*, January–February, 2000, p. 40.

47. Hucker, Charles O., *China's Imperial Past*, p. 171.

48. Bertaud, Alain, "China—Urban Land Use Issue," 1992, p. 5.

49. Steven Stares and Liu Zhi, "Theme Paper 1: Motorization in Chinese Cities: Issues and Actions," p. 68.

50. Ibid., p. 35.

51. Zhou Ganshi, "Keynote Address 3: Urban Transport Problems in Three Cities: Causes, Trends and Options," p. 36.

52. *China Daily*, August 30, 1999

53. Ibid., August 30, 1999.

54. World Bank, *China 2020, China's Environment in the New Century: Clear Water, Blue Skies*, pp. 77–78.

55. *China Daily*, November 10, 2000.

56. *Washington Post*, March 12, 2000.

57. Zhou, "Keynote Address 3," p. 36.

58. World Bank, *China 2020, China's Environment in the New Century: Clear Water, Blue Skies*, p. 75.

59. Walsh, "Transportation and the Environment," pp. 35–36.

60. Ibid., p. 79.

61. Ma, *Urban Development in Modern China*, p. 228.

62. Ibid., p. 230.

63. Chen Aimin, "China's Urban Housing Market Development: Problems and Prospects," p. 44.

64. R.J.R. Kirkby, *Urbanization in China: Town and Country in a Developing Economy, 1949–2000 A.D.*, p. 165.

65. Ibid., p. 173.

66. Ibid., p. 174.

67. Ibid., p. 176.

68. Wang Ya Ping and Alan Murie, eds., "The Process of Commercialization of Urban Housing in China," p. 972.

69. Ibid., p. 977.

70. World Bank, *China—Enterprise Housing and Social Security Reform Project*, p. 8.

71. Ibid., p. 3.

72. Minxin Pei, "Political Economy," p. 337.

73. Chen, "China's Urban Housing Market," pp. 53–55.

74. Joshua Cooper Ramo, "The Shanghai Bubble," p. 65.

75. *China Daily*, September 18, 1998.

76. *Economist*, September 30, 2000, p. 34.

77. *China Daily*, August 21, 1999.

78. *China Daily*, October 3, 2000.

79. *Far Eastern Economic Review*, May 25, 2000, p. 81.

80. Ibid., p. 81.

Chapter Five

1. Baruch Boxer, "China's Three Gorges Dam: Questions and Prospects," pp. 95–96.

2. Han Suyin, *A Mortal Flower*, p. 16.

3. Spence, *Search for Modern China*, p. 434.

4. Luk Shiu-Hung and Joseph Whitney, eds., *Megaproject: A Case Study of China's Three Gorges Project*, p. 101.

5. *China Daily*, May 8, 1998.

6. *Beijing Review*, September 21–27, 1998, p. 10.

7. *China Daily*, August 13, 1998.

8. World Bank, *Yangtze Dike Strengthening Project*, p. 3.

9. *China Daily*, September 8, 1998.

10. *China Daily*, October 6, 2000.

11. *China Today*, May 1992, p. 41.

12. Luk and Whitney, *Megaproject*, p. 8.

13. Ibid., p. 27.

14. Ibid., p. 127.

15. Simon Winchester, *The River at the Center of the World*, p. 229.

16. Dai Qing, *The River Dragon Has Come! The Three Gorges Dam and the Fate of China's Yangtze River and Its People*, p. 196.

17. Luk and Whitney, *Megaproject*, p. 123.

18. Jun Jing, "Rural Resettlement: Past Lessons for the Three Gorges Project," p. 87.

19. Ibid., p. 90.

20. Chan Kwai-Cheong, "The Three Gorges Project in China: Resettlement Prospects and Problems," p. 100.

21. International Rivers Network/Human Rights in China, "Major Problems Found in Three Gorges Dam Resettlement Program," p. 2.

22. Ibid., p. 99.

23. *China Daily*, August 10, 2000.

24. International Rivers Network, press release, February 14, 1999, p. 4.

25. *China Daily*, August 10, 2000.

26. International Rivers Network, "Major Problems," p. 6.

27. Jun Jing, "Rural Resettlement," pp. 85–86.

28. Luk and Whitney, *Megaproject*, p. 25.
29. International Rivers Network, press release, February 14, 1999.
30. *Washington Post*, January 7, 2001.
31. Elizabeth Childs-Johnson and Lawrence R. Sullivan, "The Three Gorges Dam and the Fate of China's Southern Heritage," p. 55.
32. Luk and Whitney, *Megaproject*, p. 147.
33. *Beijing Review*, December 1997, p. 5.
34. International Rivers Network, press release, April 3, 1999.
35. International Rivers Network, press release, July 20, 1999.
36. International Rivers Network, press release, May 6, 1999.
37. *China Daily*, March 17, 1999.
38. *China Daily*, June 21, 1999.
39. Boxer, "China's Three Gorges Dam," p. 98.
40. *Far Eastern Economic Review*, July 19, 2001.
41. International Rivers Network, "Major Problems," p. 8.

Chapter Six

1. Milton Mueller and Tan Zixiang, *China in the Information Age: Telecommunications and the Dilemmas of Reform*, p. 14.
2. *Far Eastern Economic Review*, September 30, 1999, p. 69.
3. Mueller and Tan, *China in the Information Age*, p. 64.
4. Eric Harwit, "China's Telecommunications Industry: Development Patterns and Policies," p. 179.
5. Mueller and Tan, *China in the Information Age*, p. 41.
6. *China Business Review*, March–April 1993, p. 19.
7. Ibid., pp. 31–32.
8. Harwit, "China's Telecommunications Industry," p. 187.
9. China State Statistical Bureau, *China Statistical Yearbook*, 1995.
10. *China Daily*, July 14, 2000.
11. Mueller and Tan, *China in the Information Age*, p. 26.
12. *China Daily*, September 4–10, 2001.
13. Mueller and Tan, *China in the Information Age*, p. 48.
14. Ibid., p. 47.
15. *China Business Review*, March–April 1996, p. 12.
16. *Asian Wall Street Journal*, February 7–13, 2000.
17. *Far Eastern Economic Review*, August 31, 2000, p. 36.
18. *China Daily*, November 6, 2000.
19. Mueller and Tan, *China in the Information Age*, p. 72.
20. Ibid., p. 63.
21. *Far Eastern Economic Review*, September 30, 1999, p. 71.
22. *Financial Times*, October 18, 1999.
23. *Far Eastern Economic Review*, December 28, 2000–January 4, 2001, p. 96.
24. *Washington Post*, February 28, 2001.
25. *Wired*, February 2000, p. 146.
26. *China Daily*, December 4, 2000.
27. *China Business Review*, March–April 1993, p. 28.
28. *China Business Review*, March–April 1996, p. 26.

29. *Asian Wall Street Journal*, April 30–May 6, 2001.
30. *China Business Review*, March–April 1993, p. 27.
31. Ibid., p. 27.
32. *China Daily*, October 26, 2000.
33. *Far Eastern Economic Review*, October 19, 2000, p. 85.
34. *Asian Wall Street Journal*, October 26, 2000.
35. *Upside*, January 2001, p. 62.
36. *Far Eastern Economic Review*, October 26, 2000, p. 77.
37. *Far Eastern Economic Review*, December 7, 2000, p. 62.
38. *China Daily, Business Weekly*, June 19–25, 2001.
39. *Asian Wall Street Journal*, August 20–26, 2001.
40. *Far Eastern Economic Review*, August 17, 2000, p. 40.
41. *Far Eastern Economic Review*, December 7, 2000, p. 69.
42. *China Daily*, February 10, 2000.
43. *China Business Review*, March–April, 2000, p. 20.
44. *Far Eastern Economic Review*, May 11, 2000, p. 34.
45. *China Daily*, June 26, 2000.
46. *China Daily*, September 25, 2000.
47. *Far Eastern Economic Review*, September 30, 1999, p. 70.
48. *Washington Post*, April 20, 2001.
49. *China Business Review*, July–August 2000, p. 37.
50. *China Business Monthly*, July 1998, p. 22.
51. *Far Eastern Economic Review*, February 1, 2001, p. 46.
52. *Asian Wall Street Journal*, November 13–19, 2000.
53. *China Daily*, November 13, 2000.
54. *Asian Wall Street Journal*, November 13–19, 2000.
55. *Far Eastern Economic Review*, September 21, 2000, p. 72.
56. *Far Eastern Economic Review*, August 24, 2000, p. 42.
57. *Asian Wall Street Journal*. December 12–18, 2000.
58. *Asian Wall Street Journal*, November 13–19, 2000.
59. *Far Eastern Economic Review*, August 24, 2000, pp. 32–33.
60. *Far Eastern Economic Review*, September 7, 2000, p. 52.
61. *Asian Wall Street Journal*, October 30–November 5, 2000.
62. Ibid.
63. *Far Eastern Economic Review*, June 8, 2000, p. 42.
64. *China Daily, Business Weekly*, July 17–23, 2001.
65. *China Business Review*, July–August, 2001, p. 34.
66. *Asian Wall Street Journal*, October 8–14, 2001.

Chapter Seven

1. Nicholas D. Kristof, and Sheryl Wu Dunn, *China Wakes*, p. 14.
2. Andrew J. Nathan, *China's Transition*, p. 226.
3. Edward S. Steinfeld, "Governing the Chinese Market," p. 272.
4. *Asian Wall Street Journal*, November 4, 1999.
5. *Asian Wall Street Journal*, November 8, 1999.
6. *China Daily*, October 12, 2000.
7. *Asian Wall Street Journal*, November 1–7, 1999.

8. *Washington Post*, June 1, 2001.

9. *China Daily*, October 30, 1999.

10. *China Daily*, July 4, 2001.

11. The Economist Intelligence Unit, *Country Report: China.* August 2001, p. 24.

12. *Asian Wall Street Journal*, July 30–August 5, 2001.

13. *Asian Wall Street Journal*, November 11, 1999.

14. Andrew J. Nathan, *China's Transition*, p. 219.

15. W.J.F. Jenner, *The Tyranny of History: The Roots of China's Crisis*, p. 145.

16. Ibid., p. 115.

17. *China Daily*, September 23, 1997.

18. Minxin Pei, "Is China Unstable?" p. 5.

19. Kenneth Lieberthal, *Governing China: From Revolution Through Reform*, p. 329.

20. Arthur Waldron, "After Deng the Deluge," p. 149.

21. Minxin Pei, "Racing Against Time," p. 28.

22. *Far Eastern Economic Review*, October 26, 2000, p. 34.

23. *International Herald Tribune*, June 2–3, 2001.

Bibliography

Almanac of China's Finance and Banking 1995. Beijing: China Financial Publishing House, 1995.

Ash, Robert F. "The Performance of China's Grain Sector: a Regional Perspective." In *Agricultural Policies in China*. Washington, DC: Organization for Economic Co-operation and Development, 1998.

Ash, Robert F. and R.L. Edmond, "China's Land Resources, Environment, and Agricultural Production." *China Quarterly* (December 1998).

Banker 147 (July 1997): p. 140.

Beijing Review (21–27 September 1998): p. 10.

Beijing Review (December 1997): p. 5.

Bertaud, Alain. "China—Urban Land Use Issue." 1992. Unpublished manuscript.

Bottlier, Pieter. "Killing Two Birds with One Stone: Using State Assets to Help Finance 'Old' Pension Debt and Develop Domestic Capital Markets During Transition." Unpublished manuscript for The China Development Forum, August 20–21, 2000, Beijing.

Boxer, Baruch. "China's Three Gorges Dam: Questions and Prospects." *China Quarterly* (1987): pp. 95–96.

Brown, Lester R. and Bryan Halweil. "The Drying of China." *World Watch* 11, no. 4 (July–August 1998): p. 13.

Brown, Lester R. *Who Will Feed China? Wake-up Call for a Small Planet*. New York: Norton, 1995.

Chan Kam Wing. *Cities With Invisible Walls*. Hong Kong: Oxford University Press, 1994.

Chan Kwai-Cheong. "The Three Gorges Project in China: Resettlement Prospects and Problems," *Ambio* (Stockholm) 4, no. 2 (March 1995): p. 100.

Chen Aimin. "China's Urban Housing Market Development: Problems and Prospects," *Journal of Contemporary China* 7, no. 17 (1998): pp. 43–60.

Cheng Li. *Rediscovering China: Dynamics and Dilemmas of Reform*. Lanham, MD: Rowman and Littlefield, 1997.

Childs-Johnson, Elizabeth and Sulllivan, Lawrence R. "The Three Gorges Dam and the Fate of China's Southern Heritage," *Orientations* (July–August 1996): p. 55.

China Business Monthly (July 1998): p. 22.

China Business Review (March–April 1993): pp. 19, 27–28, 31–32.

China Business Review (March–April 1996): pp. 12, 26.

China Business Review (January–February 2000): pp. 20, 40.

China Business Review (March–April, 2000): p. 20.

China Business Review (July–August 2000): pp. 22, 37.

China Business Review (November–December 2000): pp. 19–25.

China Business Review (May–June 2001): pp. 13–15.

China Business Review (July–August 2001): p. 34.

China State Statistical Bureau. *China Statistical Yearbook.* 1995.

China Today (May 1992): p. 41.

Crook, Frederick W. "An Analysis of China's Food Grain Security Policy." In *Agriculture in China and OECD Countries: Past Policies and Future Challenges.* Washington, DC: Organization for Economic Co-operation and Development, 1999.

Crosson, Pierre. *Perspectives on the Long-term Global Food Situation*, no. 2. Washington, DC: Federation of American Scientists Fund, spring 1996.

Economist (September 30, 2000).

The Economist Intelligence Unit. *Country Report: China* (August 2001).

Embassy of the United States, The Peoples Republic of China. *Agreement on Market Access Between The People's Republic of China and the United States of America.* Section I-A, *Tariffs.* November 15, 1999.

Fairbank, John King. *China: A New History.* Stanford CA: Stanford University Press, 1992.

Far Eastern Economic Review (October 16, 1997): p. 62.

Far Eastern Economic Review (September 30, 1999): p. 69.

Far Eastern Economic Review (April 27, 2000): p. 26.

Far Eastern Economic Review (May 11, 2000): p. 34.

Far Eastern Economic Review (May 25, 2000): p. 81.

Far Eastern Economic Review (June 8, 2000): p. 42.

Far Eastern Economic Review (August 17, 2000): p. 40.

Far Eastern Economic Review (August 24, 2000): pp. 32–33, 42.

Far Eastern Economic Review (August 31, 2000): p. 36.

Far Eastern Economic Review (September 7, 2000): p. 52.

Far Eastern Economic Review (September 21, 2000): p. 72.

Far Eastern Economic Review (October 5, 2000): p. 46.

Far Eastern Economic Review (October 19, 2000): p. 85.

Far Eastern Economic Review (October 26, 2000): pp. 34, 77.

Far Eastern Economic Review (November 30, 2000): pp. 15–18.

Far Eastern Economic Review (December 7, 2000): pp. 62, 69.

Far Eastern Economic Review (December 14, 2000): p. 14.

Far Eastern Economic Review (December 28, 2000–January 4, 2001): pp. 96, 106.

Far Eastern Economic Review (February 1, 2001): p. 46.

Far Eastern Economic Review (March 1, 2001): pp. 46–50.

Far Eastern Economic Review (July 19, 2001).

Global Environment Facility. *China: Efficient Industrial Boilers*. Washington, DC: Global Environmental Facility, 1996.

Gregory, Neil, Stoyan Tenev, and Dileep Wagle. *China's Emerging Private Enterprises*. Washington, DC: International Finance Corporation, 2000.

Han Suyin. *A Mortal Flower*. London: Jonathan Cape, 1966.

Han Suyin. *The Crippled Tree*. London: Jonathan Cape, 1970.

Harwit, Eric. "China's Telecommunications Industry: Development Patterns and Policies." *Pacific Affairs* 71, no. 2 (summer 1998): pp. 175–193.

Hucker, Charles O. *China's Imperial Past, An Introduction to Chinese History and Culture*. Stanford, CA: Stanford University Press, 1975.

International Herald Tribune, June 2–3, 2001.

International Rivers Network / Human Rights in China. "Major Problems Found in Three Gorges Dam Resettlement Program." Joint Report. March 12, 1998.

International Rivers Network. Press releases, 1999.

James, Estelle. "How Can China Solve Its Old Age Security Problem? The Interaction Between Pension, SOE, and Finance Market Reform." *Journal of Pension Economics and Finance* 1, no. 1 (Janaury 2002).

Jenner, W.J.F. *The Tyranny of History: The Roots of China's Crisis*. London: Penguin Books, 1994.

Johnson, Michael. "The Vices—and Virtues—of Corruption." *Current History* (September 1997): pp. 270–273.

Jun Jing. "Rural Resettlement: Past Lessons for the Three Gorges Project." *China Journal* no. 38 (July 1997): p. 87.

Kirkby, R.J.R. *Urbanization in China: Town and Country in a Developing Economy, 1949–2000 A.D.* London: Croom Helm, 1985.

Kristof, Nicholas D. and Wu Dunn, Sheryl. *China Wakes: The Struggle for the Soul of a Rising Power*. New York: Vintage Books, 1995.

Lardy, Nicholas R. *Agriculture in China's Modern Economic Development*. Cambridge: Cambridge University Press, 1983.

———. *China's Unfinished Economic Revolution*. Washington, DC: Brookings Institution, 1998.

——— "China and the Asian Contagion." *Foreign Affairs* (July–August1998): p. 86.

——— "The Challenge of Bank Restructuring in China." In *Strengthening the Banking System in China*. Basel: Bank for International Settlements,1999.

Lieberthal, Kenneth. *Governing China: From Revolution Through Reform*. New York: Norton, 1995.

Luk Shiu-Hung and Whitney, Joseph, eds. *Megaproject: A Case Study of China's Three Gorges Project*. Armonk, NY: M.E. Sharpe, 1993.

Ma, Laurence J.C., ed. *Urban Development in Modern China*. Boulder, CO: Westview Press, p. 253.

Meisner, Maurice. "The Other China." *Current History* (September 1997): p. 265.

Mueller, Milton and Tan Zixiang. *China in the Information Age: Telecommunications and the Dilemmas of Reform*. Westport, CT: Praeger Publishers, 1997.

Nathan, Andrew J. *China's Transition*. New York: Columbia University Press, 1997.

Naughton, Barry. "The Third Front: Defence Industrialization in the Chinese Interior." *China Quarterly* (1986): pp. 351–386.

Nyberg, Albert and Scott Rozelle. *Accelerating China's Rural Transformation.* Washington, DC: World Bank, 1999.

Ogilvy, John. *Embassy from the East-India Company of the United Provinces, to the Grand Tartar Cham, Emperor of China, Delivered by Their Excellencies, Peter de Gruyer and Jacob de Keyser, at his Imperial City of Peking, Wherein the Cities, Towns, Villages, Ports, Rivers, etc. in Their Passages from Canton to Peking All Ingeniously Described by Mr. John Nieuhoff, Steward to the Ambassadors.* London: Printed by the author, 1673.

Oi, Jean C. "Two Decades of Rural Reform in China." *China Quarterly,* no. 159 (September 1999): p. 7.

Pei, Minxin. "Is China Unstable?" *Foreign Policy Research Institute WIRE* 7, no. 8 (July 1999): p. 5.

———. "Racing Against Time." In *China Briefing, Contradictions of Change.* Ed. William A. Joseph. Armonk, NY: M.E. Sharpe, 1997.

———. "The Political Economy of Banking Reforms in China, 1993–1997." *Journal of Contemporary China,* 7 (1998): p. 328.

Qing Dai. *The River Dragon Has Come! The Three Gorges Dam and the Fate of China's Yangtze River and Its People.* Armonk, NY: M.E. Sharpe, 1998.

Ramo, Joshua Cooper. "The Shanghai Bubble." *Foreign Policy* (summer 1998): p. 65.

Schell, Orville, and David Shambaugh, eds. *The China Reader: The Reform Era.* New York: Vintage Books, 1999.

Spence, Jonathan D. *The Search for Modern China.* New York: W.W. Norton, 1990.

Stares, Steven and Liu Zhi. "Theme Paper 1: Motorization in Chinese Cities: Issues and Actions." In *China's Urban Transport Development Strategy, Proceedings of a Symposium in Beijing, November 8–10, 1995.* Washington, DC: World Bank, 1996.

Steinfeld, Edward S. *Forging Reform in China, the Fate of State-Owned Industry.* Cambridge: Cambridge University Press, 1998.

Steinfeld, Edward S." Governing the Chinese Market." *Current History* (September 1999): p. 272.

Sun, Peter, ed. *Multipurpose River Basin Development in China.* Washington, DC: The Economic Development Institute of World Bank, 1994.

Tuan, Francis C., and Bingsheng Ke. "A Review of China's Agricultural Policy: Past and Present Developments." In *Agriculture in China and OECD Countries: Past Policies and Future Challenges.* Washington, DC: The Organization for Economic Co-operation and Development, 1999.

Twitchet, D. and J.K. Fairbank, eds. *The Chin and Han Empires, 221 B.C.–A.D. 220. The Cambridge History of Modern China,* vol. 1. Cambridge: Cambridge University Press, 1978.

Upside (January 2001): p. 62.

Waldron, Arthur. "After Deng the Deluge." *Foreign Affairs* (September–October 1995): p. 149.

Walsh, Michael P. "Transportation and the Environment." In *China Environment Series,* Issue 3. Washington, DC: Woodrow Wilson Center, 1999/2000.

Wang Ya Ping and Murie, Alan, eds. "The Process of Commercialization of Urban Housing in China." *Urban Studies* 33, no. 6 (1996): p. 972.

World Bank. *China—Enterprise Housing and Social Security Reform Project.* Washington, DC: World Bank, 1994.

———. *China, Updating Economic Memorandum: Managing Rapid Growth and Transition.* Washington, DC: World Bank, 1993.

———. *China 2020, China's Environment in the New Century: Clear Waters, Blue Skies.* Washington, DC: World Bank.

———. *China 2020, Development Challenges in the New Century.* Washington, DC: World Bank, 1997.

———. *China 2020, Food Security Options: At China's Table.* Washington, DC: World Bank, 1997.

———. *China 2020, Pension Reform in China: Old Age Security.* Washington, DC: World Bank, 1997.

———. *China's Management of Enterprise Assets: the State as Shareholder.* Washington, DC: World Bank, 1997.

———. *The Chinese Economy: Fighting Inflation, Deepening Reforms,* vol. 1. Washington, DC: World Bank, 1996.

———. *Chongqing Industrial Pollution Control and Reform Project.* Washington, DC: World Bank, 1996.

———. *Rural China: Transition and Development.* Washington, DC: World Bank, 1999.

———. *China: Air, Land, and Water—The Environmental Priorities for a New Millennium.* Washington, DC: World Bank, 2001.

Winchester, Simon. *The River at the Center of the World.* New York: Holt, 1996.

Wired (February 2000): p. 146.

Yang Zhong. "Studying Chinese Local Government: Searching for a Paradigm." Paper presented at the annual meeting of the American Political Science Association, Boston, September 1998.

Yusuf, Shahid and Wu Weiping. *The Dynamics of Urban Growth in Three Chinese Cities.* New York: World Bank and Oxford University Press, 1997.

Zhou Ganshi. "Keynote Address 3: Urban Transport Problems in Three Cities: Causes, Trends and Options." In *China's Urban Transport Development Strategy, Proceedings of a Symposium in Beijing, November 9–10, 1995.* Washington, DC: World Bank, 1996.

Zhao Xiaobin and Zhang Li, "Urban Performance and the Control of Urban Size in China." *Urban Studies* vol. 32, 4–5 (1995).

Zweig, David. "Rural People, the Politicians, and Power." *The China Journal* no. 38 (July 1997): p. 154.

Index

Neil Hughes has spent twenty-eight years working in twenty-five countries as an industrial and financial specialist and project manager with the World Bank. During 1992–1999, he helped Chinese officials and state enterprise managers implement economic reforms and restructure enterprises. He has an M.A. in international economics and politics from The Fletcher School of Law and Diplomacy, Tufts University, an M.A. in anthropology from The George Washington University and a B.A. in history from The College of Wooster.